Overseeing Rights in Prison

Drawing on Ireland as its primary case study, this book is an in-depth critical examination of how rights protection bodies and mechanisms are experienced by those in prison in Ireland.

Through its analysis of the Irish experience, the book considers the implementation of, and challenges faced by, human rights protection within the prison context, and explores some of the reforms that Ireland has undertaken in this area over the past 15 years, including the introduction of a new complaint system and establishment of an Office of the Inspector of Prisons. Using a wealth of information gathered through interviews and surveys of participants in three male prisons, the book sets out personal experiences of such mechanisms and identifies the key barriers to effective rights protection.

Offering a detailed presentation of the international framework for the protection of prisoners' rights through oversight mechanisms, and proposing methods for overcoming common barriers, *Overseeing Rights in Prison: The Irish Experience of Human Rights Protection in Prisons* will be of interest to students and scholars of criminology, particularly in relation to prisons and human rights.

Sophie van der Valk is a postdoctoral researcher with the School of Social Policy, Social Work and Social Justice on the project Transforming Justice: An All-Island Examination of Justice Responses to Historical Institutional Abuse. She is a socio-legal researcher who received her PhD from Trinity College Dublin as part of the ERC funded Prisons: the Rule of Law, Accountability and Rights (PRILA) project. Her PhD examined the experiences of those in prison of human rights protecting mechanisms, specifically complaint procedures, inspection and monitoring and the courts. Her findings have been used to inform the new framework of the Office of the Inspector of Prisons in Ireland and been disseminated through workshops, training days, conference presentations, reports, blogs and academic publications. Her research has been published both internationally and domestically in journals such as the *European Journal of Criminology* and the *Law and Society Review*. She has previously conducted research in the field of counterterrorism, specifically examining issues concerning the prosecution and other measures used against foreign fighters.

Routledge Frontiers of Criminal Justice

Corporate Criminal Liability and Sanctions
Current Trends and Policy Changes
Edited by Michala Meiselles, Nicholas Ryder and Arianna Visconti

Crime Prevention by Exclusion
Ethical Considerations
Edited by Sebastian Jon Holmen, Thomas Søbirk Petersen & Jesper Ryberg

Occupational Stress Injuries
Operational and Organizational Stressors Among Public Safety Personnel
Edited by Rosemary Ricciardelli, Joy C. MacDermid and Lorna Ferguson

Mass Data Surveillance and Predictive Policing
Contested Foundations and Human Rights Impact
Plixavra Vogiatzoglou

Rational Anger
An International Comparison of Legal Systems
Stina Bergman Blix and Nina Törnqvist

The Quest for Reparations for Indian Residential School Abuse
Confronting the Legacy of the Independent Assessment Process
Konstantin Petoukhov

The Role of Food in Resettlement and Rehabilitation
Good Food and Good Lives
Edited by Julie Parsons and Kevin Wong

Overseeing Rights in Prison
The Irish Experience of Human Rights Protection in Prisons
Sophie van der Valk

For more information about this series, please visit: www.routledge.com/Routledge-Frontiers-of-Criminal-Justice/book-series/RFCJ

Overseeing Rights in Prison

The Irish Experience of Human Rights Protection in Prisons

Sophie van der Valk

Routledge
Taylor & Francis Group
LONDON AND NEW YORK

First published 2025
by Routledge
4 Park Square, Milton Park, Abingdon, Oxon OX14 4RN

and by Routledge
605 Third Avenue, New York, NY 10158

Routledge is an imprint of the Taylor & Francis Group, an informa business

British Library Cataloguing-in-Publication Data
A catalogue record for this book is available from the British Library

ISBN: 9781032761886 (hbk)
ISBN: 9781032761909 (pbk)
ISBN: 9781003477471 (ebk)

DOI: 10.4324/9781003477471

Typeset in Sabon
by Newgen Publishing UK

Contents

Acknowledgements

I wish to express my sincerest gratitude to Prof Mary Rogan for her supervision, guidance, encouragement and unfailing support in conducting the research for this book. I would also like to express my gratitude to my assistant supervisors Dr Ciara O'Connell and Dr Eva Aizpurua who provided invaluable experience and made the overall experience of researching a fun and enjoyable experience. I would like to thank the European Research Council that, through the European Union's Horizon 2020 research and innovation programme under grant agreement No 679362, provided funding for the research which forms the basis for this book.

Thanks are also due to the other members of the PRILA team, who provided feedback and moral support throughout the journey, as well as the Consultative Council that helped develop research instruments and pilot them.

I would like to thank the interviewee and survey participants who generously gave their time and thoughts to help me conduct my research. Without them, this book would not exist.

I would like to thank the staff of the Irish Prison Service who facilitated access to research participants, provided relevant information and answered my queries.

1 Introduction

1.1 Introduction

Prisoners, like other individuals, are entitled to have their rights respected. Upholding the rule of law, ensuring oversight for decisions taken by administrative bodies and the protection of fundamental rights are crucial aspects of European democracy. These foundational principles of public law take on increased importance in the prison environment, where the potential for abuse has been well documented (Sparks et al. 1996; Carrabine 2004; Dolovich 2009), where the legitimacy of authority can be fragile (Sparks and Bottoms 1995: 45), and where prisoners may be drawn from marginalised and vulnerable groups (Behan and Kirkham 2016). As noted by Calavita and Jenness (2015: 17):

> Imprisonment carries with it the circumscription or loss of many rights as being necessary to accommodate the institutional needs and objectives of prison facilities, particularly internal security and safety.

A key feature of rights protection within prison as promoted by international human rights doctrine is the establishment of bodies tasked with supporting the protection of rights for individuals in the prison system. Oversight bodies, specifically complaint procedures, inspection and monitoring bodies, as well as the ability to access the courts play an important role in the protection of prisoners' rights and are promoted by international treaties as 'crucial mechanisms to ensure that the provisions of these [European prison] rules are respected'.[1]

This book provides an empirical analysis of prisoners' perceptions of and experiences with certain oversight bodies in Ireland, exploring whether they are in fact understood and accessible to those whose rights they are designed to protect. As will be discussed further in Chapter 2, oversight itself is a complex term and used interchangeably with terms such as accountability and governance. For the purposes of this book, the focus is on oversight and accountability in so far as they form a part of protecting the rights of those in prison, otherwise known as human rights protecting mechanisms.

DOI: 10.4324/9781003477471-1

Calavita and Jenness (2015: 95) found 'multiple, conflicting views of law and legal practices' in their study of complaints in Californian prisons. Literature is beginning to emerge on this in the European context (van der Valk and Rogan 2021; Daems and Larrauri 2024). Drawing upon the extant prisoner literature, as well as rights consciousness and procedural justice scholarship, the primary aims of this book are to explore prisoners' understanding and experiences of oversight bodies in prison, their sense of rights consciousness and the challenges for engaging with oversight in the prison environment. This book has four main interrelated aims:

1 To describe how prisoners experience oversight structures in Irish prisons and specifically;
   a To describe how prisoners experience and view complaints-receiving bodies;
   b To describe how prisoners experience and view inspection and monitoring bodies;
   c To describe how prisoners experience and view judicial oversight of prisons;
2 To examine prisoners' views of being a holder of rights and how these views interact with their views of oversight structures;
3 To explore factors which may influence prisoners' views of oversight structures in Irish prisons;
4 To provide recommendations by which inspection and monitoring bodies may better operate in Irish prisons so as to ensure greater oversight, drawing on prisoners' experiences and perceptions of good oversight structures.

1.2 International Legal Framework for Oversight

International and European frameworks such as the UN Mandela Rules, the Council of Europe (CoE) European Prison Rules (EPRs) and Optional Protocol to the Convention Against Torture (OPCAT) highlight the importance of rights-protecting mechanisms for those in custody. Both the Mandela Rules and the EPRs promote a three-pronged approach to the protection of rights in prison, incorporating both retroactive and preventative elements. As will be set out further in Chapter 3, this approach entails the establishment of an independent complaint mechanism with a right of appeal, although the nature of this appeal varies across different jurisdictions, inspection and monitoring by external bodies, as well as the possibility of access to the courts. As highlighted by Behan and Kirkham (2016: 439) this 'model is designed to uphold prisoner rights on an ongoing basis, using a framework which supplements, and is supported by, the pre-existing judicial process'. However, as noted by Kemp and Tomczak (2024: 3), the use of regulatory standards to preserve human rights in prison needs to address the 'fundamental limitations of rules-based prison-regulation'.

1.3 Prison Oversight and Ireland

Prison oversight has a long history in Ireland, though little is known about its operation in practice. Visiting Committees (VCs), comprised of laypeople who are assigned to individual prisons to carry out visits and listen to prisoner complaints, have been part of the Irish prison system since at least 1925.[2] Although over time their powers have changed and they have been subject to criticisms (O'Mahony 1997: 126–127), their primary role has been providing the public with a view inside the walls of Irish prisons. Recent years have also seen a growth in oversight bodies operating in Irish prisons and elsewhere. In line with the international frameworks on prisons to which Ireland is a party under the United Nations (UN) and CoE, Ireland has developed a tripartite model of human rights protection for those in prison which will be explored with respect to people in custody in this study. Since 2007, Ireland has had an Office of the Inspector of Prisons (OiP) on a statutory basis. Ireland is also subject to visits by the European Committee for the Prevention of Torture, Inhuman and Degrading Treatment or Punishment (CPT) since 1989. While Ireland has signed the UN OPCAT, which would require Ireland to establish a National Preventative Mechanism for all places of detention and be subject to visits from the Subcommittee, discussions on how this would be implemented and ratification of the OPCAT is ongoing. Alongside these domestic and international inspection and monitoring bodies, the international human rights monitoring framework promotes an accessible complaints procedure, as well as access to the courts. Ireland introduced a formal complaint procedure in 2013 with respect to its prisons; however, this mechanism continues to lack an independent appeals component and prisoners have brought a variety of court cases on their treatment and conditions in prison. Prisoners face significant challenges in accessing the courts and these cases are limited with most cases brought by longer-term prisoners or those subject to significant disciplinary proceedings.

1.4 Prisons and Oversight: The Challenges

The existence of oversight bodies, in and of themselves, does not mean that an effective oversight system exists. As highlighted by Deitch (2010: 1762), in the case of the United States, although there are various oversight bodies for aspects of imprisonment, 'formal and comprehensive external oversight – in the form of inspections and routine monitoring of conditions that affect the rights of prisoners' is rare. An effective oversight structure, consisting of a regular inspection and monitoring procedure and a complaints system, is key to ensuring the human rights of prisoners are protected and that any violation is remedied promptly. As stated by Owers (2010: 1536–1537), former Prison Inspector for England and Wales, an 'independent administrative protection of prisoners' rights designed to be preventative and proactive, as well as to expose and deal with abuse or malpractice' is needed to complement the role of the courts. The various aspects of oversight promise to provide comprehensive protection for prisoners' rights, while also recognising the role of staff in ensuring rights are respected. An effective complaints mechanism allows prisoners to voice their concerns and grievances, while the inspection and monitoring carried out by external bodies, such as an inspector or the Committee against Torture, seek to prevent ill-treatment through visiting places of detention and providing recommendations.

Prisoners' engagement with oversight bodies remains poorly understood, with Crewe (2009) noting a distinct lack of trust or faith in VCs, since renamed Independent Monitoring Bodies, by prisoners in an English prison and the Ombudsman for Children's Office (2011) noting similar issues amongst young prisoners in Ireland. Similarly, Behan (2016) noted the lack of trust of participants in his study in the VC, as well as concerns about reprisals for speaking up. In recent years, research has begun to emerge on how prisoners view the visits of monitoring bodies, including the CPT (O'Connell and Rogan 2023).[3] Oversight is about providing insight into prison conditions in order to ensure the rights of those in custody are respected, as well as empowering prisoners to speak up about perceived harm and not feel silenced by virtue of imprisonment. Therefore, the climate in which oversight bodies operate are key to promoting information on rights and oversight bodies, as well as ensuring access to these bodies. As highlighted by Calavita and Jenness (2015: 47) in relation to complaints, structural inequality becomes more pronounced in the case of prisons due to the full control exercised by the authorities in prisons over the prisoners.

Literature is scant on how prisoners feel about themselves as citizens, or how domestic and international human rights laws apply to them. As highlighted by Sexton's (2015) work on penal consciousness, prisoners have varying degrees of expectation regarding their treatment in prisons. Hulley et al. (2012: 20) argue that 'some prisoners are well informed about their rights, making them highly sensitive to matters of fairness'. There is also considerable literature on why people choose to litigate (Ewick and Silbey 1998), much of which argues that vulnerable populations retain a belief in the possibility of legal justice, even though the odds are stacked against them, but very little exists on how this operates in prisons. Some discussion of these issues is found in Calavita and Jenness (2015) in their work on the use by prisoners in California of the 'grievance' process, that is, a formal system for filing complaints. Calavita and Jenness (2015: 20) frame their analysis within the notion of prison as a total institution, but one in which law is a 'hypervisible organizing force', and that this hypervisibility trumps the social and psychological factors that in other populations dampen the likelihood of 'claims making'. The men interviewed in their study embraced views ranging from deep cynicism to faith in the power of the law and truth (Calavita and Jenness 2015: 95).

In order to address the gaps identified in the literature, participants in this study were asked about their experiences of oversight through three specific mechanisms: the complaints system; inspection and monitoring; and the role of the courts. Through understanding prisoners' experiences of oversight, this book contributes to our understanding of effective rights protection and how to provide prisoners with the tools to feel worthy of rights and rights protection. This book aims to address the dearth of domestic and international research on prisoners' experiences of oversight in prisons by providing insight informed by interviews and surveys with prisoners in Ireland.

An exploratory and mixed-methods research design was utilised to answer these questions. In-depth, semi-structured interviews were conducted with 45 randomly selected prisoners and 508 completed surveys were gathered from across three Irish prisons. The participants represent a broad range of sentence lengths, age and prison experience. Additionally, the author took part in a rapid ethnographic study of a CPT visit to Ireland including further interviews with those in custody and has spent numerous hours engaging with various stakeholders across the prison service. However, while this additional experience has added weight to the findings discussed in this book, the data used in this book is drawn solely from the initial interviews and surveys conducted by the author as part of her PhD research.

1.5 Structure of the Book

The book is comprised of eight chapters. Following on from this introductory chapter, the initial chapters set out the literature to date and domestic and international legal frameworks which govern prison oversight. Chapter 2 discusses the literature on the concept of oversight and its relationship to terms such as accountability and regulation, followed by an examination of field work conducted in the field of oversight, which in an institution such as a prison may need to take certain factors into account. Chapter 3 sets out the policy and legal landscape of the bodies which are focused on in this study. In particular, the historical development of the bodies, the legal frameworks both nationally and internationally which guide their operations and provide some insight through existing reports and studies as to how they are perceived. Chapter 4 addresses existing literature on the specific nature of the prison environment, which can alter perceptions of legitimacy, fairness and justice. The literature on rights consciousness of vulnerable groups and prisoners will be explored. While literature on the rights consciousness of those in prison is limited, drawing on the literature of those from similar demographics provides insight into how rights may be perceived by those in prison. However, as highlighted by Calavita and Jenness' (2015: 48) study on the prisoner complaints system in California, the hypervisible nature of law in the prison environment can prompt those in prison to assert their rights and hold the prison service to account based on their own rules.

Chapter 5 introduces the empirical findings from the study. It focuses on the first research question by describing how prisoners experience and view inspection and monitoring bodies, complaints-receiving bodies and judicial oversight of prisons. It focuses on key findings on awareness, prisoners' engagement with the bodies and their views on the bodies' operations. It also sets out key powers which participants noted as important for good complaints and inspection bodies. Chapter 6 considers various factors of prison life which can create additional challenges for oversight bodies in prison and how these factors in turn influence prisoners' views of oversight structures in Irish prisons, for example, by hindering their ability to learn about and to access the bodies. In particular, the rights consciousness of those in prison will be explored as well as their views of themselves as right holders while in prison. This is followed by a discussion of aspects of penal culture such as prisons as low trust environments, relationships and survival tactics. Chapter 7 brings the findings from Chapters 6 and 7 together under three key themes identified in the data and contextualises them within the existing literature: the relationship between rights consciousness and oversight; misalignment of oversight bodies and prisoners' lived experiences; and the implications of trust in prison on the experiences of oversight. Each of these themes is explored in turn, further contextualising the analysis within the wider literature. These chapters together provide an understanding of how prisoners themselves view the oversight options available to them and themselves as holders of rights while in prison, whether they are fully aware of how to go about making a complaint or speaking to inspection and monitoring bodies and whether they feel satisfied that the mechanisms are fair, transparent and independent in coming to a decision.

Chapter 8 brings the book to a conclusion and considers the implications of these findings for policy and future research. This chapter provides recommendations for potential means by which inspection and monitoring bodies may better operate in Irish prisons to ensure greater oversight, drawing on prisoners' experiences and perceptions of good oversight structures, as well as for the prison service to promote human rights protection in prison. It is important to ensure that prisoners do make complaints when it is necessary, and this can only be achieved through encouraging trust in the system at the prisoner level. Receiving complaints can serve as a way of collecting information to improve the prisoner system itself and ensure any abuses are dealt with at an early stage. Chapter 8 also includes reflections on the research process and the role of researchers when in the field and disseminating findings. This self-reflection on the research process and the researcher's role in the field, is important to increase transparency in the process and acknowledge the researcher as part of the process.

Notes

1 Draft Recommendation Rec(2006)2-rev of the Committee of Ministers to member States on the European Prison Rules Commentary https://cdn.penalreform.org/wp-content/uploads/2020/07/EPR-Commentary.pdf

2 Prison (Visiting Committees) Act 1925.

3 As part of the PRILA project in which the data for the book was gathered, the researcher took part in a rapid ethnography of a CPT visit to Ireland in 2019. Ciara O'Connell and Mary Rogan, 'Monitoring Prisons in Europe: Understanding Perspectives of People in Prison and Prison Staff' (2023) 48(1) *Law & Social Inquiry* 205–235. https://doi.org/10.1017/lsi.2021.86

References

Cormac Behan, *Citizen Convict: Prisoners, Politics and the Vote* (Manchester University Press 2016).

Cormac Behan and Richard Kirkham, 'Monitoring, Inspection and Complaints Adjudication in Prison: The Limits of Prison Accountability Frameworks' (2016) 55(4) *The Howard Journal of Crime and Justice* 432.

Kitty Calavita and Valerie Jenness, *Appealing to Justice: Prisoner Grievances, Rights and Carceral Logic* (University of California Press 2015).

Eamonn Carrabine, *Power, Discourse, and Resistance: A Genealogy of the Strangeways Prison Riot* (Ashgate 2004).

Ben Crewe, *The Prisoner Society: Power, Adaptation and Social life in an English Prison* (Oxford University Press 2009).

Tom Daems and Elena Larrauri, *Just Prisons: Requests and Complaints in Prisons in Europe* (Palgrave MacMillan 2024).

Michele Deitch, 'Independent Correctional Oversight Mechanisms Across the United States: A 50-State Inventory' (2010) 30 *Pace Law Review* 1754.

Sharon Dolovich, 'Cruelty, Prison Conditions, and the Eights Amendment' (2009) 84(4) *New York University Law Review* 881

Patricia Ewick and Susan S Silbey, *The Common Place of Law: Stories fFrom Everyday Life* (University of Chicago 1998).

Susie Hulley, Alison Liebling and Ben Crewe, 'Respect in Prisons: Prisoners' Experiences of Respect in Public and Private Sector Prisons' (2012) 12 *Criminology and Criminal Justice* 3.

Tom Kemp and Philippa Tomczak, 'The Cruel Optimism of International Prison Regulation: Prison Ontologies and Carceral Harms' (2024) 49(3) *Law & Social Inquiry* 1683–1714.

Ciara O'Connell and Mary Rogan, 'Monitoring Prisons in Europe: Understanding Perspectives of People in Prison and Prison Staff' (2023) 48(1) *Law & Social Inquiry* 205–235.

Paul O'Mahony, *Mountjoy Prisoners: A Sociological and Criminological Profile* (Citeseer 1997).

Ombudsman for Children and Young People, *Young People in St. Patrick's Institution: A Report by the Ombudsman for Children's Office* (Ombudsman for Children's Office 2011).

Anne Owers, 'Prison Inspection and the Protection of Prisoners' Rights' (2010) 30 *Pace Law Review* 1535.

Lori Sexton, 'Penal Subjectivities: Developing a Theoretical Framework for Penal Consciousness' (2015) 17(1) *Punishment & Society* 114.

Richard Sparks and Anthony E Bottoms, 'Legitimacy and Order in Prisons' (1995) 46(1) *British Journal of Sociology* 45–62.

Richard Sparks, Anthony E Bottoms and Will Hay, *Prisons and the Problem of Order* (Oxford University Press 1996).
Sophie van der Valk and Mary Rogan. 'Experiencing Human Rights Protections in Prisons: The Case of Prison Monitoring in Ireland' (2021) 18(1) *European Journal of Criminology* 101–119.

2 Oversight and Prisoners' Views of Oversight Bodies

2.1 Introduction

Oversight plays an important role in providing insight into prison life and an opportunity for those in prison to speak up about their experiences. Effective oversight has benefits for the overall transparency of prison conditions and can create pressure at a political level to adhere to minimum standards. Additionally, it allows for open dialogue on solutions for the multi-faceted challenges of those in prison, which is not limited to within the prison walls (Stojkovic 2010). However, oversight is a complex term and as will be discussed in this chapter is often considered alongside related but distinct terms such as accountability, governance, rights protection and regulation. This chapter reviews the existing literature on prisoners' views of oversight bodies. Chapter 4 sets out the contextual factors which impact upon the operation and experience of oversight bodies in prison, specifically prisoners' legal consciousness and aspects of penal culture such as relationships and power. This chapter starts with a consideration of the definition of accountability and accountability literature, examining theories on regulation and oversight more generally and their applicability to the prison context. Regulatory theory such as Ayers and Braithwaite's (1992) sanctions pyramids provides a framework to explain the need for multiple accountability and oversight bodies. This assessment will be followed by existing studies of prisoners' views of oversight bodies. In particular, the literature on procedural justice and its role in prisoners' perceptions of oversight bodies will be discussed. As will be explored further below, procedural justice principles such as trust, neutrality, voice and respect play an important role in shaping perceptions and perceived legitimacy of disciplinary procedures, complaint mechanisms and the courts (Jackson et al. 2010; Butler and Maruna 2016; Jenness and Calavita 2018). A key study in this regard is Calavita and Jenness' ground-breaking work on the Californian prisoner complaints system and differences in how procedural justice impacts experiences of complaining in prison in contrast to other environments (Calavita and Jenness 2015; Jenness and Calavita 2018). As will be set out below, this book has settled on the term 'oversight structures' or 'oversight bodies' to describe inspection and

DOI: 10.4324/9781003477471-2

monitoring, complaints structures and access to legal remedies. In particular, the bodies which are part of this study are grounded in the international human rights framework surrounding the protection of rights in prison.

2.2 Oversight: Why Do We Need It?

As discussed in the introduction to this book and further in Chapter 4, rights in prison are vulnerable and can be subject to abuse. Therefore, as stated by Owers (2010: 1536–1537), a former Prison Inspector for England and Wales, 'independent administrative protection of prisoners' rights designed to be preventative and proactive, as well as to expose and deal with abuse or malpractice' is needed to complement the role of the courts. While this book focuses on oversight in the form which seeks to ensure humane treatment and the upholding of human rights in the prison context, oversight has a broad range of other functions in the prison system and beyond both in the public and private domain (Deitch 2009).

This section examines accountability broadly, drawing on regulation theory, especially the work of Ayres and Braitwaite (1992) on 'responsive regulation'. While empirical research on prisoners' experiences of oversight is limited to date, the latter half of this section explores studies of oversight bodies in practice, in particular, Calavita and Jenness' (2015) study of complaints in the prison context. As will be shown in other sections, the penal context is a unique environment which can present specific challenges for oversight in achieving its aims. As discussed by Karamalidou (2017: 154), '[i]n an accountable prison, prisoners are able to express themselves freely, to be actively listened to, and have recourse to a remedy, such as a hierarchical grievance procedure'. Therefore, access to effective oversight bodies are an important part of rights respecting prisons and, through drawing on regulation theory, this section highlights the basis upon which these bodies were developed. Of particular concern in this section is identifying a workable definition of oversight which encompasses the various goals sought to be achieved. A body of literature has developed regarding oversight, accountability and regulation which are regarded as overlapping and sometimes indistinguishable terms. The repercussions of this in the criminal justice context will be explored and whether a meaningful difference exists in this context.

2.2.1 Oversight, Accountability and Regulation

Oversight, accountability and regulation are all used to describe the process through which prisons are monitored both internally and externally. Scott (2000: 40) defines accountability as a 'duty to give account for one's actions to some other person or body'. However, as noted by Seddon (2010: 264) this limits accountability to a backward-looking focus while in practice recommendations are drawn from bodies established to promote accountability. Braithwaite (2011: 510) distinguishes between passive and active responsibility in discussing responsive regulation. Passive responsibility involves 'holding actors responsible for wrongs they have done in the past'. This definition fits in with Scott's understanding of accountability. However, active responsibility goes further in 'challenging actors to take responsibility for making things right into the future' (Braithwaite 2011: 510). This encompasses the learning process of accountability through recommendations by inspection and monitoring bodies and the sharing of best practices. This holistic approach ensures that all of the various actors are given an opportunity to engage, and promotes future learning.

Deitch (2009: 1438) considers the related concept of oversight as a 'means of achieving the twin objectives of transparency of public institutions and accountability for the operation of safe and humane prisons and jails'. The principles of accountability and transparency encompass the different bodies which will be considered further in this book. As outlined by Deitch (2020: 230), oversight involves 'an effective accountability model' through the courts and litigation and also a 'meaningful transparency model' via 'routine preventive inspections with public reporting of findings'. Arguably under the CoE and UN models for right protection in prisons, an effective accountability model also includes a complaints mechanism, when effective and independent. These components encompass both reactive and preventative elements to ensure high standards are consistently maintained while allowing for a quick reaction in circumstances where it may be more appropriate. This provides a protection from harm and also an assurance that rights will be vindicated when violations do arise.

In contrast to oversight, accountability is focused on being answerable and providing a justification for actions taken, while regulation, as suggested by Seddon, is a broader term. As outlined by Seddon (2010: 264) the precise scope of what is meant by regulation has been the subject of extensive debate. He highlights that while the terms accountability and regulation are often used in overlapping concepts that they are interlinked but still separate. The clear concern with being answerable in accountability is not always evident or part of the regulatory framework and it may not be desirable in all regulatory arenas.

Scott (2000) discusses the 'redundancy' model of accountability. As discussed by Seddon (2010) this approach ensures that 'effective regulation does not stand or fall on the performance of a single actor'. As noted by Behan and Kirkham (2016: 439), '[t]his approach has the perceived advantage that it reduces the potential for flaws in provision falling through gaps in accountability and is particularly important where the risks of abuse of power going undetected are high'. This model aligns with Ayres and Braithwaite's (1992) discussion of tripartism, whereby different bodies exist to ensure others remain accountable, which forms an integral part of their responsive regulation theory. This further feeds into the concept of networked regulation, whereby during the escalation of an organisation up the sanctions pyramid, other bodies can get involved to apply additional pressure. The sanctions pyramid, as discussed by Braithwaite and Ayers (1992), provides for a gradual escalation of powers based on the response of the body being inspected to previous encounters. This is especially important in the case of potentially under-resourced regulatory bodies.

However, there may be risks involved in having an overly complex system as bodies may presume that the job is already covered by someone else or those seeking to use the system may be unclear as to the specific mandate of each body. An overly complex system could be confusing for those working with or engaging with oversight bodies such as staff and prisoner, where clear expectations of what specific bodies are intended for and what they can achieve is important to avoid further compounding feelings of futility and isolation by virtue of imprisonment (Carrabine 2005). As highlighted by Hood et al. (1999: 65) in the context of accountability in English and Welsh prisons, the layers which have been added overtime have led to 'a crowded and largely uncoordinated regulatory system'.

Braithwaite and Ayres (1992: 50) outline the elements of 'effective regulation' and perceive that it is 'about finesse in manipulating the salience of sanctions and the attribution of responsibility so that regulatory goals are maximally internationalized, and so that deterrence and incapacitation works when internationalization fails'. This allows the bodies to focus on mediation and longer-term goals and relationships, which in the prison context are important to ensure smooth access in the future and encourage compliance and embedding a rights receptive atmosphere.

The roles of the various bodies which make up the oversight framework which is the subject of this book will be examined in the next chapter. To enforce regulation, a regulatory body may be established to enforce the rules. Regulation is not necessarily concerned with enforcing or protecting human rights but can go beyond that depending on the area in which it is being used. While the specific powers that inspectors may have and some examples thereof will be discussed later in the legal and policy analysis chapter, in discussing accountability and regulation the enforcement powers of inspectors will be briefly addressed in this chapter. Generally, inspectors do not have direct enforcement powers in relation to recommendations arising from their reports. While they can carry out follow-up visits and further comment on areas which have or have not been dealt with in the interim, they cannot 'directly require "behaviour modification" and are instead reliant on softer, indirect methods to achieve change'. This can be viewed as a 'significant gap from the perspective of regulatory theory' (Seddon 2010: 266).

Given the nature of imprisonment, the duty to ensure that rights are protected and provided for falls to the staff of the prison and the Governor but ultimately lies with the Department of Justice. Prison services are delegated powers by the executive to enforce judicial orders to imprison someone for committing an offence under laws drafted by the executive. Democratic rules imply that governments have a duty of accountability towards their citizens which calls for transparency in public decision making and policies (van

Zyl Smit and Snacken 2009: 66). As part of the democratic commitment, state power is subject to a system of checks and balances in exercise of state power, which feeds into the concept of democratic accountability. Therefore, accountability plays a fundamental role in the legitimacy of penal systems as an exercise of state power. In the case of prisons these powers and associated authorities are granted to the prison service and in turn prison officers through the criminal justice system. Prison officers are placed in the position of custodians of prisoners and are responsible for ensuring their needs are met within in the prison. Democratic accountability promotes trust which in turn reinforces the legitimacy of the prison officers' authority (Liebling 2004: 242). The willingness to undergo scrutiny through either being the subject of complaints or inspections by an independent authority demonstrates to prisoners that the authorities are open to critique and that these can be legitimate.

Vagg (1994: 1) describes accountability as the idea that:

> certain individuals have a duty to report on, explain, and justify to others actions they have taken or decisions they have made ...this duty is imposed because those individuals have authority, powers and perhaps budgets which are not theirs by right, but which form part of their occupational role.

Public bodies have increasingly become subject to independent monitoring and mechanisms for complaints as there is a duty to the public to ensure they function in accordance with their purpose. Additionally, the power given to those within prison settings, necessities checks and controls over its use.
As highlighted by Fullan (2010: 66):

> Accountability is needed in order to reassure the public that the system is in good hands and progressing well; it is also needed to help implementers know how well they are doing while providing the feedback and help to do even better.

This public insight into life in prison is important, as the prison service acts on behalf of the public and standards within prison should be of interest to those in whose name they act.

English (2013: 53) explores the concept of intelligent accountability developed by Roberts and notes that the

> hallmark of intelligent accountability is its questioning of the notion of absolute truths and established benchmark standards, its focus on actors and their experiences; and its rejection of verifying routine procedures and information derived from a hierarchical organization's instrumental internal data management and reporting system.

Further as discussed by Fullan (2010: 66) '[i]ntelligent accountability in essence involves building cumulative capacity and responsibility that is both internally held and externally reinforced'. This fits in with Braithwaite's (2011: 475) responsive regulation principles which include a willingness on the part of the regulator (or inspector as the case may be) to learn from those in the industry and be flexible in engaging with the different actors. Inspection and other forms of oversight need to take context, both physical and historical, into account in approaching their tasks and this can often only be learnt from practice. In ensuring that oversight fulfils its purpose and goes beyond merely a box-ticking exercise it needs to engage with and impact on the culture in the institution under scrutiny.

Drawn together these different definitions and relationships between accountability, regulation and oversight there are clear differences in their understandings and usage. However, for the purposes of this book some clear principles emerge. Oversight, specifically external oversight, is adopted as the preferred term drawing on Deitch's (2009) work which emphasises the importance of different bodies complementing each other to provide the most comprehensive protection of rights in custody and are reflected in the UN and CoE frameworks on prisons. Flexibility in responding to potential harms is important to ensure different actors can be brought on board and accountability does not become a mere box-ticking exercise. The next section outlines some of the structural components of different interrelated oversight bodies before exploring studies of oversight in practice.

2.2.2 Oversight Structures

Braithwaite and Ayres (1992) discuss the concept of responsive regulation and suggest a generic design for an enforcement pyramid which can then be adapted in various regulatory areas as needs arise (Figure 2.1). They note that different kinds of sanctions may be more appropriate in certain arenas than in others. Responsive regulation considers when it may be necessary to punish and when to persuade those involved in inspections. As noted by Braithwaite (2008: 88), 'regulators should be responsive to the conduct of those they seek to regulate in deciding whether a more or less interventionist response is needed'. Additionally, as highlighted by Simon (2018: 167), an overreliance on the courts to force change in prisons can result in battle mode responding and 'undercut the normative influence that human rights mandates and effective monitoring should promote'.

The main premise of the enforcement pyramid is the minimal sufficient principle whereby 'the more sanctions can be kept in the background, the more regulation can be transacted through moral suasion, the more effective regulation will be' (Ayers and Braithwaite 1992: 19). This principle promotes the internalisation of a desire to comply rather than forcing compliance on a short-term basis. This is in line with the preference for informal resolution amongst officers with prisoners and the reference to informal alternative

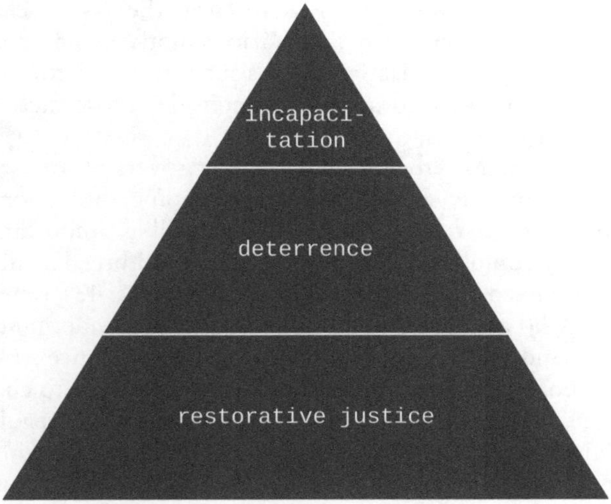

Figure 2.1 Broad principles applicable to each level of sanctions.

resolution where possible in the EPRs.[1] At the base of the pyramid, restorative justice aligns with virtuous actors and those who will be willing to engage on moral grounds and who have a genuine desire to improve. At the next level, deterrence works for rational actors who may weigh the pros and cons of receiving a fine in comparison to seeking to remedy issues identified by the regulator. Finally, at the top level we see incapacitation, as some actors are simply irrational and therefore, we need alternatives open to us to deal with them (Braithwaite 2011: 485).

Ayers and Braithwaite (1992: 36) note that 'defection from cooperation is likely to be a less attractive proposition for business when it faces a regulator with an enforcement pyramid than when confronted with a regulator having only one deterrence option'. This remains true even when they are given the highest power of enforcement. As with the enforcement pyramid, regulators are reluctant to use strong powers of enforcement, especially for what are considered more minor infractions. However, these minor infractions are important to change in order to promote best practice and therefore gradual measures allow for these to be addressed more appropriately. They argue that the more severe the final penalty, the more likely firms will remain in the lower penalty area and forms of compliance such as persuasion will be used to enforce regulations.

However, the minimum sufficient principle presumes the rationality and unitality of actors which in practice can demonstrate a broad degree of variances and motives. Braithwaite and Ayres (1992: 36) call for dynamic institutions for regulatory oversight. These institutions will allow for lower-level responses and persuasion in the case of citizens who are willing to comply, while also ensuring those who seek to cheat the system can be escalated quickly and forced to comply (p. 53). Various motives and interests are inevitably part of any large organisation and as such the regulatory body seeking compliance should be able to adjust and consider those factors in overseeing adherence to regulations.

In considering punishments, they warn against overuse of severe punishments. Inspections are generally part of an ongoing discussion for reform and maintenance of a relationship and goodwill is important to ensure ongoing voluntary compliance. Overregulation could breed a subculture of resistance. As discussed by Ayers and Braithwaite (1992: 43), repeated punishment of citizens who are complying with the law 'will undermine the legitimacy of the state and thereby threaten voluntary compliance'. In the prison context, it is important to bear in mind who has the power to change the area of concern and who will be subject to punishment if the regulator uses their enforcement powers. Certain aspects of concern may be difficult to change within the prison without external support or additional funding. The prison services are only one of the criminal justice agencies in a state and a public body delegated with exercising state power in a particular domain. Continuously criticising and punishing at a prison level without consideration of the external circumstances can be damaging to internal goodwill and cooperation (Braithwaite 2011: 475). While regulatory bodies do often produce reports and such reports can create a public awareness and political pressure to change, this is not a guarantee and the regulatory response should not be overly punitive towards the prison service if they genuinely wish to comply but are operating under constraints.

2.3 Oversight in Practice

While the legal frameworks for oversight bodies are important, Carver and Handley (2016) emphasis the role of implementation in the prevention of torture in places of detention. Practice is at the heart of prevention and the main factor in determining effectiveness. Practice is determined by the law itself, 'as well as considerations such as the political and social environment and the level of knowledge and skills that auctioneers acquired through training' (Carver and Handley 2016: 27). Additionally, oversight bodies rely on interactions as one way of gathering information on the institutions they are inspecting or against which complaints have been made. Goffman (1974: 511) notes that in replying an individual 'will draw on facts as he sees them, the facts stored or hidden in his head. He may elect to reply frankly or fully or to withhold information or to lie knowingly'. In the context of prison oversight, interactions will be shaped by prisoners' expectations of their environment. As discussed further in Chapter 3, the low trust nature of prisons and culture of hypermasculinity may lead to curt interactions and an unwillingness to expose vulnerabilities to strangers.

While limited studies have taken place in prison, studies of oversight in policing have found that those involved in handling complaints were not entirely satisfied with the system in place and that dealing with complaints was viewed as superfluous to the job rather than an inherent responsibility and part of their duty (May et al. 2008; Prenzler et al. 2013). This attitude could have a potentially negative effect on the benefits of the complaints system as the willingness to learn from it is likely to be undermined by those who consider it unnecessary. Furthermore, Galovic et al. (2016) found that complaints were a source of workplace stress and impacted on relationships. Ongoing investigations became the source of rumours as general discussion of complaints was banned and while this is understandable it can have a significant impact on a close relationship-based work environment (Galovic et al. 2016). The complaint system also bred a reluctance towards proactive policing due to a fear of being complained about. This attitude can act as a barrier to motivation and prevent development of innovative methods. Participants also felt that complaining could impact on career progression (Galovic et al. 2016). This is similar to the attitudes found in Calavita and Jenness' (2015) study on complaints in prison where some prisoners wanted to keep their heads down and serve out their sentence rather than engage in matters which could impact on their release date or get them labelled as troublemakers. Additionally, as noted by Prenzler et al. (2013: 155) various factors were cited by complainants as being a cause for their dissatisfaction with the complaint procedure, including a lack of communication and timeliness in dealing with the complaint, as well as a distrust of investigating police, whereby complainants felt that the police sided with colleagues and investigations conducted by the police themselves could not be trusted. The issues identified by studies on complaining in the police environment could act as barriers to seeking to engage with the system.

2.3.1 Oversight and Prisons

Carver and Handley (2016), in their study as to whether torture prevention works, found that international and national monitoring mechanisms do have an effect on reducing torture in places of detention. Additionally, while complaint mechanisms were not associated with a decrease in torture, as victims did not generally turn to complaint mechanisms, linking complaint procedures to the prosecution process was seen as being associated with a decline in incidences of torture (Carver and Handley 2016). However, there are limited studies to date of prisoners' perceptions of accountability in prisons. The studies that have been undertaken focus on bodies involved in dealing with prisoner complaints both internal written procedures and appeals to independent bodies such as Ombudsmen.

Complaint mechanisms form part of the accountability structure as they give a voice to prisoners, as one of the key stakeholders, and call on decision makers to reconsider and justify their decisions. However, as discussed by

Kerr (2014: 49), '[p]risons have a stark advantage at the outset of a complaint due to an element of Foucauldian power/knowledge imbalance that is more extreme than in other contexts of judicial review of government action'. As noted by Calavita and Jenness (2015), this has led to a practice of deference by the courts to the expertise of prison staff in the work of prisons. Studies on complaints in prison have found a number of recurrent themes in how people in prison engage with such bodies. As with the studies of policing complaints discussed above, these include a lack of faith in bodies, as well as the exclusion of specific groups from interacting. For example, in an ethnographic study of a UK prison, Crewe (2009) found a significant lack of trust amongst prisoners concerning VCs – since renamed Independent Monitoring Boards (IMBs). These bodies are mandated to meet prisoners and seek to resolve any issues brought to them informally. Similarly, prisoners in Martin and Godfrey's (1994) study of the England and Wales system felt that the Boards were invisible, irrelevant, aligned with the prison management, and ineffective. A similar lack of faith was found amongst juveniles in a correctional facility in Ireland by the Ombudsman for Children and Young People (2011). Edgar et al. (2003), in a mixed-methods study in England, found that prisoners feel very let down when no action was taken in response to complaints. Both O'Mahony (1997), in his study with prisoners in Mountjoy and Behan (2016), in his study of prisoners' right to vote in Ireland, found a lack of faith in the Irish VCs amongst the participants in their research.

Carver and Handley (2016: 92) note that while the Ombudsman and complaint mechanisms are widely used by the public, they are 'seldom used by members of the public who have suffered serious violations of their fundamental human rights, such as freedom from torture'. Complaints to the Ombudsman tend to be concerned with social and economic rights which can be resolved through administrative action (Carver and Handley 2016). This raises important questions as to who is making use of rights protecting mechanisms and whether these bodies are being used by the most vulnerable in society, including those in custody.

Previous studies have found that age and education are factors of significance when considering usage of the Ombudsman (Buck et al. 2010). Van Roosbroek and van de Walle (2008), in a Belgian study of the general population, found that the majority of those who complained to the Ombudsman were older, middle-class men, with the majority having a Bachelors' or Masters' level of education. This was in line with other research analysing complaints from the Netherlands, the United Kingdom, and Belgium (van Zutphen 2002). Further studies have also found that awareness of the office of Ombudsman is lower amongst groups with lower levels of education (Loois and Sieben 2003).

Studies have also explored the backgrounds of people who engage with accountability bodies. Morgan and Liebling (2007) have found that long-term, high-security prisoners were more likely to bring complaints to the Prisons and Probation Ombudsman, than their short-term, low-security counterparts, suggesting that such prisoners are not deterred by the delays which can occur in this process being one possible reason for the difference. As noted by participants in a qualitative study conducted in Australia, significant delays in responses to complaints can impact upon short-term prisoners, who may view it as unlikely that they will receive a response before the end of their sentence, and therefore feel apathy about making a complaint (Naylor 2014). Dâmboeanu et al. (2021) studied prisoners' experiences of complaining in a Romanian prison and found that developing rights consciousness was a lengthy process, identifying the role of complaints in increasing awareness of rights and developing the language of rights among prisoners.

The potential for reprisals or being labelled as a troublemaker for using the complaint system or helping others use it was evident in research conducted in the United Kingdom with female and juvenile offenders in England and Wales. One young person helped others to fill out their forms and felt that he was labelled 'Mr. Complaints' by staff as a result (Prisons and Probation Ombudsman 2015: 12). Given the dependence inherent in the prison environment and the keep your head down attitude encouraged by the 'prisoner code', drawing attention to yourself in this way could be a deterrent for those seeking to use the system.

2.4 Conclusion

While accountability and regulation are oft discussed terms, a large proportion of the existing work is theoretical or in areas outside of criminal justice, especially prisons. It is important to examine this work in practice in specific contexts to gain a better understanding of the nuances and factors which may hinder or support accountability bodies. It is important to gain the perspective of those who the mechanisms are to be used by and intended to protect. As evident from the literature surveyed above, the prison environment itself and the challenges prisoners face can provide significant hurdles for effective accountability. This study adds to the existing by exploring prisoners' experiences of these bodies in Ireland to understand their experiences and views of the bodies active in Irish prisons. As noted by van Zyl Smit (2010: 510),

> in general more work needs to be done towards understanding how prison regulation interacts with the very different social climates found in prison in different societies in order to understand how effective such regulation may be perceived by prisoners themselves.

This call is reiterated by Seddon (2010: 280) in the context of prison inspections and the need for empirical research to understand the work of inspectors to identify best practices and areas for improvement. To date there has been limited insight into prisoners' experiences of these systems in particular engaging with inspection and monitoring bodies. However, the studies to date suggest that while these bodies play a role in developing rights consciousness, they have not been overly positive in terms of access and adhering to principles of independence.

2.5 Procedural Justice

This section considers procedural justice and the role it plays in determining experiences and perceptions of institutions and accountability bodies. Key principles of procedural justice such as voice, neutrality, respect and trust play an important role in encouraging engagement with accountability bodies, which to date have been predominately explored in the context of complaining. As discussed by Karamalidou (2017: 154), '[in prison, fairness translates into accountability with regard to the way the institution operates and manages its affairs, measured inter alia by its adherence to the rules in force and consistent application'. Prisons are environments which have a series of formal and informal rules and codes and the prison service including frontline staff make decisions every day on the treatment of those in custody. As observed by Ryan (1992: 50–51), 'no number of formal rules will secure justice unless the prison officers deliver it in their daily rounds, in their intimate relationships with those over whom they exercise great and sometimes regrettably, unyielding power'. In this section, the procedures surrounding decision making will be discussed and the impact of this on perceptions of bodies as fair and just. While procedural justice is usually associated with dispute resolution mechanism, procedural justice plays a key role in accountability structures more broadly, such as the complaint mechanism and the body of the Inspectorate. As discussed by Aitken (2021: 13), the legitimacy of independent oversight bodies is derived from the transparent and rules-based procedures they use to reach their decisions. Complaint mechanisms need to be perceived as procedurally fair by prisoners to promote engagement with same and greater acceptance of their outcomes even when they are not necessarily decided in the prisoner's favour. Procedural justice studies have linked procedurally just processes to increased legitimacy and acceptance of outcomes even if not favourable to the applicant (Tyler 2010). On the other hand, Bierie's (2013) study of complaints in prison reveals that in the absence of procedural justice or a perceived legitimate means to resolve complaints, violence can rise in prisons. This section deals with procedural justice in the wider field of criminal justice and then move on to its application specifically in the prison context. While research is limited on procedural justice in the case of accountability mechanisms in prisons, studies of complaint mechanisms in the policing context can provide helpful insight as to the role of procedural justice in prisons. Additionally, studies of disciplinary procedures can add to our understanding of procedural justice in prisons and the impact of the prison environment on perceptions of justice. However, an overt focus on the process itself is also considered and the potential this can have for injustice.

2.5.1 Procedural Justice: The Key to Engagement?

> [P]rison is a unique kind of institution, in which law is a hyper visible presence, formal rules ostensibly regulate every aspect of behaviour of both the captives and the captors, and otherwise disempowered inmates school themselves in the policies that govern them, including how to contest violations of those policies.
>
> (Calavita and Jenness 2015: 48)

The law regulates every aspect of life in the prison context from the enforcement of a legal sanction in bringing a prisoner to the prison through to the rules and regulations which govern life in the institution – thus perceptions of the law play an important role. Prisoners are no longer subconsciously aware of the law which governs individuals in the outside world but have actively experienced the effects of such and consequently are in an environment where the law is relentlessly apparent. Such institutions have been referred to as 'total institutions', where authorities oversee and organise almost every aspect of inhabitants, in this case prisoners, daily activities (Goffman 1961). Drawing on Goffman's work, van Zyl Smit and Snacken (2009: 38) highlight several key characteristics of total institutions, which make them different from normal life. These are that 'inmates have to conduct the different aspects of their lives in the same place and under the same authority, in the company of other people they have not chosen and following a structured scheme of activities'. This, as demonstrated by Calavita and Jenness' (2015: 72) study, can also create an environment where prisoners expect staff to act according to departmental policy as they are expected to 'abide by the myriad of rules and regulations that apply to them'. Prisoners see their compliance with the rules as part of a larger frame of compliance with the outlined rules, staff must lead by example to ensure prisoners' perception of their authority is upheld. This can have a bearing on prisoner's willingness to comply with rules and the staff's authority within the prison.

The role of rules in prison life was also discussed by Mathiesen (1965), in relation to alleviating the effects of imprisonment such as prisonisation, whereby prisoners accept the culture and social life of prison society. Mathiesen developed the concept of *censoriousness*, which recognises the need for prisoners to have a method of censoring staff behaviour to reduce the relationship of reliance inherent in prisoner staff relationships. This gives prisoners a sense of control over their environment and the rules to which they and the staff must adhere. Prisoners can hold staff to account by appealing to established principles and deviance from such. Two principles identified as of particular importance by Mathiesen are those of justice and efficiency. The concept of censoriousness could support the use of a complaint mechanism, as this could serve to provide prisoners with an easily accessible outlet to voice their concerns over staff adherence to the rules. As discussed by

Calavita and Jenness (2015: 72), prisoners in their study emphasised that 'if they [the prisoners] have to abide by the myriad of rules and regulations that apply to them, staff should comply with their departmental policies too'. This reinforces the importance of staff behaviour in maintaining the legitimacy of the prison.

Procedural justice can therefore influence perceptions of justice, legitimacy and fairness in prisons. Events, such as a disregarded concern of a prisoner may have broader repercussions in the context of prison life than outside of it. The specific limits placed on prisoners' freedom and liberty can create an environment where events normally considered minor may play a larger role in the life of the prisoner. Carrabine (2005: 897) described imprisonment as a situation where:

> [P]risoners are confined against their will, with people they would normally not choose to be with, in circumstances they can do little to change and are governed by custodians who police practically every aspect of their daily life.

This can significantly impact on their perceptions of the events around them and the potentially deeper impact of injustice or unfairness. Studies have found a link between perceptions and experiences of procedural justice and prison violence, as well as likelihood of reimprisonment and mental health in custody. Beijersbergen et al. (2016) found that prisoners who felt that they were treated fairly and respectfully by correctional authorities during imprisonment were less likely to be reconvicted up to 18 months after release. Additionally, those who reported higher levels of procedural justice reported fewer mental health problems (Beijersbergen et al. 2014) and were less likely to engage in misconduct (Beijersbergen et al. 2015). Bierie (2013), using data over a seven-year period from 114 federal prisons in the United States found that violence within a prison increases significantly with the volume of late replies to complaints, as well as substantive rejections of complaints.

As can be seen from these studies, procedural justice plays an important role in prisoners' experience of imprisonment and their perceptions of the prison overall. Procedural justice principles are fundamental to a wide range of decision-making processes in prisons, including accountability bodies. The next section outlines the research to date on the key principles of voice, trust, respect and neutrality to provide an overview of how these operate in practice.

2.5.2 Principles of Procedural Justice: Respect, Trust, Voice and Neutrality

Oversight can play an important role in promoting prisoners' perceptions of legitimacy in prisons. Tyler (2010) defines legitimacy as 'the widespread belief among members of the public that the police, the courts, and the legal system are authorities entitled to make decisions and who should be deferred to concerning matters of criminal justice' (Franke et al. 2010: 127). He asserts that 'procedural justice' is key to achieving such legitimacy, which is based on processes rather than outcomes. Tyler considers

> respect to be one of four key factors that can generate procedural justice in prisons, alongside 'voice' (providing opportunities for prisoners to explain their point of view), 'neutrality' (consistent and fair rule application) and 'trust in authority' (prisoners' perceiving that officers are behaving sincerely, based on what is right rather than personal well-being).
>
> (Hulley et al. 2012: 19)

'Respect' can play an important role in a prisoner's life during their sentence. If prisoners feel they are being treated with respect, they may respond better to less favourable decisions and contribute to the overall good order necessary for a prison to run. As highlighted by Hulley et al. (2012: 12) '[o]ften, what prisoners wanted was a response that was fair and unambiguous, one that removed them from a state of uncertainty'. Therefore, it is the way the request or complaint is dealt with which influences how prisoners respond to the decision and feel as though they were treated with respect. This in turn impacts on prisoner morale and possibly their willingness to comply with prison rules in general and not seek to take justice into their own hands. Hulley et al. (2012: 14) found that, generally, staff who provided a justification for their outcome even if unfavourable were more likely to be respected by prisoners. This highlights the important role of providing a clear reasoned outcome for a decision within an effective complaint mechanism. This is further emphasised by the study carried out by Bierie (2013: 15) of the grievance procedure for federal prisoners in the United States where he found that violence within a given prison increased 'significantly with the volume of late replies as well as substantive rejections of complaints'. Through communicating a reasoned response to prisoners, the prison service is showing a sign of respect and having taken their concerns seriously.

However, given the nature of the prison environment and the confines of prison life, the concept of respect is slightly altered from that in the outside world. Respect as understood in the context of prisons was examined by Hulley et al. (2012) and through questioning prisoners on the concept they developed a broader understanding of the term than merely the interpersonal relationship with staff. They established a notion of respect which 'involved a willingness and ability among staff to assist and support prisoners in relation to their daily needs and requests' (p. 11). It is this aspect of respect which is affected by accountability mechanisms and flows from Tyler's understanding of respect in procedural justice. Ensuring prisoners' complaints are dealt with and responded to effectively assures prisoners that their complaints are being heard and recognised. This concept referred to as 'organisational respect' by Hulley et al. (2012), could also play a role in monitoring bodies, where prisoners can feel and see that steps are being taken to ensure they are properly treated and not simply locked up and forgotten about by society.

In the context of respectful treatment, it has been noted that '[r]espect becomes particularly important in prisons when one has little else' (Edgar et al. 2003). This highlights the implications of overlooking basic prisoner needs in prisons, which can feed into existing anger and frustration at the system and a prisoner's own situation. Miller (2001: 530) also discusses the concept of respect in creating a sense of value and worth for an individual. He notes that 'people care whether their treatment (and not simply their outcomes) is fair because fair treatment indicates something crucially important to them – their status within their social group'. The implications of this group value theory could have clear implications for prisoners who may already feel devalued, due to difficult life experiences and the circumstances of incarceration itself. As outlined by Brouwer et al. (2018: 627), Group Value Belonging views the police as representatives of the social majority and as such fair treatment towards citizens signifies their inclusion in the same group. In prisons, officers may be viewed as the embodiment of state power in their custodial position and as such representatives of the majority social group (Sparks and Bottoms 1995: 45). Through treating prisoners in a respectful and fair manner officers can ensure that prisoners still feel attached to that group during the period of their imprisonment and that they are not further excluded from society.

Calavita and Jenness (2015: 121) noted in their study of the Californian grievance mechanism in prisons that the denial of an appeal even for complaints with less dramatic consequences 'inflict a measure of pain on those whose autonomy is severely impaired and whose lives are lived in a mind-numbing routine'. Butler and Drake (2007: 120) highlighted that, 'if respect is shown in a consistent and reliable way it exemplifies the reasonableness of the people demonstrating respectful behaviour, this in turn assists in building a sense of security within the prison'. Providing reasons for a decision can help to soften the blow and show respect for the time the person has put into voicing their complaint.

Tyler (2010: 127) defines voice in the context of procedural justice as providing people with 'an opportunity to tell their side of the story'. Bottoms and Tankebe (2013: 129) consider that 'legitimacy needs to be perceived as always dialogic and relational in character'. In discussing disciplinary processes, Butler and Maruna (2016: 135) found that prisoners distinguished between being 'heard' and being 'listened' to in the processes. There was a feeling amongst prisoners in their study that speaking up for themselves resulted in harsher punishments and this bred a sense of futility amongst participants to engage with the process. Further, their study demonstrated a conflicting view amongst staff and prisoners as to the quality of the procedures. While staff viewed the procedure as uniform, transparent and accountable due to the taping of procedures, prisoners felt intimidated and that the procedure was merely a formalisation of a predetermined verdict. Staff recognised that some prisoners could find the process difficult due to learning disabilities, mental health issues and low literacy. This reinforced the feeling amongst prisoners of an alienating process which was more a formality than a real attempt to discover what had happened and to 'listen' to the prisoner's side of the story. Prisoners in the study referred to it as a 'kangaroo court' where you were also found guilty. This underlines the importance of including the prisoner's voice in a meaningful way for a procedure to be perceived as just.

Another key principle of procedure justice is trust, more specifically trust in authorities. As discussed by Jackson et al. (2010: 5) this means considering the authorities involved in the procedures as sincerely interested in the well-being of prisoners. As highlighted by Hawley (2012), in deciding to place trust in somebody, we make an assessment of their motives, capabilities and expertise based on our knowledge or drawing upon prior experience. Placing trust in someone is an act of social power and can create a relationship of dependency between the two parties. The trusted person has power in how they use that information. Social power has 'dimensions of privilege, security, resources and comfort ... [which] include emotional stability, health, strong relationships and access to reliable information' (Hawley 2017: 70). Furthermore, the withholding of trust should also be regarded as an exercise of social power, one that in the prison context may be an act of resistance when the person has limited agency over other aspects of their life and decision making. Research on prisons, such as that by Liebling (2004), demonstrates that prisons can be low trust environments. Different aspects of prison life can communicate trustworthiness in prison authorities. Calavita and Jenness (2015: 83–84) note that in their research, prisoners swayed between seeing staff as representatives of the organisation as a whole and as individuals. Tait (2008: 48) discusses the role of care and justice in her work on prison officers and care in the prison environment highlighting the link 'between care and fairness'. She emphasises the role of care in considering the application of specific rules and communicating an interest in the well-being of those in custody. Special treatment and allowing for exceptions demonstrates 'to prisoners that their needs and circumstances were understood and important' (Tait 2008: 48). Calls for mercy as argued by Bottoms (1998: 68) are in fact a call to allow for a degree of flexibility and additional consideration in applying what at first sight can appear to be rigid rules. In Tait's (2008: 48) work she emphasises that '[j]ustice as care was largely visible in its absence: being suddenly and unexpectedly treated as a non-person. Thus, justice is constitutive of – not separate from, in opposition to, or larger than – caring staff-prisoner relationships'. Prisoners felt betrayed when officers whom they had built a relationship with wrote them up or treated them in a hostile manner – although good officers could move between their security and caring role, some were unable to manage the change between roles and this was perceived as being more unpredictable and considered worse than simply being a bad officer (Tait 2008: 44). This experience of care therefore communicated a message that officers placed value on the well-being of the prisoners and provided a basis for which prisoners could form an opinion on whether to place trust in them and the prison service more broadly.

Tyler (2010: 130) describes neutrality as 'making decisions based on the consistent application of rules rather than on personal opinions or prejudices of authorities'. As noted above in the policing context, independence was considered a fundamental component in improving satisfaction with complaint procedures (Prenzler et al. 2013). This was also evident in Butler and Maruna's (2016: 135) research of disciplinary procedures in prison where the perceived legitimacy of the procedures was redeemed somewhat in the eyes of prisoners when a member of staff was willing to testify on behalf of a prisoner. For prisoners this represented a break in the ranks and demonstrated that staff were not sticking together at all costs. Prison research to date raises questions about the perceived independence of accountability bodies, as noted above both in the United Kingdom and Ireland, where IMBs and VCs were described by prisoners as being too close to prison authorities with the result that prisoners did not trust them to follow through on promises (Crewe 2009; Behan 2016). As further discussed by Hawley (2012), overpromising can be perceived as untrustworthy.

As noted by Tyler (2010: 129), through incorporating these core principles it is sought to 'minimize the negative implications of incarceration and maximise the likelihood of positive gains'. Jackson et al. (2010: 5) in discussing research surrounding legitimacy in prisons recognises a link between legitimacy and fairness of procedures. Therefore, promoting legitimacy through ensuring procedures are perceived as just has important implications for the overall order in the prison, which will be explored in the next section.

2.5.3 Legitimacy and Procedural Justice

As portrayed by Raz's (2009) breakdown of bodies with effective power, most seek to claim legitimacy in the exercise of their power. Weber (1978) describes this as the cultivation of legitimacy. Sparks (1994: 26), in discussing legitimacy, stated that

> the question of legitimacy focuses our attention on which distributions of power we are prepared to accept and which we come to define as divisive, exploitative or oppressive in the light of norms of justice which we regard as valid and with which we hope to persuade others to agree.

Gidden (1984: 16) developed the concept of the 'dialectic of control' which encompasses a range of possible modes or dimensions of influencing other agents in a social system. Sparks et al. (1996: 84) see this as being of fundamental importance as it can influence a prisoner's choice of action when confronted with an issue. The use of formal channels over an outright show of resistance is 'likely to depend at least in part upon the prospect of obtaining some degree of success via the "legitimate" avenues'. For this reason, 'prisons cannot escape considerations of legitimacy' (Sparks et al. 1996: 84). Legitimacy within the walls of the prison may need to be approached differently due to the nature of imprisonment and the prisoner's view on the legitimacy of their imprisonment itself. If accountability mechanisms are seen as legitimate and a genuine route within prisons from the outset, then engagement with them and acceptance of their outcome is enhanced.

Sparks and Bottoms (1995: 45) sought to identify specific circumstances which can influence a prisoner's likelihood to recognise or withhold recognition of legitimacy of prison staff and regimes. In their analysis of fieldwork conducted in English maximum-security prisons, they noted certain conditions including 'regularity and efficiency of service delivery', 'perceived distributive and procedural fairness of treatment' and 'human qualities in the nature of routines', which played a role in prisoners granting of legitimacy to prison authorities. Franke et al. (2010: 93) noted the specific nature of prison life and the potential impacts on legitimacy given the prolonged close period of contact of prisoners with officers in comparison to other forms of authority.

As highlighted by Beijersbergen et al. (2015: 215), prisoners were less likely to engage in misconduct in prisons if they perceived their treatment as procedurally just. This finding was evident even with regard to age, ethnicity, educational level, self-control and those with prior experience of imprisonment. Furthermore, Beijersbergen et al. (2015: 197) also emphasised the importance in increasing 'knowledge on the mechanisms through which prisoners translate experiences with unjust treatment into subsequent misbehaviour, to explain why procedural justice may have beneficial effects on prisoners' compliance'. This underlines the importance of understanding the penal concept of procedural justice from a prisoner perspective and the factors which prompt prisoners' sense of legitimacy of a particular mechanism and compliance with both its' decisions and the wider prison regime.

Carrabine (2005: 904), however, discusses the role of fatalism in social order in the prison context and, quoting Lockwood, he notes that fatalism is where 'a sufficient condition of order is simply that the structure of power, wealth and status is believed to be inevitable'. This was referred to in Tait's (2008: 182) work on prison officers and care where she found that highly distressed prisoners were less likely to seek help from the prison authorities. This has the effect of undermining the overarching rehabilitative goals of imprisonment as prisoners are simply going through the motions and the order achieved as a result is likely to further compound any existing sense of powerlessness and hopelessness. A grudging acceptance of the prison regime as a given and unalterable reality is unlikely to promote prisoners' belief in is rehabilitative purpose and engagement with various programmes offered for self-improvement or to deal with behaviour connected to offending. Instead, this may create a sense of futility in seeking out rights protection through accountability bodies.

Liebling (2004: 291) defines order in prison as 'the degree to which the prison environment is structured, stable, predictable and acceptable'. The 'acceptable' component focuses on excluding regimes which are highly oppressive, which may lead to outbreaks of riots or other forms of unrest as prisoners' struggle with the nature of the regime. The acceptance of a regime decreases the tension between those keeping the order and those subject to its power, as its purpose and justification is supported to a certain extent, thus decreasing the pressure points and allowing the system to operate. As Beetham (1991) found only rare forms of power survived without the support of legitimacy. Liebling (2011: 486) highlighted the importance of legitimacy in the exercise of power within the prison context for staff prisoner relationships, she noted that with the increase in the perceived legitimacy of power by authorities in prisons '[o]bedience is more likely to be enduring rather than grudging, information will flow more readily between the power-holders and their subjects, trust will develop, and well-being will be higher'.

Oversight is important in ensuring the prison service maintains high standards of service and ease the 'pains of imprisonment'. Bodies which embody key principles of procedural justice and are perceived as legitimate can make important contributions to the prison environment and promote engagement with those in prison. Oversight itself presupposes a degree of acceptance on the part of the prisoner of the legitimacy of their detention and that they are capable of asserting their rights. A tripartite system of monitoring, inspection and complaint mechanism focuses on impartiality in promoting the legitimacy of its aims to prisoners. This may however be 'hindered by the institutional and cultural dynamics of prison' (Behan and Kirkham 2016: 447). Behan and Kirkham (2016: 449) see legitimacy as being dependent 'on whether there is an institutional culture that facilitates prisoners' complaints, embraces the learning from these reports and is willing to use them to improve practice in the future'. Complaints can provide an insight into reoccurring concerns of prisoners and potential areas where services need to be improved. They are a source of information for both front line staff and management of what it is like to live in the prison concerned. Complaint mechanisms in particular are based

> on the assumption that inmates needed an opportunity to be heard, to have a fair process by which decisions were made, have a process by which they could appeal a decision they disagreed with, and a system which treated all inmates equitably (e.g., everyone gets a response, and in a timely manner, no matter their race, age, or any other characteristic).
>
> (Bierie 2013: 17)

These components ring true with the factors considered central to achieving procedural justice.

2.5.4 Procedural Justice and Complaints in Prisons

Procedural justice and complaints have been explored in a range of different settings, including a number of studies on complaints in prison. A fully functional and trusted complaint mechanism could serve a role in assisting prisoners' rehabilitation for returning to the outside world. Ensuring prisoners are treated in accordance with human rights standards while in prison and having an accessible complaints mechanism while in prison could serve to develop a prisoner's respect for the system as a whole and promote their own sense of self-worth as potential good citizens in society. Beijersbergen et al. (2016) found that prisoners who perceived their overall treatment in prison as procedurally just were less likely to be reconvicted in the 18 months following their release. As noted by van Zyl Smit and Dünkel (2001: 827) in their overview of complaints procedures internationally, through recognising the legal position of prisoners in an effective complaint mechanism 'their (the prisoners') self-esteem is developed by the recognition given to their status as full citizens of a democratic society rather than subordinates dependent on the grace and favour of the prison authorities'. This could also serve to defuse elements of the tension created through the power imbalance in the staff/prisoner relationship as '[t]he inability of staff to deal with prisoners' problems could generate considerable frustration, as could staff passing on responsibility to other staff or placating prisoners to make their lives easier' (Hulley et al. 2012: 13). Woolf's report (1991) on Strangeways prison and the riots which took place there highlighted the need for a threshold quality of life in prisons and the need for the prison service to provide 'humane conditions' and 'a reasoned explanation for all decisions adversely affecting individual prisoners, and fair procedures for dealing with prisoners' grievances and alleged indiscipline' in order to maintain a sense of justice within prisons. He considered these requirements 'fundamental to the stability of the [prison] system' (Sparks and Bottoms 1995: 46).

Despite the focus on the importance of consistency in much of the literature on prisons to ensure legitimacy and good order, the extreme consistency in review decisions demonstrated by Calavita and Jenness' (2015: Ch 6) study is concerning. The focus on consistency in decision making revealed in their study resulted in a high rate of refusals of requests and complaints. While other factors may be at play such as unreasonable requests by prisoners, interviews with staff did reveal a concern with showing a united front with their peers (Calavita and Jenness 2015: 136). This was seen as necessary to maintaining good relations amongst colleagues who need to have each other's back if anything goes wrong. Furthermore, it was considered bad practice to allow prisoners to see staff disagree with each other in front of them. This meant that even if staff did disagree with a decision or action of a fellow staff member, they would support them in front of the prisoner and only express their discontent away from the prison landing. Butler and Maruna

(2016) noted this concern amongst the prisoners in their study of disciplinary processes. The hearing was viewed as a mere formality and already decided in favour of the staff. However, prisoners expressed the view that if a member of staff spoke on their behalf, they were more likely to view the procedure as fair.

Jenness and Calavita (2018) in discussing procedural justice in the penal context noted the greater role played by outcomes in prisoners' satisfaction with the grievance procedure. They noted that the large number of rejected complaints was likely to impact on satisfaction amongst prisoners and alter the procedural justice understanding with a greater emphasis on outcomes (p. 61). They also point to the higher stakes involved in filing a complaint in prison and that trivial issues took on additional meaning in the prison context where prisoners had more limited means. For example, a complaint about missing property took on additional significance when consideration is given to the limited number of items allowed by the prison rules and that clothing was a form of self-expression and identity when other facets were stripped away. This is an important finding in considering the relevance of procedural justice in other areas of research and the implications this may have. As highlighted by Boone and Kox (2014: 121), 'fairness requires a complex balance between consistency and flexibility since over-individualized decisions may lead to arbitrariness and consistency does not always result in fairness'. Both fair procedure and an equal outcome are important in the context of prison life in order to bring about fairness. This is linked to the role played by neutrality as:

> neutrality in the context of prison life means that rules should be consistently applied, but that exceptions to the rules are justified as long as such individualized decisions are neutrally applied ... and do not result in unexplainable and/or unequal differences among prisoners.
>
> (Boone and Kox 2014: 132)

The proximity of prisoners to their decision makers and the confined nature of imprisonment are key in understanding this altered perception of fairness. Awareness of previous decisions of staff and misconstrued preferential treatment are on blatant display daily in the prison environment. Bottoms and Tankebe (2013: 123) state that '[p]erceived outcome fairness as well as procedural fairness can be of great importance in the achievement of staff legitimacy in the eyes of prisoners'.[2] This is due to the enclosed context of custodial institutions and the likelihood that outcomes are widely known throughout prisons to a greater extent than in a community or broader societal setting. As noted by Rowe (2012: 110) 'prisons foster cultures of prurient interest in the affairs of others'. Perceived slights or less favourable treatment need to be justified to avoid prisoners viewing decisions as based on personal judgment and thus illegitimate. As outlined by Mathiesen (1965: 88), perceived personal rule with regard to decision making can delegitimise staff powers. The feeling of injustice experienced by prisoners as a result of rejected requests or complaints may be directed at front line officers even if the decision itself is taken by headquarters as frontline staff officers are the messengers who inform the prisoners of the outcome. As highlighted by Calavita and Jenness (2015: 83–84), prisoners swayed between seeing staff as representatives of the organisation as a whole and as individuals.

Miller (2001: 540) notes that the experiences of procedural injustice can have significant behavioural consequences. In particular, he found that those who experienced injustice displayed a 'marked disinclination to comply with authorities' and a 'diminished willingness to pursue group goals and concerns'. These behavioural responses to injustice could, according to Miller (2001), manifest itself through withdrawal reactions such as disengagement and reduced willingness to cooperate but could also manifest itself in attack reactions – for example, formally through lawsuits, or informally through violence. Crewe (2012: 36) has found this as well stating: '[i]n the absence of alternative channels for conflict resolution and rule enforcement, violence becomes the ultimate regulator and is a constant possibility'. Such repercussions could be concerning in the prison environment as the officers are highly dependent on prisoners to comply with orders in the everyday running of the prison. It also demonstrates the important role effective accountability mechanisms can play in the prison environment through providing a legitimate alternative to violent self-seeking justice.

2.6 Conclusion

While procedural justice research has been widely conducted in the field of criminal justice, it has been limited within the prison context and care needs to be taken in drawing firm conclusions from other areas due to the specific features of the prison environment as outlined above. Some research has been done into procedural justice in the case of disciplinary proceedings which is indicative of its potentially positive role in promoting trust and a belief of fairness in the system. However, an important caveat needs to be considered in promoting procedural justice and this is that it should not serve as an end goal in itself. Promoting trust in a system which does not have fairness in its outcomes does not serve to protect the rights of those attempting to assert them. This is a valid concern raised by MacCoun (2005) and is evident in Calavita and Jenness' (2015: 161) study of prisoners in the United States who became focused on the ideal complaint and getting the language right. As stated by MacCoun (2005: 189) 'authorities can use the appearance of fair procedure (dignity, respect, voice) as an inexpensive way to co-opt citizens and distract them from outcomes that by normative criteria might be considered substantively unfair or biased'. This idea of 'false consciousness' needs to be borne in mind so that prisoners' rights are effectively protected and it is not merely an illusion created by having mechanisms in place. The uniqueness of the prison environment and the additional impact of a negative finding on a prisoner's restricted world also needs to be considered as this may impact upon the importance of procedural justice in comparison to other environments. As highlighted by Calavita and Jenness (2018), the prisoners in their study often did not draw a distinction between the procedure itself and the outcome.

This section has provided an overview of the existing literature on oversight and procedural justice, identifying several gaps in the existing literature which this study as a whole will address. Studies of accountability and its operation in the penal context have been limited, in particular experiences of inspection and monitoring, as affirmed by Calavita and Jenness' (2015) research, are a unique environment for engaging with rights protection. In particular a greater understanding is needed of prisoners' awareness of their positions and their expectations of accountability mechanisms, as this can impact upon their satisfaction with outcomes. Additionally, their understanding of the various mechanisms and their distinct roles and how it feels for a prisoner to interact with these bodies. Through exploring these areas, an understanding of what is required of an effective mechanism can be developed for the penal context.

Notes

1 Rule 70.2 Recommendation Rec(2006)2-rev of the Committee of Ministers to member States on the European Prison Rules (Adopted by the Committee of Ministers on 11 January 2006, at the 952nd meeting of the Ministers' Deputies and revised and amended by the Committee of Ministers on 1 July 2020 at the 1380th meeting of the Ministers' Deputies.

2 See further discussion Richard Sparks, Anthony E. Bottoms and Will Hay, *Prisons and the Problem of Order* (Oxford University Press 1996).

References

Dominic Aitken, 'Investigating Prison Suicides: The Politics of Independent Oversight' (2021) *Punishment & Society* http://doi.org/10.1177/1462474521993002.

Ian Ayres and John Braithwaite, *Responsive Regulation: Transcending the Deregulation Debate* (Oxford University Press 1992).

David Beetham, *The Legitimation of Power* (Palgrave Macmillan 1991).

Cormac Behan, *Citizen Convict: Prisoners, Politics and the Vote* (Manchester University Press 2016).

Cormac Behan and Richard Kirkham, 'Monitoring, Inspection and Complaints Adjudication in Prison: The Limits of Prison Accountability Frameworks' (2016) 55(4) *The Howard Journal of Crime and Justice* 432.

Karin A Beijersbergen, Anja JE Dirkzwager, Veroni I Eichelsheim, Peter H van der Laan and Paul Nieuwbeerta, 'Procedural Justice and Prisoners' Mental Health Problems: A Longitudinal Study' (2014) 24 *Criminal Behaviour and Mental Health* 100.

Karin A Beijersbergen, Anja JE Dirkzwager, Veroni I Eichelsheim, Peter H Van der Laan and Paul Nieuwbeerta, 'Procedural Justice, Anger, and Prisoners' Misconduct: A Longitudinal Study' (2015) 42 *Criminal Justice and Behavior* 196.

Karin A Beijersbergen, Anja JE Dirkzwager and Paul Nieuwbeerta, 'Reoffending After Release: Does Procedural Justice During Imprisonment Matter?' (2016) 43(1) *Criminal Justice and Behavior* 63.
David Bierie, 'Procedural Justice and Prison Violence: Examining Complaints Among Federal Inmates (2000–2007)' (2013) 19(1) *Psychology, Public Policy, and Law* 15.
Miranda Boone and Mieke Kox, 'Neutrality as an Element of Perceived Justice in Prison: Consistency Versus Individualization' (2014) 10 *Utrecht Law Review* 118.
Anthony E. Bottoms, 'Five Puzzles in von Hirsch's Theory' in Andrew Ashworth and Martin Wasik (eds) *Fundamentals of Sentencing Theory: Essays in Honour of Andrew von Hirsch* (Oxford University Press 1998).
Anthony E. Bottoms and Justice Tankebe, 'Beyond Procedural Justice: A Dialogic Approach to Legitimacy in Criminal Justice' (2013) 102 (1) *Journal of Criminal Law and Criminology* 119.
John Braithwaite, *Regulatory Capitalism: How It Works, Ideas Making It Work Better* (Edward Elgar 2008).
John Braithwaite, 'The Essence of Responsive Regulation' (2011) 44 *University of British Colombia Law Review* 475.
Jelwer Brouwer, Maartje van der Woude, Joanne van der Leun, 'Border Policing, Procedural Justice and Belonging: The Legitimacy of (Cr)immigration Controls in Border Areas' (2018) 58(3) *The British Journal of Criminology* 624.
Trevor Buck, Richard Kirkham and Brian Thompson, *The Ombudsman Enterprise and Administrative Justice* (Routledge 2010).
Michelle Butler and Deborah H Drake, 'Reconsidering Respect: It's Role in Her Majesty's Service' (2007) 46(2) *Howard Journal of Criminal Justice* 115.
Michelle Butler and Shadd Maruna, 'Rethinking Prison Disciplinary Processes: A Potential Future for Restorative Justice' (2016) 11(1) *Victims & Offenders* 126.
Kitty Calavita and Valerie Jenness, *Appealing to Justice: Prisoner Grievances, Rights and Carceral Logic* (University of California Press 2015).
Kitty Calavita and Valerie Jenness, 'Race, Grievance Systems and Prisoners Perceptions of Justice in Three California Prisons' (2018) 15(1) *Du Bois Review: Social Science Research on Race* 153.
Eamonn Carrabine, 'Prison Riots, Social Order and the Problem of Legitimacy' (2005) 45(6) *British Journal of Criminology* 896.
Richard Carver and Lisa Handley, *Does Torture Prevention Work?* (Oxford University Press 2016).
Ben Crewe, *The Prisoner Society: Power, Adaptation and Social Life in an English Prison* (Oxford University Press 2009).
Ben Crewe, 'The Prisoner Culture and the Prisoner Society' in Ben Crewe and Jamie Bennett (eds) *The Prisoner* (Routledge 2012).
Cristina Dâmboeanu, Valentina Pricopie and Alina Thiemann, 'The Path to Human Rights in Romania: Emergent Voice(s) of Legal Mobilization in Prisons' (2021) 18(1) *European Journal of Criminology* 120.
Michele Deitch, 'Distinguishing the Various Functions of Effective Prison Oversight' (2009) 30 *Pace Law Review* 1438.
Michele Deitch, 'But Who Oversees the Overseers?: The Status of Prison and Jail Oversight in the United States' (2020) 47(2) *American Journal of Criminal Law* 207–273.
Kimmett Edgar, Ian O'Donnell and Carol Martin, *Prison Violence: The Dynamics of Conflict, Fear and Power* (Willan 2003).

Linda English, 'The Impact of an Independent Inspectorate on Penal Governance, Performance and Accountability: Pressure Points and Conflict "in the Pursuit of an Ideal of Perfection"' (2013) 24 (7–8) *Critical Perspectives on Accounting* 532.
Derrick Franke, David Biere and Doris MacKenzie, 'Legitimacy in Corrections: A Randomized Experiment Comparing a Boot Camp With a Prison' (2010) 9(1) *Criminology and Public Policy* 89.
Michael Fullan, *All Systems Go: The Change Imperative for Whole System Reform* (Corwin Press 2010).
Sally Galovic, Philip Birch, Margaret H Vickers and Micheal Kennedy, 'Procedural Justice and Frontline Policing: The Effects of the Police Complaints System' (2016) 18 *Journal of Forensic Practice* 170.
Anthony Giddens, *The Constitution of Society: Outline of the Theory of Structuration* (University of California Press 1984).
Erving Goffman, *On Asylums: Essays on the Social Science of Mental Patients and Other Inmates* (Doubleday 1961).
Erving Goffman, *Frame Analysis: An Essay on the Organization of Experience* (Harvard University Press 1974).
Katerine Hawley, *Trust: A Very Short Introduction* (Oxford University Press 2012).
Katherine Hawley, 'Trust, Distrust and Epistemic Injustice' in IJ Kidd, J Medina and G Pohlhaus (eds) *The Routledge Handbook of Epistemic Injustice* (Routledge 2012).
Christopher Hood, Oliver James, George Jones, Colin Scott and Tony Travers, *Regulation Inside Government: Waste Watchers, Quality Police, and Sleaze-Busters* (Oxford University Press 1999).
Susie Hulley, Alison Liebling and Ben Crewe, 'Respect in Prisons: Prisoners' Experiences of Respect in Public and Private Sector Prisons' (2012) 12 *Criminology and Criminal Justice* 3.
Jonathon Jackson, Tom Tyler, Ben Bradford, Dominic Taylor and Mike Shiner, 'Legitimacy and Procedural Justice in Prisons' (2010) 191 *Prison Service Journal* 4.
Valerie Jenness and Kitty Calavita, '"It Depends on the Outcome": Prisoners, Grievances, and Perceptions of Justice' (2018) 52(1) *Law & Society Review* 41.
Anastasia Karamalidou, *Embedding Human Rights in Prison: English and Dutch Perspectives* (Palgrave Macmillan UK 2017).
Lisa Kerr, 'Contesting Expertise in Prison Law' (2014) 60 *McGill Law Journal* 49.
Alison Liebling assisted by Helen Arnold, *Prisons and Their Moral Performance: A Study of Values, Quality, and Prison Life* (Oxford University Press 2004).
Alison Liebling, 'Distinctions and Distinctiveness in the Work of Prison Officers; Legitimacy and Authority Revisited' (2011) 8(6) *European Journal of Criminology* 484.
Sandra Loois and M Sieben, 'De onbekendheid van de Nationale ombudsman: Communicatie over een andere boeg' (2003) 18(3) *Communication Cases* 7.
Robert J MacCoun, 'Voice, Control and Belonging: The Double-Edged Sword of Procedural Fairness' (2005) 1 *Annual Review of Law and Social Science* 171.
Carol Martin and David Godfrey, 'Prisoners Views of Boards of Visitors: A Question of Credibility' (1994) 34(3) *The British Journal of Criminology* 358.
Thomas Mathiesen, *The Defences of the Weak: A Sociological Study of a Norwegian Correctional Institution* (Tavistock 1965).
Tiggey May, Hamish Warburton, and Ian Hearnden, *Appellants', Complainants' and Police Officers' Satisfaction With the Independent Police Complaints Commission* (Institute for Criminal Policy Research 2008).

Dale T Miller, 'Disrespect and the Experience of Injustice' (2001) 52 (1) *Annual Review of Psychology* 527.
Rod Morgan and Alison Liebling, 'Imprisonment: An Expanding Scene' in Rod Morgan, Mike Maguire, and Robert Reiner (eds) *The Oxford Handbook of Criminology* (Oxford University Press 2007).
Bronwyn Naylor, 'Human Rights and Respect in Prisons: The Prisoners' Perspective' (2014) 31 *Law Context: A Socio-Legal Journal* 84.
Paul O'Mahony, *Mountjoy Prisoners: A Sociological and Criminological Profile* (Citeseer 1997).
Ombudsman for Children and Young People, *Young People in St. Patrick's Institution: A Report by the Ombudsman for Children's Office* (Ombudsman for Children's Office 2011).
Anne Owers, 'Prison Inspection and the Protection of Prisoners' Rights' (2010) 30 *Pace Law Review* 1535.
Tim Prenzler, Mateja Mihinjac and Louise E. Porter, 'Reconciling Stakeholder Interests in Police Complaints and Discipline Systems' (2013) 14(2) *Police Practice and Research* 155.
Prisons and Probation Ombudsman, *Learning From PPO Investigations: Why Do Women and Young People in Custody Not Make Formal Complaints*? (Prisons and Probation Ombudsman 2015). Available at: www.ppo.gov.uk/document/learning-lessons-reports/.
Joseph Raz, *Between Authority and Interpretation: On the Theory of Law and Practical Reason* (Oxford University Press 2009).
Abigail Rowe, 'Women Prisoners' in Ben Crewe and Jamie Bennett (eds) *The Prisoner* (Routledge 2012).
Mick Ryan, 'The Woolf Report: On the Treadmill of Penal Reform?' (1992) 62(1) *Political Quarterly* 50.
Colin Scott, 'Accountability in the Regulatory State' (2000) 27(1) *Journal of Law and Society* 38.
Toby Seddon, 'Rethinking Prison Inspection: Regulating Institutions of Confinement' in Hannah Quick, Toby Seddon and Graham Smith (eds) *Regulation and Criminal Justice: Developing a New Framework for Research and Policy Development* (Cambridge University Press 2010).
Jonathon Simon, 'Penal Monitoring in the United States: Lessons From the American Experience and Prospects for Change' (2018) 70(1) *Crime, Law and Social Change* 161.
Richard Sparks, 'Can Prisons be Legitimate? Penal Politics, Privatization, and the Timeliness of an Old Idea' (1994) Special Issue 34 *British Journal of Criminology* 14.
Richard Sparks and Anthony E Bottoms, 'Legitimacy and Order in Prisons' (1995) 46(1) *British Journal of Sociology* 45–62.
Richard Sparks, Anthony E Bottoms and Will Hay, *Prisons and the Problem of Order* (Oxford University Press 1996).
Stan Stojkovic, 'Prison Oversight and Prison Leadership' (2010) 30 *Pace Law Review* 1476.
Sarah Tait, 'Prison Officer Care for Prisoners in One Men's and One Women's Prison' (DPhil thesis, University of Cambridge 2008).
Tom R. Tyler, 'Legitimacy in Corrections' (2010) 9(1) *Criminology & Public Policy* 127.

Jon Vagg, *Prison Systems: A Comparative Study of Accountability in England, France, Germany, and the Netherlands* (Clarendon Press 1994).
Steven van Roosbroek and Steven Van de Walle, 'The Relationship Between Ombudsman, Government, and Citizens: A Survey Analysis' (2008) 24(3) *Negotiation Journal*, 287.
Nan van Zutphen, 'Profiel van de verzoekers van de ombudsdiensten 1975–2000: Fen literatuurstudie' in Robert Andersen and Bernard Hubeau (eds) *De ombudsman in Belgie na een decennium: Een zoektocht naar de meerwaarde van de ombudsfunctie in de samenleving* (Die Keure 2002).
Dirk van Zyl Smit and Frieder Dünkel (eds) *Imprisonment Today and Tomorrow: International Perspectives on Prisoners' Rights and Prison Conditions* (2nd edn, Kluwer Law International 2001).
Dirk van Zyl Smit and Sonja Snacken, *Principles of European Prison Law and Policy: Penology and Human Rights* (Oxford University Press 2009).
Dirk van Zyl Smit, 'Regulation of Prison Conditions' (2010) 39 *Crime and Justice: A Review of Research* 503.
Max Weber, *Economy and Society: An Outline of Interpretive Sociology* (Vol. 1, University of California Press 1978).
Harry Woolf, *The Woolf Report: A Summary of the Main Findings and Recommendations of the Inquiry Into Prison Disturbances* (Prison Reform Trust 1991).

3 Legal and Policy Review at International and Domestic Level

3.1 Introduction

Prisoner rights and oversight mechanism are subject to legal frameworks at both an international and domestic level. This chapter considers these with a focus on complaints mechanisms, inspection and monitoring and the role of the courts in protecting prisoners' rights while in custody. It provides a brief overview of the international discussion focusing on the United Nations Mandela Rules, otherwise known as the United Nations Standard Minimum Rules for the Treatment of Prisoners, and the Subcommittee for the Prevention of Torture established under the UN Optional Protocol to the Convention against Torture (OPCAT). Following this, the operation of a regional body will be explored, in this case the European approach. The Council of Europe (CoE) has developed extensive rules on prisons, similar to the UN approach, and has also created a regional monitoring body, the European Committee for the Prevention of Torture and Inhuman or Degrading Treatment or Punishment (CPT). Finally, Ireland will be considered at a regional level as it is subject to visits from the CPT and discussions are underway towards the creation of a National Prevention Mechanism (NPM) under the OPCAT. The development of the current position in Ireland will be discussed through a review of the domestic legislation predominately found in the Prison Act 2007 and the accompanying statutory instruments, the Prison Rules 2007, the prison cases in this jurisdiction and the reforms which the various accountability bodies have undergone.

3.2 International Framework

The international community has taken numerous steps over the years, especially in the aftermath of World War II, to protect detained persons. Early developments focused on the rights of those detained in times of conflict, particularly prisoners of war (Evans and Morgan 2001; Rodley and Pollard 2009). Under Article 13 and Article 14 of the Third Geneva Convention states are required to adhere to principles of humane treatment and respect

DOI: 10.4324/9781003477471-3

for the detained person, respectively. These concepts as outlined in Chapter 4 on penal culture still play an important role in detention today.

Article 78 GC III is concerned with the right of prisoners of war to make complaints. This provision highlights core principles which are reiterated in later conventions and rules concerned with the treatment of prisoners, such as the express reference to the fact that even if complaints are unfounded, the prisoner should not be subject to consequences, a right of appeal to an independent body and that complaints are dealt with without delay.[1] While the type of inspection, which will be outlined below, does not appear in the Convention, medical inspections are provided for under Article 9 to monitor the condition of the prisoners on a monthly basis. The aforementioned Article 78 also provides for report writing by prisoner representatives on the general condition of the detention site.

Twenty-six years after the adoption of the Geneva Conventions, the United Nations Standard Minimum Rules for the Treatment of Prisoners were adopted by the First United Nations Congress on the Prevention of Crime and the Treatment of Offenders in 1955 and subsequently approved by the Economic and Social Council in 1957.[2] These Rules are concerned with the treatment of detained persons outside of conflict zones. However, while the Geneva Conventions are binding documents on State Parties, the UN Rules are non-binding guidelines (van Zyl Smit and Snacken 2009). Regional guidelines have also since been adopted by regional human rights bodies, most notably the EPRs of the CoE first adopted in 1973. Both the United Nations Standard Minimum Rules for the Treatment of Prisoners (otherwise known as the Mandela Rules) and the EPRs provide a strong emphasis on human rights in their guidelines for prison oversight mechanisms. This perspective is evident from Rule 1 of the Basic Principles which, in both cases, notes the requirement to treat prisoners 'with respect for their human rights'[3] and 'respect for their inherent dignity and value as human beings'.[4] This sets the overarching tone for the guidelines that follow. These guidelines cover a broad range of issues relevant to the prison environment and emphasise the importance of inspection and complaints. It is these provisions which will be considered below in this section.

3.2.1 'Mandela' Rules

The United Nations Standard Minimum Rules for the Treatment of Prisoners were first adopted in 1955 and renamed the 'Mandela Rules' when revised in 2015. While not legally binding, they provide extensive guidance to states on the rights of prisoners and best practice in a broad range of areas (van Zyl Smit 2023). They are expressly referred to in the General Comment by the Human Rights Committee on Article 10 of the ICCPR.[5] This comment discusses the reporting mechanism under the Covenant and indicates that concrete measures taken to implement the rules should be included in country reports. Article 10 of the ICCPR is concerned with humanity and respect for dignity in the prison environment and notes that compliance with the Rules would assist states in maintaining a humane environment (Mackay 2017: 372). From their original adoption in 1955 until their most recent revision in 2015, there has been a significant increase in the standards expected of states and the provisions relating to accountability have been expanded on. However, it is important to draw attention to the proviso in Preliminary Observation 2 of the Rules which states that the 'great variety of legal, social, economic and geographical conditions in the world [and therefore] not all of the rules are capable of application in all places and at all times'. While the spirit of the Rules should be maintained at all times, this proviso detracts from the Rules and the need to maintain the minimum standards.

3.2.1.1 Inspection and Monitoring

The Rules contain specific provisions on inspection and monitoring, as well as complaints. Regarding inspection, a twofold system is provided for under Rule 83 of the Mandela Rules 2015, consisting of an internal and an external component. The objectives of both are to 'ensure that prisons are managed in accordance with existing laws, regulations, policies and procedures, with a view to bringing about the objectives of penal and corrections services and that the rights of prisoners are protected'.[6] This is the inspection mandate with which the definition of oversight for the purposes of this book is concerned, one which focuses on the monitoring of prisoners' rights while in prison. The current Rule 83 is much more detailed than the original provision adopted in 1955 and maintained in the subsequent revisions. Rule 55 of the original Rules stated that

> [t]here shall be a regular inspection of penal institutions and services by qualified and experienced inspectors appointed by a competent authority. Their task shall be in particular to ensure that these institutions are administered in accordance with existing laws and regulations and with a view to bringing about the objectives of penal and correctional services.[7]

The 2015 revision shows a strengthening of inspection standards and recognition of the role of internal and external inspectors.[8] An additional reference to prisoners' rights demonstrates a broader consensus amongst member states that rights should be guaranteed even during imprisonment. As will be discussed below, the concept of prisoners' rights has been developed through case law from a theory of inherent limitation of rights to a focus on the principle of normalisation and rights only being restricted when necessary. These rules reflect that evolution through their initial development and subsequent revisions.

Rule 82.1 sets out the powers which inspectors should have for carrying out their inspections. Rule 84.2 outlines the various authorities, composition and activities with which the external inspection body should be vested. These are similar to those given to the Subcommittee and NPM under the OPCAT, which will be discussed below, and demonstrates the broad acceptance of these criteria in the international community.[9] The UN have also complied guidelines for assessing compliance with the Rules in the case of internal inspections and note that some powers such as interviewing prisoners may raise ethical dilemmas for internal inspection bodies.[10] In their inspection guidelines the UN Office on Drugs and Crime (UNODC) notes that internal and external inspections should serve to complement one another with the focus of internal inspections on daily functioning and management and 'fostering sound, fair and transparent prison management from within the administration'.[11] Finally, Rule 85 places an obligation on inspection bodies to provide written reports on their work with due consideration given to making such reports public. Rule 85.2 also indicates that prison authorities or other authorities should 'indicate, within a reasonable time, whether they will implement the recommendations from the external inspection'. In general inspection bodies do not have enforcement powers but their recommendations should be taken into consideration by the relevant authorities and provide a flexible dialogue for reform.

3.2.1.2 Complaints under the 'Mandela' Rules

Guidelines in relation to complaint mechanisms are contained in Rule 56 which places a clear obligation on States to provide such mechanisms and furthermore for the possibility of an appeal to 'a judicial or other authority' under Rule 57.1. The 1988 version of the Rules defines such a body as being 'an authority under the law whose status and tenure should afford the strongest possible guarantees of competence, impartiality and independence'. This was revised in the 2015 rules to include specific reference to the authority being 'vested with reviewing or remedial powers'.[12] Due to the nature of the prison environment and prisoner demographics, accessing a written form may at times be challenging due to concerns about literacy and the ability to express themselves, as well as the culture of the prison environment stigmatising complaining. Rule 55.1 refers to the provision of information on the prison rules, including the complaint system, orally; however, no express reference is made to submitting complaints orally or providing assistance in completing the complaint form.

Special mention is made of complaints concerning torture or other cruel, inhuman or degrading treatment or punishment under Rule 57.3 with reference to the need for a 'prompt and impartial investigation conducted by an independent national authority'. As with the provisions for inspections, those concerning complaints were significantly expanded on in the 2015 revisions and the previous Rule 36.4 regarding frivolous or groundless complaints was removed.[13] This is an important step in removing additional barriers from accessing the complaint system while in prison.

3.2.1.3 Additional Provisions

In addition to the specific Rules on inspection and complaints, several rules need to be considered, which can contribute to the effectiveness of the mechanisms. Rule 54 (b) Mandela Rules indicates that prisoners will be provided with written information on the procedures for making requests or complaints in the prison. Rule 55 includes reference to the information being provided in a language which can be understood by the prisoner and the need for additional supports in the form of interpreters or orally providing the information to address illiteracy issues or any alternative method necessary to convey the information in the case of prisoners' with a sensory disability.[14] This highlights the growing recognition of prisoners' needs and the imprisonment of foreign nationals in prisons in other countries (Ugelvik 2017), which is in line with the aim of the revision of the Mandela Rules to make them relevant for the 21st century.

These Rules provide a comprehensive overview of the general requirements of inspection and complaints body for member states to the UN. In light of the adoption of these rules, the CoE drafted the EPRs which reflect the main principles reiterated in the Mandela Rules and previous versions of the UN Rules of Minimum Treatment (Anagnostou and Skleparis 2017: 42).

3.2.2 European Prison Rules

The EPRs were adopted by the CoE as a non-binding document to provide guidance to its member states on best practice in the running of their prisons. They were first adopted in 1973 and have since been revised three times, most recently in 2020. The Rules are accompanied by extensive commentary on their interpretation. While the Rules themselves are soft law, they are mutually reinforced by the European Court of Human Rights (ECtHR) and the CPT and have been used by the Court in its judgements and the reports of the CPT (van Zyl Smit and Snacken 2009). They have also to be used in interpreting Article 10 of the ICCPR and the UN Convention against Torture (Easton 2013: 477). As a result of this, some of the Rules have been elevated beyond soft law (van Zyl Smit and Snacken 2009). They also have significant political support within the CoE which can be seen in the 2006 Resolution adopting revisions of the Rules.[15] Additionally, a number of states have made express reference to the EPRs in the drafting of their prison legislation, for example, in France and Germany (van Zyl Smit and Snacken 2009). A Swiss Court found that while the EPRs (or the European Standard Minimum Rules of Treatment as they were referred to at the time of the judgement) are not legally binding under international law, they did contain foundations of common legal convictions of member states of the CoE and therefore the court would not easily depart from them (van Zyl Smit and Snacken 2009: 20). In the Irish context, the government has noted that the State had subscribed to the EPRs and they are amongst the international human rights documents which 'place solemn obligations on the Government not just to prevent abuse but to take positive steps to provide humane and caring treatment and to prevent physical and mental deterioration' (The Irish Commission for Justice and Peace 1994: 5). However, they are not expressly referred to in the Irish Prison Rules or Prison Act.

3.2.2.1 Inspection and Monitoring

Reference to the role of inspection in prisons can be found in the initial Basic Principles of the EPRs under Rule 9. This provision refers to both regular internal inspection and external monitoring. The prominent position of this provision clearly indicates the view of the necessity of such mechanisms within European States, as emphasised in the commentary on the Rules '[t]he first nine rules set out the fundamental principles that are to guide the interpretation and implementation of the rules as a whole'.[16] Although not referred to in the original Rules, inspection has appeared in the basic principles section of the Rules since 1987.

The specific characteristics of inspection are expanded on in Rule 92 and 93 of the 2006 Rules. As with the Mandela Rules, the EPRs promote a two-tier approach to inspection. However, although inspections have been a component of the EPRs since their inception in 1973 the Rules are not as expansive as the Mandela Rules in detailing the powers which inspectors should have. The two-tier system is a welcome development in the latest revision of the Rules; however, the Rules only provide general guidance on the roles of these two inspection bodies and not the powers or methods to carry out inspections. Rule 92 indicates that 'Governmental Inspections' should be assessing 'whether [the prisons] are administrated in accordance with the requirements of national and international law, and the provisions of these rules', while Rule 93.1 indicates that the role of independent monitors is to assess '[t]he conditions of detention and the treatment of prisoners'. Rule 93.2 also refers to cooperation with international agencies, which in the case of CoE States is primarily concerned with the CPT, the specific role of which will be discussed below. As with the Mandela Rules, the EPRs encourage making findings of inspections public.[17]

The commentary on the Rules provides some further guidance as to the operation of inspectors and the criteria to ensure they can fulfil their objective. It is necessary for monitoring bodies to be supported by qualified staff and have access to independent experts. Further, the commentary refers to making reports public and that reports may contain proposals and observations concerning existing or draft legislation. It reiterates the need for cooperation with international bodies and the complementary role of these bodies through forwarding of reports and responses to bodies such as the CPT. The commentary recognises the important complementary role and the growing demands on limited CPT resources. While the commentary supports monitoring through boards of visitors, such as the Visiting Committees

(VCs) in Ireland, which consist of interested laypeople, these boards are not considered necessary especially in smaller jurisdictions. The commentary highlights the variety of approaches to monitoring taken by member states and that a broad variety of approaches can fulfil the basic criteria referred to in the Rules.[18]

3.2.2.2 Complaints

The EPRs provide for a right to complaint and request procedures under Rule 70.1, and this includes, as outlined in Rule 30.1, a requirement that prisoners be given the necessary information to enable them to make complaints and requests in respect of all matters that affect them. The EPRs, however, do not specify how or by whom this process should be conducted (van Zyl Smit and Snacken 2009: 309). This grants member states a broad degree of discretion in their model of complaints procedure. A reference to the possibility of mediation was added in the 2006 version of the Rules, alongside the possibility to seek legal advice if necessary. This was amended to 'an informal alternative method' of resolving the complaint in the 2020 revision to the rules. This recognises the important role of relationships in prisons and the harm formal mechanisms can potentially cause. Informal resolution of complaints can prevent the hostile dynamic which can develop when parties enter a dispute. However, the rules note the limitations of such approaches especially in the case of complaints made regarding ill-treatment or other serious human rights violations, in which case Rule 70.3 of the 2020 revisions states that 'informal methods shall not be considered'. This informal approach is not contained in the Mandela Rules outlined above and show a divergence in the international and European approaches to complaints in prison.

While previous versions of the Rules referred to speaking to the 'inspector or to any other duly constituted authority'[19] in relation to complaints, this reference was removed in the 2006 version of the Rules. This suggests a separation of the inspection and complaints appeals process. As has been outlined by Buck et al. (2010: 149), a role in both the complaint process and inspection can potentially impact on trust afforded to the relevant authorities and place an inspection body in an awkward position if a complaint arises in relation to an issue subject to inspection. However, as noted by Linos and Pegram (2017: 628) 'complaint-handling powers allow [National Human Rights Institutions] to build community support based on their public profile as accessible and accountable institutions, and thus resist budget cuts and other challenges'. Both the CPT and SPT recommend maintaining a separation between bodies which handle complaints and those that carry out inspections (SPT 2016; CPT 2018).

As with the Mandela Rules, reference to frivolous and groundless complaints, previously referred to in Rule 36.4 of the 1973 version of the Rules was removed in 1987. The 2006 version of the EPRs added an explicit reference to prisoners not receiving punishment for bringing a complaint under Rule 70.4 and was retained in the 2020 version of the rules under Rule 70.9. This demonstrates a growing recognition of the unequal power dynamics in the prison environment and the potential for abuse which may act as a barrier to bringing complaints.

3.2.2.3 Additional Rules Related to Inspection and Complaints

As with the Mandela Rules, it is also important to consider the Rules in relation to the obligation on prison authorities to provide information on the prisoners' rights and duties and regulations governing prison life. This duty is contained in the Basic Principles under Rule 15.2 and expanded on in Rule 30.1. Information should be provided as often as necessary, highlighting the concerns of potential shock upon entry and information retention on arrival, as well as in writing and orally in a language understood by the prisoner. In addition, prisoners should be allowed to keep a written version of such information in their possession as contained in Rule 30.2.

Furthermore, Rule 50 provides that '[s]ubject to the needs of good order, safety and security, prisoners shall be allowed to discuss matters relating to the general conditions of imprisonment and shall be encouraged to communicate with the prison authorities about these matters'. This provision is discussed by the CPT in their 2017 report on the Netherlands on their May 2016 under the section on complaints procedure and expression of prisoners' views. The grouping of these topics by the CPT highlights the important role prisoners play in providing information on the conditions of detention and that having an open dialogue in prisons supports a healthy environment for both staff and prisoners.

3.2.3 European Committee for the Prevention of Torture and Inhuman or Degrading Treatment or Punishment

The European Committee for the Prevention of Torture and Inhuman or Degrading Treatment or Punishment (CPT) is a body established under the European Convention for the Prevention of Torture and Inhuman or Degrading Treatment or Punishment.[20] The Convention came into force in 1989 and it builds on Article 3 of the ECHR, which contains an absolute prohibition on torture or to inhuman or degrading treatment or punishment. This body consists of international experts and the Convention has been ratified by all 47 CoE countries. The CPT has a mandate to carry out inspections of all places of detention in order to assess how people are deprived of their liberty with a view to strengthening the protection where necessary.[21] It is a non-judicial body with a preventative focus on torture, inhuman and degrading treatment or punishment as its mandate.

The Convention contains extensive guidance on the powers of the Committee and for the composition of each Committee. The Committee consists of one member from each member state.[22] The Convention requires that members of the Committee be of 'high moral character' and have 'competence in the field of human rights or ... professional experience in the areas covered by the Convention'.[23] The Convention does not indicate specifically the composition from each field in visiting delegations but suggests that lawyers, prison administrators and those from medical fields should be included in delegations. Article 4.4 indicates that members of the Committee are elected to serve in their independent and impartial capacity and not as representatives of their states. As such any conflict of interest should be declared prior to election to the Committee and members do not take part in delegations visiting their home country.

State permission is required to publish findings of the CPT; however, it has become practice to allow publication and some states have provided prior consent for the publication of all inspection reports.[24] After the inspection, the State is provided with a detailed report on the inspection findings, comments, recommendations and requests for information. The State is then requested to provide a detailed Government response to the report and through this builds a dialogue on the potential adoption of recommendations contained in the report. In the case of a state failing to cooperate or refusing to improve the situation of detained persons, the CPT can issue a public statement after the State has had an opportunity to consider the views of the CPT. This requires a two-thirds majority of member states to agree to issuing a statement.[25] In addition to country-specific reports, the Committee also provides the Council of Ministers with an annual report on its activities for the previous year.[26] The 2017 Annual Report of the CPT highlights the exceptional nature of the public statement power (CPT 2018). In their report of that year, the CPT made a public statement regarding the situation in Belgium and the ongoing issue of strikes by prison staff. This was an issue which had been ongoing for 12 years in Belgium and the statement outlines the various attempts previously taken by the CPT to assist Belgium in resolving this issue. The CPT had given recommendations in a series of reports and also met with the relevant authorities to find a solution. The final statement published is a measured last resort to improve the situation of those imprisoned in Belgium, who have been seriously impacted by the strikes.

The Committee publishes a list of countries they will visit each year and periodic inspections occur in each Member State once every four years. Ad hoc visits can take place if the circumstances require additional visits from the Committee. The State is notified of the visit but once notified the CPT delegation should be allowed to visit any place of detention at any time without further notice.

Article 8 outlines the information and access which should be provided to the Committee, which includes interviewing detained persons in confidence and the provision of any information the Committee feels is necessary to carry out its tasks. Article 9 provides for limited circumstances where the State can seek to object to a visit at specific times. Article 9 refers to representations being made on 'grounds of national defence, public safety, serious disorder in places where persons are deprived of their liberty, the medical condition of a person or that an urgent interrogation relating to a serious crime is in progress'. States may also in exceptional circumstances refuse access to Committee members to their jurisdiction.

Article 17 notes that the standards expected by the Committee are minimum standards for the prevention of the prohibited treatment and punishment and higher standards of protection will not be objected to by the Committee. This is in line with the principles outlined in the Mandela Rules and EPRs, which are minimum standards and as such higher principles should be striven to be achieved in states where this can be facilitated. The CPT also respects the work of the ICRC as they do not visit places which the Committee under that Convention effectively visit regularly.[27] While the ICRC is predominately focused on conditions of detention in times of armed conflict or unrest they have, as will be expanded on below, at times been nominated to carry out inspections by the international courts and tribunals.

The CPT refers to the importance of an effective complaints mechanism in numerous reports and outlines the criteria for an effective mechanism in its standards. As stated in their 2004 General Report 'assessing the effectiveness of action taken when ill-treatment has occurred constitutes an integral part of the Committee's preventive mandate, given the implications that such action has for future conduct'.[28] These standards include the possibility of complaining both within and outside the prison service, including confidential access to an appropriate authority.[29] The authority should be able to hear from prisoners and inspect the premises, with the possibility of taking action if necessary.[30] These criteria have been reiterated in country reports and they have examined the availability of such remedies in various country reports. The CPT also identifies good practices in their reports and in the case of complaints mechanisms has highlighted the Netherlands' approach as being particularly good. This has been reiterated in numerous country reports including the most recent in 2017.[31] In particular, the CPT stated that the approach could be an example for other countries, showing its high regard for the process. However, following the CPTs visit to the Netherlands in 2022, concerns were raised regarding the resourcing of complaints committees (CPT 2023). As will be explored further in later chapters, this highlights the need for continued oversight and the complementary nature of different forms of oversight, as systems can change over time, impacting access and effectiveness.

3.2.4 The Convention against Torture and Other Cruel, Inhuman or Degrading Treatment or Punishment and the Optional Protocol

The Optional Protocol to the Prevention against Torture and Other Cruel, Inhuman or Degrading Treatment or Punishment (CAT) provides another layer of protection to those in prison (Daems and Robert 2017: 3). Although proposals had been put forward at the UN for a visiting body prior to the establishing of the CPT, the practice of the CPT provided important groundwork when the UN revisited the drafting of the optional protocol (Murray et al. 2011: 10–11). The Optional Protocol for the Prevention against Torture and Other Cruel, Inhuman or Degrading Treatment or Punishment (OPCAT) extends CAT and establishes a Subcommittee (SPT) as a monitoring body to evaluate the Convention objectives in Party States. The Subcommittee commenced operation in 2007. OPCAT also requires States to establish an NPM to monitor domestically the State's implementation of OPCAT. The Special Rapporteur for Torture under CAT has also commented on the importance of domestic complaints procedures in prisons.[32]

Prior to OPCAT, CAT had no specific monitoring body and was primarily reliant on states submitting reports to the Committee established under the Convention to determine the domestic implementation of the Convention obligations. Under Article 19 states are required to submit initial reports following one year of entry into force of the Convention in the state concerned and supplementary reports every four years. These are then examined by the Committee who refers comments back to the State Party. Article 20 allowed the Committee to request state cooperation in cases where it received reliable information of systematic torture allegations in the jurisdiction of the state. This investigatory process is focused on confidentiality and state cooperation. It is a voluntary procedure and states could decide not to recognise the Committee's competence under this Article. Upon completion of the inquiry procedure, a summary of the work done under this Article can be included in the Annual Report of the Committee. This is the only element of this procedure which can be made public. Article 21 also provides for an optional complaints system, whereby states could report on allegations of torture in other states and the state subject to complaint can enter into a confidential inquiry procedure with the Committee, while Article 22 provides for an optional individual complaints mechanism. While the inquiry procedure has been accepted by many State Parties, the individual complaint procedure has not been as widely accepted. The prominence of the ECtHR in the CoE States means that individuals may be more familiar with its operation than the procedure under CAT.

In addition to the above, OPCAT now provides for additional monitoring under CAT. This optional protocol was adopted in 2002 and came into force in 2006 upon receipt of the 20th ratification of a state of the protocol. Upon entry into force, a monitoring body known as the Subcommittee for the Prevention of Torture (SPT) was established and commenced its work. This protocol is not as widely ratified as CAT and ratification has been subject to significant delays in some signatory states such as Ireland. In general, European states have dominated in the ratification of OPCAT and most CoE States have ratified the optional protocol and established NPMs (Bicknell and Evans 2017: 14). Ireland while signing the protocol at an early stage has had a significant delay in ratifying the protocol and some of the reasons for this, as well as local discussions regarding implementation, will be outlined below.

The SPT has a preventative mandate and similar powers to the CPT. The composition of the SPT is outlined in Part II of OPCAT, while Part III outlines the mandate of the monitoring body. The SPT conducts regular visits to member states, with the possibility of follow-up visits if necessary.[33] Findings and recommendations are communicated to states and a dialogue is entered into. This report along with state commentary can be published if requested by the state.[34]

The protocol also requires states to establish an NPM, which is intended to cooperate with the SPT at a domestic level as explicitly outlined in Article 11(1)(b). States have an obligation within one year of ratification to designate an NPM, as outlined in Article 17. Once an NPM is established the SPT should be notified of such. This obligation has proven difficult for some states and in the case of Ireland it has delayed the ratification of the treaty for a significant period of time. The SPT regularly reviews the list of countries which have yet to establish an NPM and as outlined in their 34th session in February 2018 failure to establish an NPM within four years of ratification is considered a serious violation of states' obligations under the Optional Protocol.[35]

States have designated a broad range of bodies the role of NPM with some assigning the role to an existing body or bodies, while others have established new bodies. As outlined by Bicknell and Evans (2017: 15), most European countries have adopted the 'Ombudsman's Plus' model, which involves expanding an existing Ombudsman office to include all aspects of the NPM mandate. Other countries such as France and Switzerland established new bodies to carry out the function of NPM, while countries such as the UK assigned the role to a number of existing bodies with one being designated as the coordinating body (Bicknell and Evans 2017: 15). The protocol does not require a specific body to carry out the work but outlines certain requirements for the bodies to fulfil the mandate. Their mandate and their role are outlined in Article 4 of the protocol. This is further expanded on in Part IV of the protocol and outlines the various powers and functions which should be invested in the NPM. These bodies should be independent (Article 18), have a minimum number of powers (Article 19) and shall publish annual reports on their activities (Article 23). State parties are required to publish and disseminate these reports, a step further than the CPT where reports can only be published with state consent. Article 22 further requires states to enter into a dialogue with the NPM on any proposed recommendations and possible implementation of such.

3.2.5 European Convention on Human Rights

The European Convention on Human Rights (ECHR) outlines a broad range of rights applicable to those within the jurisdiction of its member states. The Court has over time interpreted its jurisdiction broadly to include those in territories in the control of the Member State or agents of the State. Therefore, the Convention rights apply to those detained in locations controlled by the State even if outside the traditional borders of the State territory such as in military detention.[36] The ECHR and the case law of the ECtHR will be discussed in this section with specific attention being paid to the investigation requirements under Article 3 and the right to an effective remedy under Article 13 as these can serve as an indication as to what is expected of oversight mechanisms. The CPT, ECHR and EPRs, while not bound by each other, have shown a willingness to cross reference one another in the development of standards and in the Courts assessment of cases. For example, in the cases of *Kalashnikov v Russia*[37] and *Modarca v Moldova*[38] the ECtHR relied heavily on reports of the CPT to establish violations in those cases. In the case of *Kalashnikov*, it examined CPT reports and standards to assess the amount of space each prisoner should have, and in the case of *Modarca* referred to the criticisms of the CPT of the quality of food in the Moldovan prison.

The Convention is the main human rights treaty adopted by the CoE and the Court functions as its monitoring body as outlined in Article 19. Complaints can be brought from individuals in member states or by other states as stated in Article 34 and 33, respectively. A number of criteria for bringing a case are outlined in Article 35 in relation to admissibility, one of which is the exhaustion of domestic remedies. This criterion is particularly relevant for oversight, as the courts' assessment of domestic bodies for such and likelihood of success can impact on access to the court. Findings in such cases are binding on states; however, Article 47 also allows the Court to provide advisory opinions in certain instances. The ECHR was strengthened in Ireland by the adoption of the ECHR Act 2003. This incorporated the Convention into domestic law and required domestic courts, as far as possible, to interpret laws in line with the Convention obligations.[39] Furthermore, the High Court or Supreme Court can under Section 5 of the Act make a declaration of incompatibility that the relevant law or statutory provision is incompatible with Convention obligations. This order is then required to be presented before each House of the Oireachtas 21 days after it has been made. This Act highlights the prominent position of the ECHR provisions in Irish law.

3.2.5.1 ECtHR Recognition of Prisoners' Rights: Domestic Protection

A core feature of rights protection under the ECtHR, as outlined in Article 35 of the ECHR, is that states should be responsible for remedying rights violations in the first instance and therefore the court has provided guidance on the requirements for effective domestic protection of rights, such as key principles for complaints and court procedures and the importance of inspection and monitoring (van Zyl Smit and Snacken 2009).

Article 3 of the ECHR is often invoked in prison condition cases as it is an absolute right and cannot be limited, even during imprisonment. Article 3 prohibits torture, cruel, inhuman or degrading treatment or punishment. As has been discussed the substance of this right is subject to monitoring both by the CPT and the NPMs established under OPCAT. Article 13 provides those under the Convention with a right to an effective remedy. The interpretation of effective remedy has provided the court with an opportunity to examine complaint mechanisms for prisoners in a number of jurisdictions. Other rights such as Article 8, the right to respect for private and family life, have been argued in prison cases. In considering domestic complaint procedures, the courts have noted the importance of providing information on internal prison rules, as well as the need to take prisoner requests and complaints seriously (van Zyl Smit and Snacken 2009: 308).

In the case of *Golder v the UK*,[40] the Court at para 33 distinguished between Article 6 and Article 13 (right to an effective remedy), highlighting that Article 13 does not necessitate a court or tribunal in the determination or provision of an effective remedy. Following on from this, the case of *Silver v the UK*[41] examined the UK prisoner complaint mechanism under Article 13. At the time, there were several bodies which a prisoner could complain to regarding prison matters. These included to the Board of Visitors for the specific prison, make petitions to the Home Secretary or complain to a prison officer. Prisoners could also complain to the then Parliamentary Commissioner for Administration, since replaced by the Prisons and Probation Ombudsman, or apply to the courts (Rogan 2012: 9). The Courts made it clear that they would examine the available remedies on a case-by-case basis to determine if they were an effective remedy in the case before them. In the case at hand, they found that the incidents which gave rise to violations under Article 8 did not have a domestic remedy.

A number of key principles were outlined in the case of Silver regarding effective complaint procedures under the ECtHR and expanded upon in further case law. In the case of Silver, the Courts focused on the lack of binding decision making or enforcement powers in the case of complaints received by the Board of Visitors or the Parliamentary Commissioner. The Home Secretary would in certain instances be called upon to review Instruments or Orders issued by its own office and as such would lack independence in examining such complaints. Finally, the courts had a certain supervisory jurisdiction over the exercise of the powers of the Home Secretary and the prison authorities under the Prison Act and Rules. However, this jurisdiction was limited to determining whether those powers were exercised arbitrarily, in bad faith, for an improper motive or in an ultra vires manner. As such because the applicants were not concerned with the interference being contrary to domestic English law, the routes available could not be deemed by the Courts to constitute an effective remedy.[42]

The criteria for an effective complaint mechanism outlined in Silver were further expanded on in subsequent cases (Jacobs and van Kalmthout 2017: 56). In the case of *Ananyev & Others v Russia*,[43] the court highlighted the importance of an independent authority. They also indicated that there should be a possibility of a hearing and that the procedure should be adversarial. The binding nature and enforceability of decisions made by complaint bodies was discussed in *Ananyev v Russia*, along with the need for a reasonably short time limit in dealing with complaints. This case also referred to the role of an effective complaint mechanism as an important safeguard for preventing violations of Article 3. In *Alimov v Turkey*, the Court referred to Article 70.7 of the EPRs and access to legal remedies.[44]

Varga v Hungary discussed the difference between de facto and de jure complaints mechanisms and that states will be required to demonstrate the operation of a complaint mechanism at a domestic level to show the courts that it operates effectively in practice.[45] This is of particular importance given the need for complainants to exhaust domestic remedies prior to referring to the ECtHR as outlined in Article 35 ECHR. However, as indicated in *Egmez v. Cyprus* this does not require complainants to exhaust all avenues available, especially those which are proven to be inadequate or ineffective.[46] The courts will also deal with complaints which have been subject to an inordinate delay, as this is a barrier to an effective remedy. *Pugzlys v Poland* expanded on the criterion in discussing the need for an accessible complaints mechanism, which is capable of offering redress for the alleged violation and that there is a reasonable prospect of success.[47] *Varga v. Hungary* outlined the different types of relief which should be available to complainants. In this case, the court determined that there should be a possibility of improving conditions in the prison and for compensation in order for an effective remedy under the Convention to be available. This highlights a preventative and compensatory aspect to the meaning of effective remedy. These should be complementary in nature and compensation alone will not be deemed sufficient, as this could allow for states to carry out substantial violations without any commitment to improving the initial cause of the violation.

In the case of *Mathew v the Netherlands*, the Court emphasised that while they would take previous compensation received at domestic level into consideration, they would also examine whether the domestic authorities had acknowledged, either expressly or in substance, a breach of the Convention.[48] They noted that only when both of these conditions were satisfied would the applicant be precluded from having their complaint heard by the Court. The reduction in sentence could be understood as a form of compensation under the Convention and that there was a considerable reduction in sentence in this case.[49] This highlights the vigorous approach taken by the Court in examining domestic remedies and that providing some form of compensation in and of itself will not preclude an applicant from having their complaint considered by the Court.

With regard to principles applicable to inspection and monitoring bodies, the Courts have provided little guidance to date on what these bodies should look like; however, as noted above they do rely on inspection reports at times in assessing the conditions in domestic prisons, as well as the standards applied by the CPT (van Zyl Smit and Snacken 2009: 9). This highlights that the Courts, while not seeing such bodies as an effective remedy, do perceive inspection and monitoring as a part of the rights protection framework.

3.2.6 Conclusion: What Are the Common Principles for Oversight?

A broad range of rules and treaties have been outlined above which pertain to prisons and which provide guidance on oversight mechanisms. Some clear common principles emerge from these. The prohibition of inhuman and degrading treatment is a common concern across the various rules and treaties and, as has been demonstrated above, a strong approach is taken to protecting prisoners from being subject to such conditions. The availability of objective information is valued by the courts, which emphasises the need for independent monitoring bodies as contained in the rules. A preference for domestic resolution of complaints is evident both in the rules and the court judgements and the effectiveness, as opposed to the mere existence, of these mechanisms is of key importance to the courts. The above rules and court decisions highlight that imprisonment should only restrict physical liberty and that rights should only be restricted to as limited an extent as possible. Allowing greater scrutiny by external bodies and prisoners themselves to speak to such bodies is a significant step towards ensuring those rights are protected and upheld.

3.3 Ireland

This section outlines some key features of the Irish prison system and the development of oversight bodies in Ireland. Additionally, it discusses criticisms which have been directed at the system and proposed reforms to the existing rights protection mechanisms. Ireland has an imprisonment rate of 76 persons per 100,000.[50] The Irish prison campus consists of 12 prisons, one of which is a female prison and one with a female unit within the prison, meaning the majority of the campus consists of male prisons.[51] The Irish Prison Service (IPS) operates two open centres which are low-security prisons and one high-security prison. The rest of the prison campus is medium security with various internal units and regimes. As noted by the Joint Committee on Justice and Equality Report on Penal Reform and Sentencing 'Ireland's prison population is characterised by mental health issues, addictions, homelessness, poverty, unemployment, education disadvantage, chaotic family background and social marginalisation', furthermore while Ireland has a high committal rate many people serve very short sentences (Joint Committee on Justice and Equality 2018: 10).

As a member of the United Nations and the CoE, Ireland has taken steps to implement the Mandela Rules and the EPRs and to establish oversight bodies for Irish prisons. These guidelines promote a multi-layered approach for the protection of prisoners' human rights through inspection, monitoring and an independent complaints procedure. This multi-layered approach provides a comprehensive means of protecting rights at a general and individual level and promotes best practice in the running of prisons through regular and routine monitoring. The main domestic legislation for prisoners' rights in Ireland are the Prison Act 2007 and Prison Rules 2007. These have both been subject to amendments but contain the key provisions regulating Irish prisons. The oversight of prisons in Ireland, of which the complaints system forms a part, has, as Behan and Kirkham (2016) demonstrate, limitations.

3.3.2 Inspection

There are two external bodies in Ireland responsible for inspections, the VCs and the Inspector of Prisons (OiP). These will be discussed in turn below, along with the criticisms and their compliance with the international criteria outlined above. This will be followed by a discussion of the international bodies, outlined above, which Ireland is subject to visits from and a consideration of their experiences and reports on Ireland.

3.3.2.1 Visiting Committees

As part of the prison inspection framework in Ireland each prison has a VC consisting of 6 to 12 members. The powers of the committees are outlined in the Prison (VCs) Act 1925 and their early establishment highlight that external inspection has long been a part of prison oversight in Ireland. The committees are composed of members from the community, who express an interest to the Minister to undertake the role and no guidelines exists regarding the frequency or methods for their visits. Members are responsible for undertaking visits to their prison, as well as listening to prisoner complaints and investigating them, although the final power to decide on the action to be taken remains with the governor of the prison concerned. Previously VCs also played a role in the disciplinary procedures in prison, but this has been revoked.

These committees have been the subject of criticism as their reports vary widely in quality and frequency. As discussed by O'Mahony (1994), while the VC for Mountjoy has a tendency to express criticisms of the prison in their reports, this is in contrast to other committee reports. He also notes that there are inconsistencies in the information recorded with a large amount of useless information making its way into reports while important statistics 'which should be routinely monitored by an efficient and caring system because of obvious relevance to the quality of life and treatment within our prisons and essential to a proper level of accountability' are not included (O'Mahony 1994: 6). IPRT (2009) note that there is insufficient training provided to members of the Committees to perform their functions as independent monitoring mechanisms. Furthermore, they lack effective powers both in their role in hearing complaints and in the absence of a mechanism for implementation of recommendations and follow-up from their reports

(IPRT 2009). The OiP (2011a: para 2.77) in a report on Limerick Prison, noted that they met with a representative of the VC for that prison and that from that meeting they came to the conclusion that the committee does not carry out its mandate as laid out in the legislation. This demonstrates a relationship between the inspection bodies but also the continuing concerns as to the effectiveness of the VCs, especially in certain prisons.

Another issue with the VCs concerns the independence of the bodies in the performance of their role. While the VCs consist of laypersons and are not employees of the prison service, they are appointed by the Minister for Justice and Equality and have been subject to controversy at times as the appointments have been viewed as political favours and a way of gaining support for the party. In particular, a number of members on VCs were assigned to prisons at a significant distance from their homes, and this resulted in higher expenses claims (Rogan 2009: 298). This can also impact on the availability of the VCs to attend the prison when a request is made by a prisoner to see them. The importance of the perceived independence of VC members both from a public and prisoner perspective cannot be overstated. As highlighted by Rogan (2009: 301), VCs can play an important role in addressing prisoners concerns about the conditions of their confinement and while they do not have enforcement powers, they can make recommendations and investigate matters brought to their attention by the prisoner. The frequency of their visits can contribute to higher levels of visibility and awareness.

It is also of note that these committees which were kept on post-Independence and have equivalent committees in England and Wales were, in those jurisdictions, subject to significant reforms and rebranded Independent Monitoring Boards (IMBs). In particular, steps were taken to ensure that balance was achieved on the boards in terms of gender, age, occupation, education and social background, as well as to coordinate the various IMBs to provide a consistent approach across the various institutions (Rogan 2009: 305). Rogan (2009: 306) has suggested some reforms to improve the effectiveness of these committees. In particular, the members of the VCs should be provided with adequate training and information as to what the role entails and what is expected of members. Guidance should also be provided on the contents of the report, so as to improve the quality and usefulness of the reports. When reports follow a similar structure regarding content covered, systemic areas of concern can be identified but also progress can more readily be seen. It would allow VCs to readily see if their recommendations and concerns raised in previous visits have been addressed, this is especially important for VCs which may change members regularly. Record keeping is highlighted throughout the EPRs as a key part of running a prison and the VCs should also be required to provide records of meetings and visits to increase the transparency of their role. This could also assist in raising the view of the VC in the eyes of the public and prisoners, as the work of the VCs would be more visible.

Some movement towards reforming these committees has been discussed in this jurisdiction. These include the VCs submitting their annual reports to the OiP for publication, rather than the Minister for Justice and Equality, and reporting to the OiP on matters of concern. The Inspector would therefore have general oversight of the work of the VCs. In addition, it was proposed to reduce membership of VCs to six members per person of suitable people with appropriate qualifications and a genuine interest in prison issues.[52] However, it is unclear to what extent these reforms will be followed through.

3.3.2.2 Office of the Inspector of Prisons

Ireland previously had an OiP in the 19th century but this fell out of practice until the early 2000s (Kilcommins et al. 2004). Attempts were made to establish a statutory office for a significant number of years with political promises as far back as 1948 to commit to a full-time inspector (Kilcommins et al. 2004). This body was first revived on a non-statutory basis in 2002. Since 2007, Ireland has had a statutory OiP (established under the Prisons Act 2007). The Inspector carries out inspections of all the prisons in the Irish prison campus and writes reports on these visits individually and on an annual basis, subject to review by the Minister for Justice. S.32(2) of the 2007 Act clearly outlines the areas to be covered in the Inspectors report. Reports should cover a broad range of areas including the:

> general management, including the level of its effectiveness and efficiency, the conditions and general health and welfare of prisoners detained there, the general conduct and effectiveness of persons working there, compliance with national and international standards, including in particular the prison rules, programmes and other facilities available and the extent to which prisoners participate in them, security, and discipline.

The Inspector also writes thematic reports and since 2012 investigates and reports on deaths in custody. The Inspector can visit any area of the prisons at any time of day or night and does not need to notify the prison before visiting.[53] The Inspector can also request any documentation from the prison and can speak in confidence with any member of staff or prisoner. The Inspector can bring any issue of concern to the attention of the Governor either after or during the inspection or can notify the Director General of the Prison Service or the Minister of Justice if necessary.[54] The role of the Inspector in relation to deaths in custody is particularly important considering the State's positive obligations under Article 2 of the ECHR outlined above. Prior to the 2012 amendment, the Governor of the relevant prison was only required to notify the Inspector of the death in custody and, as argued by Rogan (2009: 313), this notification was unlikely to achieve compliance with Article 2 due to the *ad hoc* nature of carrying out a full investigation into the death. Arguably, the expansion of the Inspector's mandate to investigate deaths in custody could support the retention of the VCs to ensure that routine inspections are not negatively impacted by this additional workload for the Office of the Inspector.

Additionally, the Inspector has an oversight role in relation to the complaints mechanism which was established in 2013, under the Prisons Act, 2007, as outlined further below. This is a general oversight role and does not involve providing recourse for individual prisoners, although they can investigate individual complaints for the purposes of their general oversight role. One key criticism of the Inspector's powers is that the Minister for Justice and Equality is responsible for the publication of the report and can omit any matter which 'may be prejudicial to the security of the prison or of the State [… .], or would be contrary to the public interest, or may infringe the constitutional rights of any person'.[55] This has contributed to significant delays in the publication of reports as other matters may take precedence in being brought before the Houses of the Oireachtas but also undermines the independence of the role. The Irish Penal Reform Trust (IPRT 2009: 9) in their paper on 'Complaints, Monitoring and Inspection in Prison' have called for direct publication of the Inspector's reports.

Furthermore, as a State which has ratified the European Convention for the Prevention of Torture and Inhuman and Degrading Treatment and Punishment in 1989, Ireland receives visits from the European Committee for the Prevention of Torture and Inhuman and Degrading Treatment or Punishment, discussed further below. This body receives information from the Inspector and also meets with the Office along with other bodies concerned with prisons for consultation and cooperation.[56] This is an important opportunity for the international body to gain additional information on the domestic situation as visits are infrequent and important issues can be identified in this way.

3.3.2.3 International Bodies

Ireland is subject to visits from international bodies such as the European Committee for the Prevention of Torture and Inhuman and Degrading Treatment or Punishment (CPT) and, once ratified, the SPT under OPCAT. While visits by the CPT are infrequent and lack the spontaneity afforded to the OiP through his ad hoc visits, the international recognition of the CPT and use of their reports by the European Court of Human Rights in their judgements creates a degree of international pressure to comply with their recommendations in party states. It also allows for the flow of best practice between various member states where different states may have higher standards of treatment in different aspects of their prison regime.

3.3.2.3.1 CPT

Ireland ratified the European Convention for the Prevention of Torture and Inhuman or Degrading Treatment or Punishment in 1988 and has been subject to eight state visits by the Committee in the intervening years. These visits took place in 1993, 1998, 2002, 2006, 2010, 2014, 2019 and 2024. The CPT reports drawn up in light of these visits have all been published along with government responses, usually roughly a year following the visit. As noted by Kriebaum (2017: 167), the publishing of these reports are an important tool in themselves for increasing transparency and creating a public record of the activities of authorities.

The CPT's visit in 2014 was its first opportunity to examine the domestic formal complaints system since its introduction. Previous reports such as that from 2010 had raised concerns at the lack of an effective complaints system in prisons. This meant that the new system was a focus of the 2014 visit, especially Category A complaints as these deal with allegations of ill-treatment the focus of the CPT's mandate. The CPT outlines in its 2014 report on Ireland three specific functions of a well-functioning complaints system:

1 it can serve as a valuable source of information for prison management about potential problems in the establishment.
2 as well as allaying tension amongst prisoners by ensuring that their concerns are treated seriously.
3 and, where appropriate, that suitable remedies are offered.[57]

A particular concern that the CPT had with the system was prisoner trust therein and adherence to the established timelines for investigating complaints. The CPT also raised concerns in relation to the quality of reports produced by the independent investigators in the case of Category A complaints, which will be discussed below. In their 2020 report following a visit to Ireland in September 2019, further concerns were raised regarding the operation of the complaint system, in stating that it 'cannot be considered as fit for purpose'.[58]

3.3.2.3.2 OPCAT

As stated above, Ireland has signed but not ratified OPCAT to date. This contrasts with most European states, which have a high rate of ratification of OPCAT. This delay is due to the requirement to establish an NPM within one year of ratification. Despite the failure to ratify, Ireland has had discussions in relation to the establishment of an NPM and considered various existing bodies alongside the possible establishment of a new body for this role. As highlighted above, prisons in Ireland are subject to regular inspections; however, OPCAT requires all places of detention to be visited and at present some gaps in inspection remain. At the time of writing, a draft Bill was being prepared to establish an NPM, with Irish Human Rights and Equality Commission as a coordinating body for the NPM and the Office of the OiP being given a broader mandate of all criminal justice detention.

3.3.3 Complaints Mechanism

The importance of a complaints' mechanism is highlighted above in the international mechanisms; however, it is necessary to note a further few points on its role here. While prisoners can access the courts in relation to prison matters, there are significant hurdles to accessing the courts some of which will be expanded on below. Machover (2002: 234) notes importantly that most pilot cases, those concerning systemic issues, are taken by long-term prisoners. There are a variety of reasons for this, namely the amount of time required to bring a case. This is of significance in a jurisdiction which as indicated above has mainly short-term sentences. While steps have been taken to provide alternatives to custody for particularly short sentences, a significant portion – 81% of sentenced committals in 2017 – serve sentences of less than 12 months.[59] Therefore, the complaint mechanism provides a quicker, more accessible mechanism for those without the expertise or time to seek access to the courts. It is also important to bear in mind that complaints in prison often concern 'daily administrative issues' and 'need an efficient on-the-spot' system.[60] Best practice from the EPRs and Mandela Rules highlight the importance of resolving disputes at the lowest level possible.

3.3.3.1 Development

Prior to the introduction of the 2013 system, prisoners could complain under Rules 55 to 57 of the Irish Prison Rules 2007; however, the Prison Act itself was silent on the matter. Rule 55 allowed, and still affords, prisoners the opportunity to complain to the Governor of the prison either at a meeting with the Governor held at the request of the prisoner or during morning parade. Rule 56 allows for complaints to be brought to the attention of the VC for the relevant prison; however, the VC members have no decision-making powers in relation to complaints. Little is known on the practice of requesting a meeting with the VC and their recommendations (Rogan 2009: 303). While some reports contain general information on complaints, this information is not recorded in a consistent and comprehensive manner across the various prisons and committees and therefore a clear understanding of the utility of this function and prisoners' views on it is impossible to ascertain. Rule 57 states that a prisoner can make a request to meet with an officer of the Minister for Justice and Equality. If the prisoner makes a complaint or request during this meeting the officer can make a recommendation to the Governor in relation to the request or complaint or suggest that the prisoner raise the issue with the Governor. If the Governor fails or refuses to give full effect to the recommendation of the officer, the Director General may direct the Governor to do so. Finally, Rule 44 of the Prison Rules 2007 and s.31 (6) Prisons Act 2007 which established the Office of the Inspector of Prisons gives the Inspector the power to receive complaints from prisoners but as indicated above the Inspector does not have the power to adjudicate on individual complaints and therefore the utility of this power for individual prisoners is limited (van der Valk and Rogan 2020).

This approach was criticised by the Inspector in several of his reports. In a report on Mountjoy prison, the Inspector (OiP 2009) noted a number of concerns in the process for dealing with prisoner complaints. The inspection identified a number of serious concerns, especially for serious allegations which had incomplete records. A key recommendation from this report was that prisoners' complaints should 'be dealt with in an open and transparent manner in accordance with law and best practice' (OiP 2009: Recommendation 6). In a follow-up visit to Mountjoy and subsequent report, the Inspector noted that steps had been taken to improve in particular the record keeping and procedure for notifying the Garda of complaints which could be related to criminal allegations (OiP 2011b). The IPS has taken steps over the last number of years to make amendments to the complaints procedure for prisoners, creating a new mechanism to deal with complaints in 2013 under s.57A and 57B in the Prison Rules (Amendment) 2013.[61] However, this amendment only deals with complaints of a serious nature and while other types of complaints are included in the IPS policy document, they are not grounded in a legislative mandate.

3.3.3.2 Current Mechanism

Under the current system there are six categories of complaints ranging from A to F, depending on the seriousness of the complaint and the subject of the complaint. Guidance concerning the categorisation and handling of complaints can be found in an IPS policy document first published in 2014. The procedure for Category A complaints can be found in the Rule 57A and 57B of the Prison Rules 2007 inserted by Prison Rules (Amendment) 2013. Category A complaints are concerned with 'complaints alleging assault or use of excessive force against a prisoner, or ill treatment, racial abuse, discrimination, intimidation, threats or any other conduct against a prisoner of a nature and gravity likely to bring discredit on the IPS'.[62] Category B complaints are 'complaints of a serious nature, but not falling within any other category of complaint'.[63] For example, category B complaints could include 'verbal abuse of prisoners by staff, inappropriate searches or any other conduct against a prisoner of a nature likely to bring discredit on the IPS'.[64] These are dealt with by a prison officer at Chief Officer grade and can be appealed to the governor. Category C complaints, of which the majority of complaints comprise, 'are basic service level complaints … [such as complaints] about visits, phone calls, reception issues, missing clothes, not getting post on time, not getting appropriate exercise'.[65] These are investigated by an officer not below Class Officer who is assigned the role by the governor. The Senior Chief Officer in the relevant prison maintains oversight of the investigations of Category C complaints and should take action if they are not resolved in 48 hours. Category D complaints 'relate to complaints against professionals such as [for example] dentists [and] doctors'.[66] Category E complaints are those made by visitors to the prison. Category F complaints are 'complaints against decisions made by IPS Headquarters in relation to the granting of temporary release and prison transfers'.[67] The category of the complaint is assigned by the member of staff who receives the complaint and depending on the categorisation is subject to different investigation procedures.

Only Category A complaints involve the appointing of independent investigators by the Governor but the decision in regards to the outcome of the complaint still ultimately lies with the Governor.[68] The Inspector (OiP 2012: para 5.9) had previously suggested that the office of the Inspector could fulfil this role of independent external complaints mechanism in the case of Category A complaints. However, as will be explored below the general Ombudsman or potentially a specialised prison Ombudsman are the proposals being considered as an external reviewer of internal complaints.

Section 57B of Prison Rules 2007 inserted by Prison Rules (Amendment) 2013 also contains some important provisions for record keeping and the management of complaints reflecting international best practice and adherence to the Rules outlined at the start of this chapter. S.57B(5)(c) requires the governor to investigate why a complaint has been withdrawn and provide a report to the Director General. This provides an important safeguard against retaliation for submitting a complaint or pressuring complainants to withdraw their complaint. As demonstrated in Table 3.1, while the system is being actively used by those in prison the majority of complaints concern Category C complaints around basic service issues such as family visits,

Table 3.1 Usage of the prisoner complaint system for 2019

Prison	*A*	*B*	*C*	*D*	*E*	*F*	*No. of Complaints*
Arbour Hill	0	3	5	0	0	0	8
Castlerea	8	11	73	19	0	0	111
Cloverhill	12	37	121	54	0	0	224
Cork	0	5	3	1	0	0	9
Dochas	8	10	41	3	1	0	63
Limerick	1	3	2	3	0	0	9
Loughan House	0	0	0	0	0	0	0
Midlands	5	43	212	4	6	0	270
Mountjoy	6	30	120	18	0	1	175
Portlaoise	9	3	25	9	4	0	50
Shelton Abbey	0	0	0	0	0	0	0
Wheatfield	11	4	76	26	1	0	118
Category/ Outcome Totals	***60***	***146***	***678***	***128***	***8***	***1***	***1037***

clothing and access to phones and there are differences in usage across the prison campus.

3.3.3.3 Criticisms

While this mechanism allowed for the development of a formal procedure for lodging complaints, it was criticised by the OiP (2016). The CPT has also commented on the Irish complaint procedure in their reports. In their reports on the 2014 and 2019 visits to Ireland, they welcomed the introduction of the mechanism but noted some ongoing concerns with the mechanism, as discussed above.[69]

These criticisms were accepted by the then Minister of Justice in 2016 and the Inspector's specific recommendation to extend the Ombudsman's mandate to cover prisoner complaints was accepted.[70] As of 2021, further delays with reforming the system have been indicated due to the Covid-19 pandemic.

3.3.3.4 Role of the Ombudsman

The general Ombudsman was established under the Ombudsman Act 1980, and it is this office which is expected to deal with prisoner complaints. Currently the office deals with complaints from a range of public service bodies, with specialised Ombudsman Offices in areas such as the Defence Forces and the Ombudsman for Children. Prisoners were expressly excluded from the remit of the Office of Ombudsman under s. 5(1)(e)(iii). This was amended under the Ombudsman (Amendment) Act 2012 in so far as the exclusion of prisoners was moved from the main body of the Act to the Second Schedule part II para (f)(ii). The General Ombudsman can review decisions concerning those in custody, who are under 18.[71]

Current reform proposals are focused on the Ombudsman acting as an external review body for decisions taken by the internal complaints system (van der Valk and Rogan 2020). This would allow prisoners who had exhausted the internal mechanism to apply to the Ombudsman for a review of the decision taken. The Ombudsman can also receive complaints which have been subject to undue delay, i.e. where the complainant has not received a response for an extended period of time. This ensures that complaints are not simply delayed indefinitely and the prompt dealing with of complaints is a key component of an effective complaint mechanism. Given the short timeframes set out in the IPS complaints policy, consideration will need to be given as to how undue delay will be defined once the Ombudsman commences the handling of prisoner complaints. While some discussion has taken place regarding the establishment of a specific Prisons Ombudsman, similar to that in place in the United Kingdom, the main focus still remains to be on the existing general Ombudsman.[72]

3.3.3.5 Courts' Relationship with the Prisoner Complaints Mechanism

A decision of the Court of Appeal suggests that more scrutiny of the internal complaints process is needed. The case of *McDonnell v Governor of Wheatfield* arose in relation to the constitutional rights of a prisoner on protection in prison due to the potential threat posed to him by being with other prisoners.[73] In the Court of Appeal, Birmingham J, Ryan P and Hogan J seemed to suggest that a prisoner's use of the internal complaints process could be examined when assessing the prisoner's claim before the court. In their judgement, the court discussed the complaint procedure in place at the time of the case and considered that the prison authorities themselves were better placed in coming to a decision regarding prisoner safety and welfare than the court.[74] This decision then, according to the court, could be the subject of judicial review. In this case, the court referred to the procedure for making a request for a meeting with the Governor, Director of Prison Services, a member of the VC or the Minister for Justice and Equality to raise a complaint. Given the substantive reform to this procedure through the more formal complaints procedure the courts may be even more inclined to promote the use of this procedure prior to making a claim to the court. While the court does not exclude having recourse to the courts, they state that 'he may decide or be advised in the future to utilise the grievance procedure or to make an application to the court'.[75] This suggests that recourse to the courts should be limited to judicial review except when constitutional or legal rights are at stake. The scheme under the Prison Rules was found by the courts to be reassuring as to the IPS commitment to provide conditions in line with the human rights of the prisoners.[76]

While the position that a prisoner would be required to go through the internal complaints procedure before taking a case has never formerly been established, if this were to become court practice in considering cases it would be essential to have a fully functioning complaint system. It highlights the deference the court accords to the prison authorities in taking care of prisoners. The court distinguishes between intervention and supervision in McDonnell, emphasising the separation of powers and that supervision is the appropriate role for the courts.[77] They found that the High Court orders which directed the IPS to end the 'unnecessarily oppressive regime' amounted to interference with the executive function of the prison service due to the specific directions given to the Governor in relation to the handling of the prisoner in his prison.[78]

The above position implied by the court in relation to the complaint mechanism contrasts with that taken by Ní Raifeartaigh J in *Kenny v Governor of Portlaoise Prison* concerning the internal appeals process for decision on disciplinary procedures.[79] Ní Raifeartaigh J states that:

> I do not think that it is an appropriate case in which the applicant should be shut out from judicial review simply because there was in existence

> a right of appeal which he did not exercise. In circumstances where a hearing is tainted by the absence of a basic fair procedure, judicial review seems to me to be an appropriate course of action to pursue.[80]

In the case of Kenny, the Governor had ordered a number of sanctions for a period of 35 days following a disciplinary hearing and Kenny sought judicial review on the basis of a breach of fair procedures in the determination by the Governor.[81]

It seems at odds that a prisoner who has been subject to a number of sanctions for violating prison rules would have greater access to the courts than someone who has lodged a complaint in this regard but who has not received a sanction due to a breach of prison rules. This is of particular concern in light of the specific concerns raised in the OiP's report on the existing system. The OiP (2016) carried out a review of the complaint mechanism over a six-month period in 2014/2015 in the six prisons involved there were 371 Category C complaints out of a total of 556 recorded. The Inspector (OiP 2016) noted in particular the delay in dealing with complaints, incomplete complaints, lack of follow-up with the prisoner when there were further questions and that outcomes resulted in recommendations rather than enforced decisions.

3.3.4 Judicial Oversight of Prison Conditions and Prisoners' Rights

In addition to the complaint procedure outlined above, prisoners have recourse to the courts for breaches of their rights. The Mandela Rules and the EPRs refer to a right to appeal decisions either to 'a judicial or other authority' or 'an independent authority'. In recent years, Ireland has seen a growth in cases concerning prison conditions (Rogan 2014a). This section outlines the types of actions which can be taken by Irish prisoners, the development of prisoners' rights in the Irish context and a consideration of some of the challenges which prisoners may face. Hogan J in the case of *Connolly v the Governor of Wheatfield Prison* held that:

> [w]hile due and realistic recognition must be accorded by the judicial branch to the difficulties inherent in the running of a complex prison system and the detention of individuals, many of whom are difficult and even dangerous, for its part *the judicial branch must nevertheless exercise a supervisory function* to ensure that the essence of these core constitutional values and rights – the dignity of the individual and the protection of the person – are not compromised ...[82]

This extract highlights the important supervisory role the courts should play in all areas of life, especially for those who have had their rights restricted as in the case of prisoners' loss of liberty. However, as will be outlined below, there are considerable challenges to accessing and navigating the courts.

3.3.4.1 Types of Actions

Prisoners have a variety of avenues under which they can seek redress for prison conditions and treatment while in prison. This section considers in particular Habeas Corpus applications under Article 40.4.2, judicial review and plenary summons.

Habeas Corpus applications are one type of action used in prison condition cases. Traditionally intended for detention which did not have a legal basis or was flawed in some way it has been argued in the context of prison conditions which due to their quality merit release or in the case of prison disciplinary procedures whereby the prisoner is viewed by being unlawfully detained in a prison inside another prison due to the extent of the restricted regime. However, as stated in *Kinsella* the release of sentenced prisoners could only be ordered on this basis in exceptional circumstances. Nonetheless, the court also noted that

> although the principal function of the High Court on an application pursuant to Article 40.4.2A of the Constitution was to inquire as to the lawfulness of the detention of an individual, it enjoyed a residual jurisdiction for the purpose of making its orders effective.[83]

As will be discussed in more detail below, the courts are reluctant to make such orders and tend to afford the authorities an opportunity to remedy the situation without expressly directing them as to how to do so.

Prisoners can also seek access to the courts through instigating judicial review proceedings. This is a process where an individual applies to the courts to have a decision of a public or administrative body overturned, in this instance a decision of IPS. While this process has the benefit of offering a speedier resolution, it is subject to strict deadlines in seeking to review a decision. It also is more constrained in the review process than other forms of proceedings and as such provides limited room to explore all issues. An example of a case taken by virtue of judicial review is that of *McMenamin v Governor of Wheatfield*, in which the applicant sought a mandamus for specific medical treatment.[84] The applicant was unsuccessful in the case as the judge found that while he was entitled to medical treatment, he was not entitled to the medical treatment of his choice.

Prisoners can also argue a breach of a constitutional right or a tort right. These rights may have an overlapping basis as discussed in Mulligan.[85] This was a case concerning the practice of slopping out in Irish prisons. While the applicant focused on the right to bodily integrity under the Constitution, as recognised under Article 40.3 in the case of *Ryan v Attorney General*, MacMenamin J noted that this right also arose in the law of tort when examining the duty of care owed to the applicant by the prison service.[86]

3.3.4.2 Access to Courts: The Challenges

While there has been a growing recognition of rights in the prison environment and rights language amongst prisoners, this cannot be equated with knowledge of the precise legal provisions and the complexity of court proceedings to recognise those rights (Durand et al. 2017: 47). Prisoners face sufficient hurdles in gaining access to the courts and a number of these will be explored below. As noted above, unlike the majority of those held in Irish prisons, the majority of prisoners bringing cases are those serving longer sentences.

Important to note as regards the issue of access to the courts as a means of asserting prisoners' rights in Ireland is the status of the EPRs. As outlined above, these are soft law and as such are not binding on states; however, certain provisions have been considered binding in some states (van Zyl Smit and Snacken 2009). In the Irish context, the EPRs were argued as the basis for a legitimate expectation for a prisoner seeking temporary release in the case of *McAlister*.[87] However, Finnegan J held that 'the European Prison Rules were not binding and did not create a legitimate expectation in the applicant that the respondent would have regard to them'.[88] The applicant argued that he had a legitimate expectation that the respondent in making the decision on compassionate temporary release would refer to the relevant provision of the EPRs. The court, following the case of *Kinahan v Minister of Justice*,[89] found that the EPRs constituted recommendations and as such there was no legitimate expectation to consider them in decision making. In *Kinahan*, the main finding regarding the EPRs was that the general nature of the provisions relied upon could not create legitimate expectations, whereas in the case of McAlister it was considered that requiring consideration of the EPRs in decision making would bring the international agreement into Irish law contrary to the requirement under Article 29.6 of the Constitution that this power lies with the Oireachtas.

Another significant hurdle for gaining access to the courts can be the financial costs involved in bringing a case. This is mediated for by the provision of legal aid. However, accessing legal aid itself can be challenging especially in the penal context. In Ireland, judicial review cases for prison conditions are excluded from criminal legal aid, therefore civil legal aid would need to be sought by prisoners seeking to bring a case. There is a two-step process for civil legal aid with regard to such cases. The first step involves a financial means test. Following on from this the board will assess the merits of the case if the case is one which needs to go to the courts. This test involves considering a number of different criteria which include questioning whether the applicant has grounds for taking the case, or defending the case the other person is taking against them; is it the best way of solving the dispute; would the applicant be likely to win the case; and what is the cost to the taxpayer against the benefit the applicant might receive if they win. This sets a high threshold for someone who has limited contact with the outside world and can be difficult to navigate. As highlighted by the ECtHR in a number of cases, evidence is essentially held by the prison service and prisoners may find it difficult to gather. As discussed in the case of *O'Donoghue v Legal Aid Board,*

> where the courts have recognised the State's obligation in non-criminal situations, it has done so in very serious situations where the constitutional rights of individuals are clearly involved and failure to grant aid in the circumstances will amount to a breach of its constitutional responsibilities.[90]

As noted by Rogan (2014b: 157), this would require an applicant to argue that 'the failure to fund him/her would result in a serious breach of a constitutional right'.

Also, of significance is the courts view as stated in *Simpson* that '[i]t would be entitled in mitigation to take into account the failure of the Plaintiff to apply for judicial review at the time of his imprisonment seeking to remedy the conditions of his imprisonment'.[91] The plaintiff at the time of the case was already released from custody and the failure to issue more timely proceedings in the form of judicial review was viewed negatively by the courts. This position fails to address the challenges of bringing a court case while in custody, both in terms of seeking legal assistance and the potential fear when the case concerns the institution responsible for all aspects of your life.

3.3.4.3 Remedies

The type of action taken will impact on the type of remedy available to the applicant. Traditionally, Habeus Corpus applications were aimed at seeking releases. However, in the *Richardson* case the court came to an interesting conclusion. Despite finding that the health and privacy rights of the applicant had been breached in the case, the Court held that as the prison authorities were willing to alter the regime, there was no necessity to make an order of mandamus, which would force the respondent to comply with their statutory to protect the rights at question in the case.[92] This demonstrates a high level of faith in the prison service on the part of the courts and a lack of respect for the meaning of granting such an order for the applicant. Mulligan, as highlighted by Rogan (2014b: 15), demonstrates the separation of powers in so far as the court should not recommend to the Executive how to run prisons and its order of priorities and recognises the limitations of practicability in the prison environment. This is further elaborated in *Walsh v the Governor of Midlands*, where Charleton J emphasised the danger of the courts overseeing the day-to-day running of the prison.[93]

In judicial review proceedings, the courts have recognised their jurisdiction to direct improvements but noted in *Mulligan* that they must consider the practicalities of the prison environment. The courts found that a mandamus is a difficult remedy to provide in the prison context but that it could be awarded in an appropriate case. This was also held in the case of *Devoy* but found that it was inappropriate in the case to issue an order quashing the unlawful decision noting the duty of the state to protect life and the security concerns which had driven the governor's decision.[94] This case concerned an individual being separated from the general population due to the perceived risk he posed but without adherence to the proscribed procedures.

Finally, in the context of remedies, the case of *Simpson* presents insight as to the courts view of prison applicants. In that the case, the High Court found that the applicant exaggerated the nature of his claims and gave untruthful evidence and held therefore that '[t]he Court could not contemplate awarding the Plaintiff damages because of his untruthful and exaggerated evidence'.[95] This is despite a finding that his right to privacy had been breached in that case. While the plaintiff was also denied his costs this was, however, revised on appeal.

3.4 Conclusion

As has been highlighted in this chapter, Ireland has a range of oversight mechanisms which have been reformed and strengthened over time. In addition to this, there is an extensive international and domestic framework for oversight in Ireland. These bodies have allowed for additional public oversight of the operation of Irish prisons. They have been openly critical of certain practices in Irish prisons, such as slopping out, and this has been taken on board with a steady move towards eliminating the practice. Ireland has also seen an increase in prison law cases despite the barriers to accessing the courts. The precise relationship of the courts to the internal complaint mechanisms remains unclear and the impact the introduction of the external element of the Ombudsman will have on this remains to be seen (van der Valk and Rogan 2020). However, in light of recent moves for reform it is clear that oversight is a concern for the IPS and attempts are being made to open the service up to external scrutiny. However, the practice of oversight remains underexplored. The next chapter draws on concepts of legal and penal consciousness, legal mobilisation and prison life, in particular relationships and trust in prison, to illustrate the contextual challenges and motivators in engaging with accountability in prison.

Notes

1 Geneva Convention III Article 78 *Complaints and requests* – Prisoners of war shall have the right to make known to the military authorities in whose power they are, their requests regarding the conditions of captivity to which they are subjected. They shall also have the unrestricted right to apply to the representatives of the Protecting Powers either through their prisoners' representative or, if they consider

it necessary, direct, in order to draw their attention to any points on which they may have complaints to make regarding their conditions of captivity. These requests and complaints shall not be limited nor considered to be a part of the correspondence quota referred to in Article 71. They must be transmitted immediately. Even if they are recognised to be unfounded, they may not give rise to any punishment. Prisoners' representative may send periodic reports on the situation in the camps and the needs of the prisoners of war to the representatives of the Protecting Powers.

2 Economic and Social Council Resolution 663 (XXIV) 31 July 1957.

3 Recommendation Rec(2006)2-rev of the Committee of Ministers to member States on the European Prison Rules. Adopted by the Committee of Ministers on 11 January 2006, at the 952nd meeting of the Ministers' Deputies and revised and amended by the Committee of Ministers on 1 July 2020 at the 1380th meeting of the Ministers' Deputies.

4 UN General Assembly (2016) United Nations Standard Minimum Rules for the Treatment of Prisoners (the Nelson Mandela Rules). Resolution adopted by the General Assembly on 17 December 2015. UN Doc. A/RES/70/175, 8 January 2016. https://undocs.org/A/RES/70/175 Accessed 18 February 2021.

5 UN Human Rights Committee, CCPR General Comment No. 21: Article 10 (Humane Treatment of Persons Deprived of Their Liberty), 10 April 1992, paragraph 5.

6 Rule 83 Mandela Rules.

7 Rule 55 UN Minimum Standard of Treatment Rules 1955.

8 UNODC, *Assessing Compliance with the Nelson Mandela Rules* (United Nations Office on Drugs and Crime 2017) 3.

9 UNODC, *Assessing Compliance with the Nelson Mandela Rules* (United Nations Office on Drugs and Crime 2017) 3.

10 UNODC, *Assessing Compliance with the Nelson Mandela Rules* (United Nations Office on Drugs and Crime 2017) 3.

11 UNODC, *Assessing Compliance with the Nelson Mandela Rules* (United Nations Office on Drugs and Crime 2017) 8.

12 Rule 56.3 Mandela Rules.

13 Rule 36.4 UN Minimum Standard of Treatment Rules 1955: 'Unless it is evidently frivolous or groundless, every request or complaint shall be promptly dealt with and replied to without undue delay'.

14 Rule 55.1 Nelson Mandela Rules 2015.

15 Recommendation Rec (2006)2 of the Committee of Ministers to member states on the European Prison Rules, Adopted by the Committee of Ministers on 11 January 2006 at the 952nd meeting of the Ministers' Deputies.

16 Recommendation Rec (2006)2 of the Committee of Ministers to member states on the European Prison Rules, Adopted by the Committee of Ministers on 11 January 2006 at the 952nd meeting of the Ministers' Deputies.

17 Rule 93.1 European Prison Rules 2006: 'The conditions of detention and the treatment of prisoners shall be monitored by an independent body or bodies whose findings shall be made public'.

18 Recommendation Rec (2006)2 of the Committee of Ministers to member states on the European Prison Rules, Adopted by the Committee of Ministers on 11 January 2006 at the 952nd meeting of the Ministers' Deputies.

19 European Prison Rules 1977 Rule 36.2: 'It shall be possible to make requests or complaints to an inspector of prisons during his inspection. The prisoner shall have the opportunity to talk to the inspector or to any other duly constituted authority entitled to visit the prison without the director or other members of the staff being present'.

20 Article 1 European Convention for the Prevention of Torture and Inhuman and Degrading Treatment or Punishment 1989.

21 Article 1 European Convention for the Prevention of Torture and Inhuman and Degrading Treatment or Punishment 1989.

22 Article 4.1 European Convention for the Prevention of Torture and Inhuman and Degrading Treatment or Punishment 1989.

23 Article 4.2 European Convention for the Prevention of Torture and Inhuman and Degrading Treatment or Punishment 1989.

24 Committee for the Prevention of Torture and Inhuman or Degrading Treatment or Punishment, *14th Annual Report on the CPT's activities covering the period 1 August 2003 to 31 July 2004* (Council of Europe 2004) para 15.

25 Article 10.2 European Convention for the Prevention of Torture and Inhuman and Degrading Treatment or Punishment 1989.

26 Article 12 European Convention for the Prevention of Torture and Inhuman and Degrading Treatment or Punishment 1989.

27 Article 17.3 European Convention for the Prevention of Torture and Inhuman and Degrading Treatment or Punishment 1989.

28 Committee for the Prevention of Torture and Inhuman or Degrading Treatment or Punishment, *14th Annual Report on the CPT's activities covering the period 1 August 2003 to 31 July 2004* (Council of Europe 2004) para 25.

29 Committee for the Prevention of Torture and Inhuman or Degrading Treatment or Punishment, 2nd *Annual Report on the CPT's activities covering the period 1 January to 31 December 1991* (Council of Europe 1992) para 54.

30 Committee for the Prevention of Torture and Inhuman or Degrading Treatment or Punishment, 2nd *Annual Report on the CPT's activities covering the period 1 January to 31 December 1991* (Council of Europe 1992) para 54.

31 Committee for the Prevention of Torture and Inhuman or Degrading Treatment or Punishment, *Report to the Government of the Netherlands on the visit to the Netherlands carried out by the European Committee for the Prevention of Torture and Inhuman or Degrading Treatment or Punishment (CPT) from 2 to 13 May 2016* (Council of Europe 2017) <https://rm.coe.int/16806ebb7c> Accessed 21 July 2021.

32 UN Special Rapporteur for Torture, *Interim report of the Special Rapporteur on torture and other cruel, inhuman or degrading treatment or punishment* (A/71/298 2016) 22ff.

33 Article 13 Optional Protocol to the Convention against Torture and other Cruel, Inhuman or Degrading Treatment or Punishment.

34 Article 16 Optional Protocol to the Convention against Torture and other Cruel, Inhuman or Degrading Treatment or Punishment.

35 34th Session of the SPT February 2018, Geneva www.ohchr.org/EN/NewsEvents/Pages/DisplayNews.aspx?NewsID=22729&LangID=E Accessed 24 May 2018.

36 For further discussion of the Courts jurisdiction and its development see Extra-territorial jurisdiction of States Parties to the European Convention on Human

Rights <www.echr.coe.int/Documents/FS_Extra-territorial_jurisdiction_ENG.pdf> Accessed 2 May 2018.
37 App no 47095/99 (ECtHR, 15 July 2002).
38 App no 14437/05 (ECtHR, 10 May 2007).
39 European Convention of Human Rights Act 2003, s. 2(1) states '[i]n interpreting and applying any statutory provision or rule of law, a court shall, in so far as is possible, subject to the rules of law relating to such interpretation and application, do so in a manner compatible with the State's obligations under the Convention provisions'.
40 Golder v UK (1976) 1 EHRR 524.
41 Golder v UK (1980) 3 EHRR 475.
42 *Silver v the UK* (1993) series A no 61, para 118.
43 App nos. 42525/07 and 60800/08, ECHR 10 January 2012.
44 *Alimov v Turkey* App no 14344/13 (ECtHR, 6 December 2016).
45 *Varga v Hungary* App no 14097/12 (ECtHR, 7 March 2019).
46 App no 30873/96 (ECtHR, 21 December 2020).
47 App no 446/10 (ECtHR, 14 June 2016).
48 *Mathew v the Netherlands* App no 24919/03 (ECtHR, 29 September 2005) para 149.
49 *Mathew v the Netherlands* App no 24919/03 (ECtHR, 29 September 2005) para 151.
50 IPRT Facts and Figures, www.iprt.ie/prison-facts-2 Accessed 17 September 2021.
51 Irish Prison Service <www.irishprisons.ie/> Accessed 21 July 2021.
52 Dail Eireann debate – Thursday 1 December 2011, Vol. 748 No. 3. https://www.oireachtas.ie/en/debates/debate/dail/2011-12-01/43/ Accessed 25 February 2025 .
53 S.31 Prisons Act 2007.
54 S. 31 Prisons Act 2007.
55 S.31(4) Prisons Act 2007.
56 CPT, *Report to the Government of Ireland on the visit to Ireland carried out by the European Committee for the Prevention of Torture and Inhuman or Degrading Treatment or Punishment (CPT) from 16 to 26 September 2014* (Council of Europe 2015) 38, para 4.
57 CPT, *Report to the Government of Ireland on the visit to Ireland carried out by the European Committee for the Prevention of Torture and Inhuman or Degrading Treatment or Punishment (CPT) from 16 to 26 September 2014* (Council of Europe 2015) para 81.
58 CPT, *Report to the Government of Ireland on the visit to Ireland carried out by the European Committee for the Prevention of Torture and Inhuman or Degrading Treatment or Punishment (CPT) from 23 September to 4 October 2019* (Council of Europe 2020) para 34.
59 Irish Prison Service Yearly Statistics, Sentenced Committals for Years 2007 to 2017. www.irishprisons.ie/wp-content/uploads/documents_pdf/COMMITTALS-Sentence-Length-by-Year-2007-to-Year-2017.pdf Accessed 17 September 2021.
60 Deputy Brendan Howlin, Seanád Eireann debates on the Ombudsman (Amendment) Bill 2008 4 October 2012. www.oireachtas.ie/en/debates/debate/seanad/2012-10-04/5/ Accessed 17 September 2021.

61 Statutory Instrument 11/2013 Prison Rules (Amendment) 2013 www.irishstatutebook.ie/eli/2013/si/11/made/en/print Accessed 27 March 2018.
62 Irish Prison Service, *Policy Document on Prisoner Complaints* (Irish Prison Service 2014).
63 Irish Prison Service, *Policy Document on Prisoner Complaints* (Irish Prison Service 2014).
64 Irish Prison Service, *Policy Document on Prisoner Complaints* (Irish Prison Service 2014).
65 Irish Prison Service, *Policy Document on Prisoner Complaints* (Irish Prison Service 2014).
66 Irish Prison Service, *Policy Document on Prisoner Complaints* (Irish Prison Service 2014).
67 Irish Prison Service, *Policy Document on Prisoner Complaints* (Irish Prison Service 2014).
68 Rule 57B Prison Rules Amendment 2013.
69 CPT, *Report to the Government of Ireland on the visit to Ireland carried out by the European Committee for the Prevention of Torture and Inhuman or Degrading Treatment or Punishment (CPT) from 16 to 26 September 2014* (Council of Europe 2015) 8; CPT, *Report to the Government of Ireland on the visit to Ireland carried out by the European Committee for the Prevention of Torture and Inhuman or Degrading Treatment or Punishment (CPT) from 23 September to 4 October 2019* (Council of Europe 2020).
70 Irish Penal Reform Trust, *Inspector of Prisons' review of prisoner complaint system* 9th June 2016. Available at: https://www.iprt.ie/latest-news/inspector-of-prisons-review-of-prisoner-complaints-system/) Accessed 25 February 2025.
71 Statutory Instrument No. 341/2013 Ombudsman Act 1980 (Section 4(10)) Order 2013.
72 Dail Éireann Debate, Tuesday 13 June 2023 www.oireachtas.ie/en/debates/question/2023-06-13/900/ Accessed 12 December 2024.
73 *McDonnell v Governor of Wheatfield* [2015] IECA 216.
74 *McDonnell v Governor of Wheatfield* [2015] IECA 216, para 96.
75 *McDonnell v Governor of Wheatfield* [2015] IECA 216, para 107.
76 *McDonnell v Governor of Wheatfield* [2015] IECA 216, para 97.
77 *McDonnell v Governor of Wheatfield* [2015] IECA 216, para 94.
78 *McDonnell v Governor of Wheatfield* [2015] IECA 216, para 91.
79 *Kenny v Governor of Portlaoise Prison* [2017] IEHC 581.
80 *Kenny v Governor of Portlaoise Prison* [2017] IEHC 581, para 17.
81 *Kenny v Governor of Portlaoise Prison* [2017] IEHC 581, para 6.
82 *Connolly v Governor of Wheatfield Prison* [2013] IEHC 334, 15–17, emphasis added.
83 *Kinsella v. The Governor of Mountjoy Prison* [2011] IEHC 235, para 4.
84 *Kinsella v. The Governor of Mountjoy Prison* [2012] IEHC 431.
85 *Kinsella v. The Governor of Mountjoy Prison* [2010] IEHC 269, para 18ff.
86 *Kinsella v. The Governor of Mountjoy Prison* [2010] IEHC 269, para 17.
87 *McAlister v Minister for Justice, Equality and Law Reform* [2003] 4 IR 35.
88 *McAlister v Minister for Justice, Equality and Law Reform* [2003] 4 IR para 3.
89 *McAlister v Minister for Justice, Equality and Law Reform* [2001] 4 IR 454.

90 *McAlister v Minister for Justice, Equality and Law Reform* [2008] IEHC 204, 15.
91 *Simpson -v- Governor of Mountjoy Prison & ors* [2017] IEHC 561, para 458.
92 *The State (Richardson) v the Governor of Mountjoy Prison* [1980] ILRM 82.
93 *The State (Richardson) v the Governor of Mountjoy Prison* [2012] IEHC 229, para 9.
94 *Devoy v Governor of Portlaoise Prison & Others* [2009] JR 165.
95 *Devoy v Governor of Portlaoise Prison & Others* [2019] IEHC 561, para 457.

References

Dia Anagnostou and Dimitris Skleparis, 'Human Rights in European Prisons: Can the Implementation of Strasbourg Court Judgments Influence Penitentiary Reform' in Tom Daems and Luc Robert (eds) *Europe in Prisons: Assessing the Impact of the European Institutions on National Prison Systems* (Palgrave Macmillan 2017).

Cormac Behan and Richard Kirkham, 'Monitoring, Inspection and Complaints Adjudication in Prison: The Limits of Prison Accountability Frameworks' (2016) 55(4) *The Howard Journal of Crime and Justice* 432.

Christine Bicknell and Malcolm Evans, 'Monitoring Prisons: The Increasingly Complex Relationship Between International and Domestic Frameworks' in Tom Daems and Luc Robert (eds) *Europe in Prisons: Assessing the Impact of the European Institutions on National Prison Systems* (Palgrave Macmillan 2017).

Trevor Buck, Richard Kirkham and Brian Thompson, *The Ombudsman Enterprise and Administrative Justice* (Routledge 2010).

CPT, *27th Annual Report of the CPT* (Council of Europe 2018).

CPT, *Report of the Government of the Netherlands on the periodic visit to the Kingdom of the Netherlands as carried out by the European Committee for the Prevention of Torture and Inhuman or Degrading Treatment and Punishment (CPT) from 10 to 25 May 2022* (Council of Europe 2023).

Tom Daems and Luc Robert, Introduction: From Prisons in Europe to Europe in Prisons, in Tom Daems and Luc Robert (eds) *Europe in Prisons: Assessing the Impact of the European Institutions on National Prison Systems* (Palgrave Macmillan 2017).

Corentin Durand, Nicolas Ferran and Hughes de Suremain, 'The European Oversight of France' in Gaëtan Cliquennois and Hughes de Suremain (eds) *Monitoring Penal Policy in Europe* (Routledge 2017).

Sarah Easton, 'Protecting Prisoners: The Impact of International Human Rights Law on the Treatment of Prisoners in the UK' (2013) 93(4) *The Prison Journal* 475.

Malcolm Evans and Rod Morgan, *Combating Torture in Europe: The Work and Standards of the European Committee for the Prevention of Torture (CPT)* (Council of Europe 2001).

Irish Penal Reform Trust, *Position Paper 7: Complaints, Monitoring and Inspection in Prison* (IPRT 2009).

Pauline Jacobs and Anton van Kalmthout, 'Monitoring Penal Policy in Europe' in Gaëtan Cliquennois and Hughes de Suremain (eds) *Monitoring Penal Policy in Europe* (Routledge 2017).

Joint Committee on Justice and Equality, *Report on Penal Reform and Sentencing May 2018* (House of the Oireacthas 2018).

Shane Kilcommins, Ian O'Donnell, Eoin O'Sullivan, and Barry Vaughan, *Crime, Punishment and the Search for Order in Ireland* (Institute of Public Administration 2004).

Ursula Kriebaum, 'Council of Europe Anti-Torture Committee and Prisons in Austria' in Tom Daems and Luc Robert, *Europe in Prisons: Assessing the Impact of the European Institutions on National Prison Systems* (Palgrave Macmillan 2017).

Katerina Linos and Tom Pegram, 'What Works in Human Rights Institutions?' (2017) 111 *American Journal of International Law* 628.

Danial Machover, 'Enforcing Prisoners' Rights' (2002) 49(3) *Probation Journal* 233.

Anita Mackay, 'Article 10(1) of the International Covenant on Civil and Political Rights (ICCPR) and Australian Prisons' (2017) 23(3) *Australian Journal of Human Rights Law* 368.

Rachel Murray, Elina Steinerte, Malcolm David Evans and Antenor Hallo de Wolf, *The Optional Protocol to the UN Convention Against Torture* (Oxford University Press 2011).

Office of the Inspector of Prisons (OiP), *Report on an Inspection of Mountjoy Prison* (Office of the Inspector of Prisons 2009).

Office of the Inspector of Prisons (OiP), *Report on an Inspection of Limerick Prison* (Office of the Inspector of Prisons 2011a).

Office of the Inspector of Prisons (OiP), *Report on an Inspection of Mountjoy Prison* (Office of the Inspector of Prisons 2011b).

Office of the Inspector of Prisons (OiP), *Suggested Prisoner Complaints Model for Irish Prisons* (Office of the Inspector of Prisons 2012).

Office of the Inspector of Prisons (OiP), *Review, Evaluation and Analysis of the Operation of the IPS Prisoner Complaints Procedure* (Office of the Inspector of Prisons 2016).

Paul O'Mahony, 'The Annual Report on Prisons and the Issue of Accountability' (1994) 12(1) *Irish Law Times* 6.

Nigel Rodley and Matt Pollard, *The Treatment of Prisoners Under International Law* (3rd edn Oxford University Press 2009)

Mary Rogan, 'Visiting Committees and Accountability in the Irish Prison System: Some Proposals for Reform' (2009) 31 *Dublin University Law Journal* 298.

Mary Rogan, *Accountability Structures and the Law Regulating Irish Prisons* (Irish Penal Reform Trust 2012).

Mary Rogan, 'Judicial Conception of Prisoners' Right in Ireland: An Emerging Field'. Academy of European Law, 'Improving Conditions Related to Detention' (Council of Europe, Strasbourg, November 2014a).

Mary Rogan, *Prison Law* (Bloomsbury 2014b).

SPT, *Compilation of Advice to NPMs*, 2016.

The Irish Commission for Justice and Peace, *Human Rights in Prison: Comments on the Draft Prison Rules Contained in "The Management of Offenders Plan" Department of Justice, June 1994* (Irish Commission for Justice and Peace 1994).

Thomas Ugelvik, 'The Incarceration of Foreigners in European Prisons' in Sharon Pickering and Julie Ham (eds) *The Routledge Handbook on Crime and International Migration* (Routledge 2017).

Sophie van der Valk and Mary Rogan. 'Prisoner Complaints Mechanisms: Assessing Human Rights Requirements and the Role of a General Ombudsman'. *European Public Law* 26 (2020): 801.

Dirk van Zyl Smit and Sonja Snacken, *Principles of European Prison Law and Policy: Penology and Human Rights* (Oxford University Press 2009).
Dirk van Zyl Smit. "Dignity unlocked? The Nelson Mandela Rules as a key to the transnational legal ordering of imprisonment: Godność uwolniona? Reguły Nelsona Mandeli jako klucz do transnarodowych rozwiązań prawnych w zakresie pozbawiania wolności." *Archives of Criminology XLV/2* (2023): 115–141.

4 Understanding Prisoners' Rights and Penal Culture

4.1 Introduction

The aim of this book is to understand prisoners' experiences of oversight bodies. To better understand this, it is necessary to consider literature on rights' consciousness of those in prison and the environment in which these bodies operate – that is, prisons. This chapter starts with a consideration of the role of rights in prison life as the exact scope of rights in prison remains open to interpretation and the embeddedness of those rights has also been considered by scholars such as Karamalidou (2017). Additionally, Kelk (1978) highlights the different components of rights necessary to ensure full protection of those rights while in prison. Scholars such as Piacentini and Katz (2017) and Armstrong (2018) note the possibility of rights being used as a form of control over those in custody and the risk and security focus in some prison systems reflects these concerns. Additionally, Kemp and Tomzcak (2024) raise questions about the utility of prison regulation and the pursuit of better prison standards as distinct from broader decarceration objectives. Beyond this, the understanding of rights can vary amongst different groups, even within the same environment. As discussed by Engel (2012), rights have a horizontal and vertical understanding, with formal recognition of rights in policies and the law not always translating to impact at lower levels. Similarly, in rights consciousness theory, people's experiences in terms of their own background and various socio-economic factors, along with their environment, play a key role in their understanding of rights and their scope. Merry et al. (2010) highlight that human rights consciousness is an essential support for human rights law. These variances in levels of rights consciousness can have implications for the ability for people in prisons to identify problems. As noted by Sexton (2015), people's expectations about their treatment can affect their experience and in turn whether they consider something as a problem. Drawn together the research to date reveals the challenges of rights in prison and this chapter discusses the relationship this has to accessing and interacting with rights-protecting bodies in prison.

Prisoners' awareness of their rights and how prisoners view themselves as holders of rights are key concerns because, in order to be effective, oversight

DOI: 10.4324/9781003477471-4

mechanisms are dependent on engaging with those whose rights are at risk. The legal protection model, discussed in this chapter, presumes that the individuals, which oversight bodies are intended to protect, can engage with the protection system. However, a lack of rights' consciousness can give rise to potential challenges for accessing and engaging with accountability bodies. To understand and assert their rights, prisoners must be aware that they are rights holders, and they must feel capable and worthy of asserting those rights or more broadly that they are entitled to make a claim in general (Ewick and Silbey 1998; Calavita and Jenness 2015).

The legal framework for rights protection needs to account for, and be examined alongside, considerations of the rights' consciousness of people in prison. In addition to this, a receptive atmosphere for rights and rights' protection is needed. Given some of the prevalent features of prison culture as noted in the literature, such as prioritising tough personas and hiding vulnerabilities, this can create additional challenges for asserting and protecting rights in prison (Crewe 2009). Therefore, this chapter discusses relevant areas of the literature on penal and prisoner culture, alongside literature on rights consciousness and rights awareness amongst vulnerable groups.

4.2 Historical Context of Rights in Prison

This section provides an overview of the historical development of prisoners' rights, as well as the theoretical basis for prisoners as rights' holders. It demonstrates how rights are conceived at an institutional level. As discussed by van Zyl Smit and Snacken (2009), over time the concept of prisoners' rights has evolved. Initially, imprisonment was viewed as 'social death' and various models of imprisonment were designed which reflected the societal approaches to dealing with prisoners (Behan 2016). However, over time, within Europe, the purpose of imprisonment shifted from an arbitrary infliction of pain to a more deliberate disciplining of offenders (van Zyl Smit and Snacken 2009). Alongside this there was a growth in the recognition of rights held by those in prison. While previously rights were considered inherently limited by virtue of imprisonment and prisoners were granted privileges rather than rights, the adoption of the European Prison Rules 'prompted a prison system that upholds human dignity with agreed limits of the restrictions that may legitimately be imposed on the individual rights of prisoners' (van Zyl Smit and Snacken 2009: 19). Vagg (1994) notes the important principle promoted by European and international guidance and the courts that imprisonment itself is punishment and not for further punishment. Karamalidou's (2017) research on embedding rights in prison, discusses the significant developments which have taken place in advancing the legal basis for rights in prisons; however, further consideration is needed as to how those rights are experienced by those in prison and access to mechanisms when rights are not protected.

4.3 Rights of Prisoners: Kelk and Prisoners as Rights Holders

Despite the legal recognition of prisoners' rights, the lived experience of rights and being a rights holder can diverge from the legal position. Kelk (1978) in developing the concept of 'Rechtsburger' (rights-bearing citizen), emphasises that having formal/legal rights is only one part of the picture and prisoners need to be able to assert those rights as well as have access to information on how to go about this to be full legal citizens. The concept of prisoners as 'Rechtsburger' and the associated 'Rechtsburgerschap' (rights citizenship) recognises prisoners as human beings who retain legal citizenship and rights during the term of their imprisonment. Kelk (1978: 70–72) provides three elements of an effective legal position regarding the protection of prisoners' rights: material rights, procedural rights and information rights about the former two types of rights. The information aspect ensures de facto protection of prisoner rights, as a 'theoretical legal position without adequate information equals no legal position at all', meaning information about rights and how to protect those rights play a key role in ensuring rights are actually enforced (van Zyl Smit and Snacken 2009: 72). As will be expanded on in other sections, incorporating these different facets of rights protection in prisons face numerous challenges.

As will be explored further in Section 4.5.1, rights consciousness and an absence of rights rhetoric amongst those in prison can act as barriers to asserting rights. As highlighted by Sarat (1990: 344), in his study of the welfare poor, law and decision making becomes hypervisible for those who seek to claim welfare, resulting in private and personal matters coming within the jurisdiction of officials who assess their basic needs. Similarly in prisons, as discussed by Calavita and Jenness (2015), the law is overtly present in people's everyday lives. This close relationship of the law to every day decision making shapes how people see themselves as well as their rights. The legal protection model discussed below presupposes knowledge and resources which may be lacking or not readily available to marginalised groups such as prisoners. Previous research on prisoners' experiences of complaining in particular outlines a lack of awareness of means to appeal complaints (Prisons and Probation Ombudsman 2015), barriers to gathering information on rights and rights protection (Sawyer 2021: 120) as well as low expectations of what rights mean in prison and what prison should be like (Sexton 2015). This suggests the central importance of paying attention to challenges in the environment itself and views of rights in understanding perceptions and experiences of rights protection in prison.

4.4 Rights versus Security: Bureaucratisation of Rights to Increase Penal Control

A key consideration in discussing the rights of those in prison is the focus in prison on the need to balance rights with security, as well as the concern raised by scholars about rights as a tool of control (Piacentini and Katz 2017; Armstrong 2018). Central to the literature on rights in the penal context is the evident tension between order and security and the provision of rights to prisoners. This tension is also relevant to complaints, inspection and monitoring and access to the courts. As expressed by Calavita and Jenness (2015: 112), some of the things prisoners complain about through 602s (the form for submitting complaints in Californian prisoners) are difficult to change because to do so would jeopardise the top priorities of the prison – 'safety and security'. In interviews with officers handling complaints, the focus in dealing with complaints was on the safety and security of the institution as a whole, an important right of prisoners and staff in itself and difficult to reconcile at times with concerns such as out of cell time and the facilitating of workshops and visits.

Calavita and Jenness (2015) highlight in their study the conflicting role of rights and imprisonment, as well as imprisonment and the prisoner complaints system. Courts can also struggle to identify and balance the impact of imprisonment on specific rights. As noted by Rogan (2014), deference to the prison service when it came to matters of security has been a feature of Irish court decisions. Additionally, Calavita and Jenness (2015: 17) note that:

> [i]mprisonment carries with it the circumscription or loss of many rights as being necessary to accommodate the institutional needs and objectives of prison facilities, particularly internal security and safety.

In taking decisions in the prison context a clear understanding of the closed nature of imprisonment and severe curtailment of prisoners' liberty in general is needed, which may as a result attach added meaning to ordinary events. As discussed by Fassin (2016), in relation to the French prison, the issue of the peephole in doors and who maintained control over it had increased meaning in a world where prisoners had limited control over their privacy. However, the same peephole was viewed as a necessary security measure by staff. This raises questions as to how rights frameworks are deployed in prisons; as highlighted by Armstrong (2018: 409), 'security is the ultimate trump card for prison authorities' in defining the discretion on how rights operate in prison. However, empirical assessments of how this operates in the lives of people in prison remain lacking and the impact of security rhetoric on prisoners' rights expectations while in prison.

According to Scheingold (2010), we have misplaced faith in rights' discourse in seeking to empower the subordinated. Rights' discourse has been plagued by failure across areas where it has sought to empower the subordinated and has not achieved the intended result. Kemp and Tomzcak (2024) question the ability of prison regulation through international human rights standards to alleviate the problems of prisons in the absence of explicit goals such as decarceration. Calavita and Jenness (2015: 14) argue that 'a focus on rights can be detrimental to social movements by channelling and stamping down their radical energies to accommodate the legal arena'. This critique of the rights revolution demonstrates the use of a rights dialogue through legal channels as a method of control. As discussed in MacCoun's (2005: 189) research on procedural justice, the false sense of justice achieved through acknowledging rights (or in MacCoun's case having fair procedures) should not be mistaken for achieving those rights. Thus, care needs to be taken to ensure cultural acceptance of the moral aspect of rights recognition, as in its absence there is a risk of undermining rights.

This tension is perhaps most keenly felt in the area of complaints. Calavita and Jenness (2015: 172) note that the logic of rights and control collides in starkly contradictory narratives evident in the views expressed by both prisoners and guards in their study. While prisoners viewed the complaint procedure as rights-protective, guards viewed it as a mechanism to increase control through identifying issues while also giving prisoners a legitimate avenue to complain, thus decreasing illegitimate forms of protest or resistance to unsatisfactory conditions. Therefore, the complaint procedure 'simultaneously affirm[s] both the validity of prisoner rights and the legitimacy of punishing control' (Calavita and Jenness 2015: 184). Through the constant denial of prisoner complaints and the reference to such, the legitimacy of the prisoner conditions may be increased. It also gives prisoners a degree of hope and frames the prison environment as one where their voices can make a difference.

This concern with expanding penal control through rights rhetoric was further discussed in Piacentini and Katz's (2017: 223) study of Russian prisons, where they explored the 'sociological intersection between prison as a place of legal rights and penal power'. Their study found that the human rights discourse was being used as a means of control for effective prison management through legal obedience and ensuring that prisoner behaviour was in line with a penal policy organised around institutional control. Human rights were used to enhance the normative state power as well as legitimatise the penal institution and culture dynamics. Further to this, Armstrong (2018) raises questions about the interaction between rights and security concerns in prisons to focus on control and safety rather than the individual rights of those held in prisons. She notes that domestic interpretation of human rights obligations focus on operational measurables which risk overly bureaucratising the prison and in turn further strengthening penal power. By framing rights obligations in this way, minimum standards may be met for perceived compliance but not necessarily meet the underlying objectives of prison rights as a whole (Armstrong 2018). These debates have particular relevance for inspection and monitoring as these bodies are regarded as examples of ways in which the state is adhering to its obligations under human rights principles, but the experience of those rights and rights-protecting structures may not chime with those aspirations. This is emphasised by Kemp and Tomzcak (2024), in their discussion on prison regulations as 'cruel optimism' and the potential for prison oversight to hinder broader objectives such as the reduction of prison numbers.

As highlighted by the studies outlined here, while scholars tend to agree that human rights principles have largely improved over the last decades in Europe, there is evidence of a disconnect between those principles and practice. In addition to this, there is an increasing scepticism about the potential of human rights, fundamentally, to improve the experience of people in prison and, moreover, to act as a restraint on penal power. While this literature is emerging, there remains a lack of empirical analysis of how people in prison experience rights-protecting structures, a critical gap considering the importance of the debates on this subject. This book addresses this by engaging with those in prison and discussing their experiences with rights protection while in custody.

4.5 Legal Consciousness and Legal Mobilisation in the Prison

In addition to the security concerns and the notion of rights as control outlined above, prisoners' awareness of their rights can create challenges to their engagement with oversight mechanisms. There is limited research on prisoners' rights awareness; however, studies of rights' awareness amongst other vulnerable groups in society provide valuable insights into how rights awareness can vary substantially (Marshall 2005; Edelman 2016). Additionally, some of the challenges posited by penal culture in encouraging prisoners to be empowered rights aware citizens will be considered here, such as the work by Behan on the voting rights of prisoners in Ireland (Behan 2016).

Legal consciousness is a well-developed term and provides a basis for understanding consciousness, especially through research on marginalised groups (Hull 2016). Legal consciousness, as defined by Merry (1985) 'is the way law is experienced and understood by ordinary citizens'. Engel (2012: 424) defines rights consciousness as 'the understandings of law and the social practices through which individuals and groups come to embrace, ignore, manipulate, remain unaware of, or consciously reject rights in relation to their everyday experiences'. While legal protections are important for providing a basis for the existence of rights, law cannot be detached from the reality of the people who it is designed to be used by. For someone to seek redress or protection of their rights, a certain degree of awareness of the existence of rights and trust in the system is necessary.

Through exploring rights consciousness of marginalised groups, a deeper understanding of those who enter the prison system can be gained. However, as highlighted by Calavita and Jenness (2015), context matters and despite the perceived vulnerability of those in prison and significant power dynamics, prisoners in their study did use the complaint system at high rates. Cunha (2014: 224) posits that prisoners do not arrive in prison completely absent of preconceived ideas, but rather have pre-existing moral and cultural forms which could inform their rights awareness. Therefore, literature on marginalised groups, which have similar socio-demographic backgrounds to prisoners, can provide an insight into the awareness and expectations they have on arrival. Further as suggested by Hull (2016: 555), 'it seems reasonable to assume that many forms of marginalisation will lead to heightened awareness of the gap between legal ideals and realities, with implications for legal consciousness'. Hull (2016: 555) argues that, through understanding the legal consciousness of one marginalised group, LGBT people, we can 'understand the processes and mechanism that link aspects of marginalisation to modes of legal consciousness'. Scheingold (2010: 77) notes that across race, gender and class the views on the ideals of the law showed different variances, in addition to views on the realities of the law which also varied significantly.

In discussing rights consciousness, a distinction needs to be drawn between high-level official rhetoric and real-life experiences. Engel (2012) draws a distinction between vertical and horizontal perspectives in considering rights' consciousness. The vertical perspective represents the global level influences of rights discourse, which may be disconnected from ground level experience of rights. It focuses on concepts as they are understood by high-level sections of an organisation, such as demonstrated by policy documents. The horizontal perspective, on the other hand, focuses on the 'ordinary person' and the manifestation of rights in everyday interactions (Engel 2012: 425). Engel concludes that focusing on one perspective without considering the other can lead to different conclusions on rights' consciousness in a particular setting. In the prison context, this means that while the concept of rights may be visible in the legal framework and official guidelines of the organisation, the permeability of these concepts into the everyday life of both staff and prisoners may be substantially different.

Calavita and Jenness' (2015: 161) study provides valuable insight into the legal consciousness of prisoners from their study of the grievance system in California. In their study, they found that prisoners had a high level of rights awareness and focused on legal rights language in their complaints. In particular, the dominant framing of sample complaint forms filled out by the participants offered narratives of a legalistic frame focused on rights and which assert basic human needs. Other framings for complaints focused on accountability, procedural justice, fairness and discrimination (Calavita and Jenness 2015: 151). In contrast to this, participants in Naylor's (2014) study in Australia lacked a clear rights rhetoric and instead spoke about issues in prison without necessarily using rights terminology. Interestingly, the absence of rights rhetoric amongst Dutch prisoners in Karamalidou's (2017: 153) study was seen by the prisoners themselves as a sign that the prison was respecting their rights and the 'absence of human rights talk was seen positively as they regarded its opposite as a sign of prisoner mistreatment and hostile prisoner'.

Legal consciousness literature, such as Marshall's (2005) work on sexual harassment grievance procedures in the workplace, also highlights key issues with complaint procedures in practice, especially when there are power dynamics between the complainer and the harasser. In prisons, both staff and prisoners hold different forms of power with staff responsible for the everyday needs of prisoners, but staff are also dependent on prisoners to maintain law and order in prisons (Sparks and Bottoms 1995). In addition to this, internal procedures can place employees in difficult positions, as the supervisor investigating can be closer to the accused than the complainer (Marshall 2005). In Butler and Maruna's (2016) study, prison staff felt that there was a need for prison staff to support one another in the case of disciplinary procedures. This was also evident in Calavita and Jenness' (2015) study, wherein staff expressed a need to show a united front when dealing with prisoners and to maintain good relations with peers. These issues emphasise the need to examine complaint procedures with vulnerable groups as, at times, complaint procedures can be a symbolic recognition rather than a practical solution to protecting rights.

4.5.1 Developing Rights Consciousness

Engel (2012: 427) notes that '[i]ndividual rights consciousness derives from the intersections of a person's life experience with the interpretive frameworks that are available in the social environment'. Additionally as discussed by Sexton (2015) in relation to penal consciousness, prisoners' expectations of prison shape their experiences and perceived severity of prison and punishment. Expectations of punishment can be based on a range of knowledge of prisons. These include 'vicarious knowledge of prison, prior first-hand experiences with punishment, and even expectations of what punishment should or ought to be in an ideal sense' (Sexton 2015: 129). Therefore, those who have lower expectations of prison are less likely to experience punishment as severely. This has implications for identifying what is 'wrong' in prisons and speaking up about issues such as prison conditions or ill-treatment.

In discussing rights awareness amongst prisoners, the implications of the 'prisoner' label itself needs to be considered, as it plays a role in how people conceive of themselves and their rights and rights worthiness. Research with other vulnerable groups has highlighted the role of labelling in people's perceptions of their identity and entitlements. A study conducted by Sarat (1990: 353) explored the question of self-identity by welfare participants and determined that self-identity and welfare status is difficult to discard in interactions. Therefore, status is inherently connected to an individual's concept of self. This sense of self is constantly being reshaped and formed by external and internal factors and in the case of prisoners, the label and status attached can play a significant role in their understanding of their own identity. During their term of imprisonment, other roles which they can still maintain become significantly constrained or may be lost and their primary identity becomes attached to their prisoner status (Hutton 2016). Scheingold (2010: 132) highlights the importance of identity in shaping our expectations and aspirations and that they are intrinsically linked to experiences and environment. There may, therefore, be an expectation of a denial of rights amongst certain groups and an alternative to this may be viewed as impossible. Life experiences can serve to harden individuals and they learn to bear their burden rather than challenge their position. He shows the role that litigation and court declarations of rights can play in political activation, serving as a form of mobilisation through asserting the existence of rights and the infringement thereof.

Sarat's (1990: 353) work highlights the persistence of the welfare status in the participants' engagement with various authorities. While welfare workers and legal services lawyers are separate entities, to the participants they were viewed as part of the same welfare bureaucracy. In Sarat's (1990: 533) study, the continuing relationship between welfare lawyers and officers made some participants wary that the lawyers' relationship with the services agency could impact on their willingness to rock the boat. As highlighted by Waldram (2009) in the prison context, while the independent status of his research was constantly reiterated, care and time was needed to enable participants to truly trust his assurances. Studies on VCs and IMBs raise concerns amongst prisoners of the distance between prison management and members of these bodies (Behan 2016; Padfield 2018). Therefore, the reality of the independence of oversight bodies and whether it is accepted as such by prisoners themselves is questionable and calls for further exploration.

In Calavita and Jenness' (2015: 5) study, they found that the internal complaint process itself contributed to rights' consciousness amongst prisoners while also being an important tool for carceral control for officers as allowing grievances creates a legitimate avenue to complain. The US complaint procedure was initially created to limit prisoners' legal access to the courts. However, the presence of the system stoked prisoners' rights consciousness. As noted by Calavita and Jenness (2015: 48), '[t]he grievance system is prisoners' concrete and daily reminder that they have rights to contest'. This serves to enhance the rights consciousness of prisoners and general awareness of the existence of rights. They observe that '[f]or ... prisoners, whose every move is "constricted", not only does filing grievances deploy the laws of the "very institution that dominate[s]" them, but it galvanises a consciousness of rights in a context in which rights are severely limited' (Calavita and Jenness 2015: 74).

Calavita and Jenness (2015: 78) found that the complaint procedure in the prison environment provides for 'rights consciousness [to be] paradoxically enhanced, as prisoners focus on how to preserve the rights they retain and defiantly contest perceived violations', while the complaint procedure systematically denied prisoners the satisfaction of resolving complaints. When viewed as a whole, these studies highlight rights consciousness as evolving throughout a prisoners' life and the duration of imprisonment. While preconceptions of imprisonment and a person's entitlements play a role in shaping rights consciousness, imprisonment itself, as well as interactions while in prison can further ingrain prisoners' sense of entitlement to rights and expectations.

4.5.2 Beyond Legal Consciousness

While legal consciousness is one factor which may explain why prisoners do not engage with rights protection in prison, studies such as Behan's (2016) point to other factors in the prison environment which may prompt disengagement with institutional systems for rights. As noted by Lovell (2012), a lack of observed resistance should not be equated with the law's hegemonic power resulting in acquiescence and compliance amongst ordinary people. Lovell (2012) instead suggests that we need to consider alternatives for a lack of resistance. In the case of prisons, the literature on penal culture and relationship dynamics goes some way to explaining why non-adherence to the legal norm is not met with outright resistance which would be expected amongst those with a high level of legal consciousness. Fighting back against prison authorities can be challenging in prisons (Calavita and Jenness 2015), and those in prison may be worn down and defeated into a state of fatalism by the prison system, whereby fighting back is seen a futile (Carrabine 2004). Fatalism, or fatalistic order, is brought about by 'dull compulsion of rituals that powerfully constrain action and signify the inevitability of the social structure' (Carrabine 2005: 904). Hull (2016: 570) calls for a need for deeper understanding of tolerance of 'the gap' between the law and reality amongst ordinary people. Silbey (2005: 338) notes that in the ethnographic work on legal consciousness, it has been demonstrated that otherwise capable citizens may be inhibited in participating in the legal sphere by issues of power and inequality. Given the dominance of power in prisons and prison culture, the implications this can have on understandings of rights and asserting rights needs to be considered.

Behan (2016), in his study of the prisoner's right to vote in Ireland, identified different categories of prisoner for the purposes of understanding the 'Abstentionist Prisoner'. His categorisation distinguished between those who actively chose not to vote (voluntary abstentionism) and those who were prevented from doing so due to practical considerations (circumstantial abstentionism). His framework identifies some of the challenges of asserting rights in prison while seeking out legal protection can be beyond certain prisoners. In engaging with oversight mechanisms, prisoners may face some of the same challenges identified in Behan's study, either through a lack of awareness with the mechanisms in place or a sense that mechanisms do not work, and rights are not accessible to those in prison. Circumstantial abstentionism referred to a broad range of reasons given by prisoners for not voting; some reflected concerns with the process of registering to vote in prison, while others reflected broader issues with the political process. Circumstantial abstentionists referred to concerns about media coverage of prisoners voting, the refusal by prisoners to give the prison as their home address, the lack of home address for registration, the lack of personal engagement, poor literacy levels, complicated processes, imprisonment post-registration, being transferred between prisons and a lack of institutional support in the registration process. In terms of voluntary abstentionism, prisoners expressed clear reasons related to politics and society which made them choose not to vote. These were apathy towards politics, political negativity towards politicians, little political engagement outside prison, sentence length, new government policies which reiterated prisoners' concerns with previous policies and alienation. The voluntary abstentionism prisoners reflected wider issues in the prison with encouraging civic identity and preventing social death through imprisonment.

Calavita and Jenness' (2015) work highlights that effective complaint systems can provide prisoners with a voice and serve to balance the powerlessness that may be inherent in the prison environment. This empowerment process is significant as, while prisoners need to have an awareness of their rights to seek to assert them, they also must feel worthy of those rights in order to seek to protect them. Therefore, the meaning prisoners attach to their rights, on a practical level, will shape and further the understanding of accountability mechanisms which seek to protect those rights and what is needed for such mechanisms to be effective.

While the research to date suggests that rights and legal consciousness may currently face challenges in prison, Karamalidou (2017) provides us with a framework for embedding rights throughout the prison system. Karamalidou discusses the benefits of a proactive human rights approach in prison, which embeds human rights standards. She highlights that a human rights approach in prison, which is based on general application through soft law instruments, can serve four purposes: educative, psychotherapeutic, humanising and has an emancipatory potential. Karamalidou (2017) discusses the educative role as one which promotes awareness of rights and an appreciation of rights and responsibilities amongst prisoners. She sees this as one which can be done through prison education which goes beyond basic skills to promote personal development. The psychotherapeutic aspect refers to a building of self-awareness and empowering prisoners to take positive action to change their circumstances. Tied in with the education aspect, prisoners are better equipped to identify rights issues and circumstances which should be addressed. In terms of humanising, rights can provide meaningful interactions with others, such as staff and other prisoners to restore self-respect, self-worth and dignity. These are all characteristics which can be stripped through the prison experience and environment, or which prisoners may be lacking due to their pre-prison lifestyle. The central role played by officers through their relational proximity to prisoners should not be wasted and officers through every day interactions can promote these traits. They can give hope and purpose to prisoners and assist them in surviving the pains of imprisonment.

Finally, the emancipatory potential of rights in prison can create a determination to return to society and skills for successful reintegration. Prison can be a dehumanising experience but an embedded human rights approach throughout can build important social skills and encourage prisoners to seek rights, as well as recognise their societal responsibility by virtue of the rights of others. The next section considers how the prison environment shapes and limits opportunities to engage with rights-protecting bodies; however, it is clear from the research to date on rights and rights consciousness amongst marginalised groups, including prisoners, that rights are not perceived or experienced as readily available or accessible.

4.5.3 Legal Protection Model: Limitations

Kelk's (1978) work highlights the importance of establishing procedural mechanisms for de facto protection of prisoners' rights; this is the focal point for oversight mechanisms. The legal protection model sets out legal tools for victims to use when they perceive their rights have been infringed. While inspection and monitoring are different in allowing external professionals to enter a prison and observe conditions, there is still a reliance on prisoners to interact and identify issues. Relying on prisoners to assert their rights through these bodies needs further consideration, as discussed by Stanley (2011: 109):

> Monitors may not see violations because they change, or are hidden – and sometimes even because prisoners do not tell them what is happening, because they feel ashamed, or they do not have an understanding that they have been violated, or they do not have faith or trust in the complaints system, or they are resigned to their fate.

Calavita and Jenness (2015) found that complaints offer a voice and a way for prisoners to rightfully resist, that is, through using a prison-created means of complaint. However, in Bumiller's (1987) study, victims of discrimination felt doubly victimised by seeking to assert their rights through the courts as it distanced them from support which they needed at that time and they were both the object of discrimination as well as a case before the law. In contrast, Calavita and Jenness' (2015: 75) study found that participants felt they were victims if they did not assert their rights. By asserting rights and seeking to call upon the law, participants are seeking to ensure the institution lives up to the expectations and standards which it claims to uphold. Standing up for rights, even if ultimately ineffective, serves as a reminder that those rights exist and even in prison rights are retained. This suggests that in the prison context the hypervisibility of law in prisons may drive prisoners to seek protection, despite their vulnerability and marginalisation (Calavita and Jenness 2015).

The legal protection model sees the law as a powerful and effective instrument for the protection of civil rights. As noted by Bumiller (1987: 422),

> [t]he law provides victims with a tool by which they can force perpetrators of unlawful conduct to comply with socially established norms. [However,] [t]he model of legal protection assumes that those who have suffered harms will recognise their injuries and invoke the protective measures of law.

This places the burden on the victim to report the alleged harm and assumes that seeking the protection of the law is unproblematic. The law in theory and the law in practice can be vastly divergent especially amongst different groups. Therefore, there is a need to question the compatibility of legal rules with the everyday life of those who it seeks to protect as

> [t]he model of legal protection would suggest that the failure of persons to use the law stems from the victims' inability to serve their own needs: lack of information and knowledge about their rights and their limited resources for utilising legal channels.
>
> (Bumiller 1987: 426)

However, this does not represent the complete picture and Bumiller identifies other factors which can have a role in preventing victims of discrimination from seeking to assert their rights. Bumiller (1987: 439) notes that

> legal strategies put unacceptable burdens on disadvantaged groups with little promise of success. The gap between the symbolic life of the law and the ineffectiveness of the law in action imposes a cost borne by the intended beneficiaries of civil rights policies.

While inspection and monitoring may mitigate this to a certain extent, as they seek out information, they still require input from those in prison to understand the environment fully and to ensure targeted and feasible recommendations.

In relying on the legal protection model, certain groups may lack the resources, knowledge and skills to gain effective protection for their rights. While limited research exists on legal protection in the prison environment, rights consciousness can create a barrier to seeking out information on and using oversight mechanisms to protect rights.

4.6 Context Matters: The Role of the Prison Environment in Accessing and Assessing Rights Protection Mechanisms

Human rights are not adopted in a vacuum but rather adapted 'to existing normative structures and specific socio-historical situations … [t]hey expand upon ideas already present as "value added" expansions of existing organizational and cultural frameworks rather than as replacements' (Merry et al. 2010: 108). This section explores penal culture and the effect this can have on the operation and perception of oversight mechanisms. As highlighted by

Sexton (2012: 50), little things matter in prison due to the stripping away of previous freedoms. In particular, it deals with literature on staff-prisoner relationships, as staff act as gatekeepers for prison services and provide for the fundamental needs of prisoners. As will be outlined below, staff can have both a negative or a positive impact on prisoners' experiences through imparting knowledge on life in prison, providing support to prisoners and can be seen as representatives of the system as a whole. Following on from this, the role of power dynamics in relationships and prison in hindering or enabling engagement with accountability bodies will be explored.

4.6.1 Prison Culture

Culture can be seen as

> a pattern of shared basic assumptions that the group learned as it solved its problems of external adaptation and internal integration, that has worked well enough to be considered valid and, therefore, to be taught to new members as the correct way to perceive, think and feel in relation to those problem.
>
> (Suntiger and Birk 2021)

In the prison context, these shared values and modes of behaviour which are adhered to are often referred to as the 'prisoner code' and as noted by Crewe (2012: 35), '[s]ome aspects of the prisoner code seem to be remarkably consistent across time and space'. Sykes and Messinger (1960: 5–19) identify the following five core rules for prisoners to adhere to while in prison:

- don't interfere with other prisoners' interests and never rat [grass] on another prisoner;
- don't lose your calm and play it cool and do your own time;
- don't exploit or steal from other prisoners;
- don't be weak/be tough;
- don't ever side with prison officers or authorities.

This section explores the role of aspects of prisoner culture and trust in prison settings in relation to seeking out rights protection in prison.

As discussed by Goffman (1986), people engage in impression management in front stage spaces to create an 'acceptable' persona of themselves in public. However, this impression management in social life is done on the presumption that privacy to drop this appearance and allow for the true self is ensured at some stage. In a prison environment where prisoners share cells and are constantly watched by staff, the private spaces for the true self are increasingly diminished. Jewkes (2005) notes the overt masculinity that prisoners often use as a 'front' in prison. This masculine front serves a number of purposes. In the situation of role stripping experienced upon entering the prison, it is a way of re-establishing a sense of masculine self-esteem, known as compensation. It also serves as a protection from exploitation and a means to develop a certain status in prison, which can be viewed as a way of earning additional resources (Crewe et al. 2014: 61–62). This overt masculinity is concentrated on extreme self-control and avoiding appearing weak to other prisoners or staff. Weakness is considered undesirable as it could be a basis for exploitation, as demonstrated by the deprivation of security discussed in Sykes (1958) 'pains of imprisonment'. However, as noted by Jewkes (2005), this extreme masculine front can be damaging to a prisoner's mental health and can cause significant emotional strain. It prevents them from dealing with the shock of imprisonment and discussing their struggles. Incarceration can be an extremely difficult experience for prisoners as further demonstrated by Sykes' (1958: 63) 'pains of imprisonment'. This tough persona can also be difficult to drop due to being deeply embedded, which may make exposing vulnerabilities to accountability bodies a challenge, as it may be felt as being the antithesis to adherence to the prisoner code of being tough and not engaging with authorities.

Prisoner relationships play a key role in shaping experiences – as noted by Sykes (1958: 8), any interaction amongst prisoners creates 'a social system of relationships, norms and hierarchies'. These may include relationships of dependency, as well as sources of genuine support amongst prisoners, prisoner 'codes of conduct' and prisoner hierarchies. While mistrust of other prisoners is a factor due to the fact that most people in prison have done something to get themselves there, Sykes (1958) emphasises that forming relationships in prison is necessary to ease the 'pains of imprisonment', which include separation from traditional sources of support and comfort such as family and friends. Prisoners can serve as a source of comfort for each other, providing safety in numbers in what can be a dangerous environment, as well as guidance to those serving shorter sentences or those in prison for their first time as to how things work. Rowe (2012: 110) illustrates that accepting support from other prisoners can be fraught with concerns of other risks such as fear of exposing vulnerability and trusting a stranger who is assumed to be untrustworthy. These concerns create barriers to the formation of 'real friendships' in prisons. Additionally, there is a hierarchy of status and stigma evident in the literature surrounding prisoners. The clearest example is the attitude towards those convicted of sexual offences, especially in relation to children, who are at the bottom of the pecking order amongst prisoners (Crewe 2012: 32).

Long-term prisoners in Crewe's (2012: 32) research highlighted the changing approach regarding staff, as previously prisoners who spoke to staff would be targeted by other prisoners or avoided as they would be viewed as a snitch, considered a serious violation of the prisoner code discussed above. This highlights a shift in penal policy which encourages engagement with staff to demonstrate a willingness to address offending behaviour and gain privileges which may be subject to staff discretion or input on assessment.

While bullying was not considered acceptable by a prisoner interviewed by Crewe (2012: 31), there was a degree of blame placed on the victims of bullying for displaying weakness and allowing themselves to be bullied. This ties in with the literature on hypermasculinity in prisons such as that by Jewkes discussed above and the need to present a tough front, as weaknesses can be exploited or there is a fear of such amongst many prisoners.

Another feature of prison culture which plays a role in shaping experiences of accountability and rights in prison is the low trust nature of the prison environment (Liebling 2004). As highlighted by Crewe (2011: 459), '[p]risons are low trust environments, holding people who experiences of trust tend not to dispose them to faith in others'. Additionally as discussed by Hardin (2002), certain features of prison space and practices are designed to destroy trust, through blocking group mobilisation. Hardin (2002) highlights how an ability to place trust in others is based upon past encounters which moulds trust in authorities and in daily life. Prisoners may also lack self-trust, whereby they are unsure whether to trust their own judgement in placing trust in others (Hardin 2002). Prior experiences of trusting others may have been misplaced and thus created a vacuum of trust for the prisoner. Hawley (2012: 18) discusses the challenges of trusting for those who have not been trusted themselves in the past, noting that those in 'positions of privilege may find it easier to take a chance with trusting, simply because the risks and stakes are lower'. As emphasised by Calavita and Jenness (2015), prisons are high stakes environments, therefore the cost of misplaced trust can be high and prisoners have limited resources to lose. Another key feature of trust centres on expectations – prisoners are required to place their trust in others in order to meet their needs or to resolve complaints. When those expectations are not met, the trust placed in the other body can be damaged. These expectations are built around the skills and intention or motivation which the person is believed to hold, and trust in both skills and intentions are necessary for full trust (Hawley 2012: 4). In the absence of knowledge to assess skills and intentions, some may choose not to engage due to perceived high risks of not having the requisite information, while others may engage with limited expectations. As discussed in Chapter 2, trust in authorities is a core component of procedural justice and a key element in whether bodies, including accountability bodies, are perceived as being just. Therefore, the low levels of trust in prisons and challenges to enhancing it can act as a hurdle to encouraging trust in accountability bodies.

4.6.2 Prisoner/Staff Relations: An Unequal Relationship with a Potentially Positive Impact?

As highlighted by Carrabine (2005: 897) imprisonment is a situation where:

> prisoners are confined against their will, with people they would normally not choose to be with, in circumstances they can do little to change and

> are governed by custodians who police practically every aspect of their daily life.

During their sentence of imprisonment, prisoners are limited to a significant extent to life within the walls, aside for visitations and external communication which are controlled by the prison authorities. This separation can exacerbate feelings of neglect and contempt (Sykes 1958). A prisoner's understanding of prison life and accountability within the prison environment is experienced, in part, through their engagement with staff, who play a pivotal role during their sentence by providing access to various facilities within the prison, as well as information on prison life itself and rules for the prison. Staff are a source of access to the outside world through facilitating visits and phone calls as well as through interacting with prisoners.

The quality of the behaviour of officers was identified by Sparks and Bottoms (1995: 55) as a relevant component for the maintenance of order and avoidance of disorder within a prison through acting as representatives of the system. As discussed in the context of procedural justice in the previous chapter, research suggests that treatment of prisoners by staff impacted on prisoners' compliance with the prison rules (Beijersbergen et al. 2015). However, Sparks and Bottoms (1995), as well as Calavita and Jenness (2015: 82) note that prisoners at times differentiate between their views of the system and staff as a whole and a particular member of staff who they got along with. Prisoners in Sparks and Bottoms study (1995: 56), 'considered [staff] in the main to be reasonable, fair, "just doing their job"'. Similarly Calavita and Jenness (2015: 83) found that prisoners viewed staff as just doing their job, with even those who had particularly bad prison experiences acknowledging that some staff could be 'cool'. This, as expounded by Sparks and Bottoms (1995: 56–57), demonstrates that staff could use interpersonal relationships to help ease the pains of imprisonment even within strict regimes, such as the UK prison in their study, and to retain a degree of legitimacy. A study by Franke et al. (2010: 89), which compares a boot camp to a prison in terms of legitimacy, showed the significance of prisoners' perceptions of staff and their desire to care for prisoners. In the boot camp, the perceived interest of staff in the development of the prisoner served to enhance legitimacy and develop motive-based trust despite the harsher conditions at the boot camp at times in comparison to the prison studied (2010: p. 112). As further stated by Liebling (2008: 38):

> Staff-prisoner relationships were significant because they constituted the framework within which decisions were made by prison officers and evaluated by prisoners. They were the route through which everything else was achieved. What officers could do was limited not by rules but by relationships (they were both a resource and a constraint).

In the context of oversight, staff provide the gateway to complaint mechanisms through support in filling out forms, registering complaints, investigating them in certain instances and communicating an outcome and justification for a decision to the prisoner. This suggests that perceptions of staff and relationships in prison may play a role in prisoners' use and perceptions of complaints mechanisms, as well as in their decisions to interact with inspection and monitoring bodies.

However, as shown by Liebling et al.'s (1999: 83) work on the concept of good versus right relationships, getting the relationship right is not always easy and 'being a good prison officer involved being good at not using force, but still getting things done'. Relationships within prisons can vary broadly and have been described as 'too close', 'too distant', 'too flexible' and 'too oppressive' (Liebling et al. 1999). Right relationships go further than good relationships in that while staff get along with prisoners, they also remain vigilant and are not afraid to use their power when a prisoner crosses the line. Additionally, Liebling (2011: 486) highlighted the importance of legitimacy in the exercise of power within the prison context for staff prisoner relationships. She noted that, with the increase in the perceived legitimacy of power by authorities in prisons, '[o]bedience is more likely to be enduring rather than grudging, information will flow more readily between the power-holders and their subjects, trust will develop, and well-being will be higher'.

Butler (2016: 343 and 244) describes the 'right' relationships as ones which are 'respectful, have clear boundaries, are consistent, recognise the power imbalances in prison, address conflict rather than avoid it, and explain deviations from the norm'.[1] This includes ensuring that the prisoner's voice is being heard, which is only fulfilled through an effective complaints mechanism that prisoners perceive as fair and just. As indicated by Boone and Kox (2014: 132), '[t]he semi-permanent relationships between prison officers and prisoners increase the impact of these officers' decisions on prisoners and intensify the need for exceptions to the rules'. Prisoners may begin to view staff as a friend of sorts, the term friend being used hesitantly in the prison environment even when it comes to other prisoners, and therefore decisions that may impact heavily on the prisoner can be difficult to deliver by staff. Tait (2008: 45) notes the increased sense of betrayal felt by prisoners when a trusted staff member wrote them up or switched between care and a hostile discipline with a lack of clear explanation. A UK study of female and youth offenders found that prisoner relationships with particular staff members played a role in the engagement with complaint mechanism, as some prisoners were able to resolve concerns informally by speaking to a trusted officer (Prisons and Probation Ombudsman 2015). In addition to this, Bierie (2013: 19) found that while violence in prisons increased with an increase in custody staff, it decreased with an increase in support staff such as teachers and counsellors. These studies highlight the role staff play in mediating both inter-prisoner conflicts and complaints.

Additionally, Tait (2008: 13) identifies a number of structural limits which can create barriers in staff prisoner relationships,

> such as fear of reprisal from managers and peers (Lombardo 1985), accusations of sexual relations with inmates resulting in an inflexible detached manner (Zimmer 1986; Owen 1988) and lack of support for officers to express their emotions about working with prisoners (Tracy 2005).

Penal culture and prisoner codes of solidarity can act as a further barrier to engagement with staff and developing relationships as approaching staff for help can be viewed as a betrayal (Tait 2008: 13). Furthermore, factors such as race, nationality and ethnicity can play a role in prisoners' perceptions of staff and relationships. Potential language or cultural barriers can impact on foreign nationals' experiences of prison and relationships with staff. As highlighted in a study by Boone and Kox (2014) of a Dutch prison used to facilitate Belgium prisoners, French-speaking prisoners felt that they were unable to seek help from staff and that Flemish (a language similar to Dutch) speakers had an advantage. This can further compound feelings of isolation and mistrust. Additionally, it can create a barrier to gaining information and knowledge on accountability bodies available to them in prison.

It is clear from the existing literature on staff prisoner relationships that they play an important role in prisoners' experience of life in prison. However, relationships can have both a negative and positive impact depending on the officers' use of power, discretion and attitude towards the prisoners in their care. As outlined by Butler and Maruna (2016: 134–135) in discussing the role of restorative justice in the disciplinary process they found that both sides felt that hearings and formal proceedings impacted on relationships in the prison and levels of trust between the parties. The role of staff relationships in prisoners' perception of and engagement with accountability bodies remains underexplored; however, it is clear that staff shape prisoner experiences and can serve as representations of trust and legitimacy of the system.

4.6.3 Inter Prisoner Relationships

While relationships between staff and prisoners are vertical in nature given the power imbalance and dependant nature of the relationship, prisoners also have horizontal relationships in prisons with other prisoners. As outlined by Sykes (1958), these relationships can play an important role in easing what he terms the 'pains of imprisonment'. In particular, as described by Crewe (2009: 301), relationships with other prisoners enhanced 'physical safety, material provision and social support'. However, these relationships can play a role in assessments carried out by staff and, as described by Crewe (2009: 147) in his interviews with prisoners, prisoners felt that they were judged by who they associated with and that it had an impact on how their progress was viewed. Associating with people from similar backgrounds or locality, while a source of comfort for prisoners in an unfamiliar environment, could be seen by management as resistance to change and refusal to deal with offending behaviour.

In addition to this, other prisoners can be valuable sources of information on life in prison and shape other prisoners' expectations of what prison should be like. As discussed by Sawyer (2021: 104), those in prison learnt from one another when preparing cases in prison and the study of law was 'inextricably linked to ... other [prisoners] ... who passed the proverbial torch on how to effectively file administrative appeals, and state petitions for writ of habeas corpus'. However, other prisoners could also exploit vulnerable prisoners and therefore carefully selecting who could be relied on without seeking something in return was an important part of letting your guard down and trusting others, even, to a limited extend, in prison (Crewe 2009).

4.6.4 Power in Prisons

This section explores the various power dynamics at play in prisons, as power can shape a prisoner's choice of action when confronted with a problem in prison. Prior research has found that a key feature of life in prison is the power differential experienced by those in custody. Prisons are not generally anarchic unregulated environments but rather they are the subject of extensive rules and surveillance not entirely evident in general society. The maintenance of order in prison is dependent on the power dynamics between the various parties as rules are under- and over- enforced to achieve a balance, as highlighted by Liebling's (2004) research on prison performance. Power in prison has been discussed extensively in the literature such as by Foucault (2012) and Weber (1978), revealing the pervasiveness of its role in prison life and interactions. Accountability can shift the power balance and allow prisoners to reclaim control over their environment, as evident by Mathieson's (1965) research on censoriousness discussed in the previous chapter. Also not speaking to an inspection and monitoring body or filing a complaint can be used as leverage to gain power and hold over staff.

As stated by Wooldredge and Steiner (2016: 130), 'power involves one person's ability to influence the behaviour of another'. Paramount in examining the power dynamics in prison is the need to consider the 'local' standards of power as prisoners are dependent on staff to fulfil their basic needs and therefore situationally power manifests itself differently than for those outside of prison. Prisoners are stripped of the traditional decision making in their routine which adults in society have become accustomed to and this stripping of power to a reversion to a childlike position needs to be acknowledged in the power dynamic of the prison environment.

4.6.5 Power, Fear and Resignation: Obstacles to Engagement

As discussed by Foucault (2012: 236) the prison 'gives almost total power over the prisoners'. The prison takes over responsibility for every aspect of the prisoner's life. As highlighted by Behan and Kirkham (2016: 446), 'the potential for abuse of power, especially with minor infractions, necessitates that safeguards are required to protect the vulnerable in the unequal power relationship that exists in prisons'. The power held by prison officers over prisoners is a key feature of their relationship and although it often goes unused, its existence remains clear in the relationship. Despite this, prison officers are to a certain extent dependent on prisoners to cooperate in the running of the prison. While prison officers do have the power and the means to use force, being entirely dependent on this as a means of gaining cooperation has its limits due to staffing levels in prisons and the potential negative implications on legitimacy. Greater reliance on coercive power was reported by prisoners in Wooldredge and Steiner's (2016: 157) study as decreasing their perceptions of an officer as fair, equitable and competent. As discussed by Sykes (1958), tolerating minor infringements in exchange for general goodwill is one way of promoting good relations but in doing so consideration needs to be given as to how far this should go so that prisoners do not become the ones in control in the prison. Staff need to find the balance between providing support and consideration of a prisoner's specific circumstances and ensuring that prison order is maintained. This was discussed by Crewe (2009: 104), who notes the positive attributes of officers' use of discretion, '[a]t times, [it] can be employed to bypass inefficiencies, enable prisoners to back down from confrontation without losing face, reduce needless tensions, and to make exceptions or prisoners who are vulnerable'.

Sykes (1958: 41) asserts that the power held by prison officials is incomparable to those in contemporary society, as it consists of a 'merging of legislative, executive and judicial functions which has long been recognized as the earmark of complete domination'. This contrasts with the basic principles of democracy which delegate these kinds of functions to different organs with interrelated systems of checks and balances. However, certain aspects of the prison institution and its daily functioning serve to counter the authoritarian appearance of such an institution. The growth in accountability which gives prisoners a distinct voice and opens the prison up to public inspection also further serves as a check on the exercise of power and discretion within the prison.

In discussing the power dynamic between staff and prisoners, it is important to bear in mind the shift in penal policy from physical power to psychological power as prisons have gone through various phases of reform. Recent years have seen a rise in policies which focus on prisoners self-regulating their behaviour and coercive control through framing better treatment as something to be earned through behaviour (Crewe 2009: 108). This has altered the kind of power held by front line staff dealing with prisoners who may affect the gaining of privileges through report writing to administrators taking decisions at a higher level. The officer/prisoner relationship has shifted as 'real' decision making has moved out of the hands of those who directly engage with the prisoners. As officers develop a friendly approach to prisoners on an interaction level, they are still involved indirectly in influencing some decisions. The need to resort to enforcing an order through more direct means of power can also be in stark contrast to general friendly behaviour by staff and can happen suddenly as issues arise in prisons. As discussed by Crewe (2011: 457), this can breed mistrust amongst prisoners as they 'struggle to reconcile the apparently conflicting responsibilities of officers to deliver decency alongside control and public protection'.

Prison rules are also often based on a degree of flexibility in their application. While this is desirable, this discretion can give rise to perceptions of prejudice and preferential treatment of specific prisoners leading to potential conflict (Butler 2016: 343). As noted by Sparks et al. (1996: 272), 'consistency is one of the chief terms that prisoners use to assess the fairness of legitimacy of treatment they receive'. This was highlighted in the study conducted by Boone and Kox (2014) in a prison in the Netherlands. This study focused on a very specific type of prison which housed Belgium prisoners in the Netherlands, due to undercrowding in the Netherlands and overcrowding in Belgium and an agreement between the neighbouring countries to transfer prisoners. While prisoners appreciated staff flexibility and discretion, the language barrier between the staff and French-speaking prisoners in particular had a significant impact on their experience of discretional power (Boone and Kox 2014). Although this study is clearly of a specific nature given the language barrier of a group of prisoners in this particular prison, the role of communication could have a more general impact on prisoners who are more willing to speak up and engage with authorities than those who lack trust in authorities and shy from seeking additional benefits. Discretional decision making requires an awareness of a prisoner's specific needs, something that can only be ascertained through communication.

Foucault (2012), Carrabine (2004) and Karamalidou (2017) point to the effects that the power of the prison over prisoners can have on them. When the exercise of power is perceived as arbitrary and unjust, this can create feelings of anger and frustration, especially when the prisoners' position of powerlessness limits possible modes of recourse (Foucault 2012). Additionally, prisoners may experience feelings of fatalism or dull compliance, as discussed by Carrabine (2004), due to the all-encompassing nature of power over them and a sense of futility at fighting back. As highlighted by Foucault (2012), the lines of power in prison can become embedded in one's sense of self and engrain feelings of powerlessness. These experiences can be further compounded by the expansion of penal power and the different types of power acting on those in prison, specially hard and soft power.

Hard powers include the use of force and legally enforceable decisions in prisons such as those made in disciplinary procedures. Soft power, however, is the subtler use of power and in the prison environment can compound feelings of powerlessness to a much greater extent than outside of prisons, such as the use of discretion in staff decision making. Rules and regulations often provide for a broad degree of discretion and can as contain proviso clauses such 'as soon as it is practicable'.[2] Of particular concern regarding soft power is what Crewe (2011) and Warr (2020) describe as psychological power. This refers to the input in report writing from prison psychologists and other officers who monitor a prisoner's 'progress' through the system. This is of particular concern for prisoners serving indeterminate sentences or those approaching parole hearings. As prison policy develops and increases the degree of self-regulation by prisoners of their own behaviour, the power dynamic shifts creating a less clear distinction of acceptable behaviour and what is required to progress through the system. This is especially so in the case of staff/prisoner interactions where prisoners may experience different levels of appropriate behaviour from various staff members before being written up. As described in Rowe's (2012: 114) study, the powerlessness felt by prisoners can be elevated by evaluations which may affect decision making in prisons by resting on 'apparently subjective judgements about … character and behaviour by officers and psychologists'. This highlights the oppressive sense of latent power which can be held by staff in prisons and the hypervisibility of law in prisons as described by Calavita and Jenness (2015: 48).

As prisons are environments where there is a substantial risk of abuse of power, oversight mechanisms provide an important tool in reducing this risk (Behan and Kirkham 2016). They give prisoners a legitimate voice which should not be subject to sanction and a safe space to challenge the sometimes-overwhelming power of prison officers. Inspectors can provide an independent voice and an insight for the public into how prisoners are treated. However, oversight has its limits. Inspectors are often dependent on the good will of prison management to accept their recommendations and lack the bite of sanctions. Complaints also serve to identify troublemakers who may fear that they will receive different treatment if they challenge staff. As highlighted above in relation to prison culture, prisoners' focus can be on getting through prison rather than seeking to challenge the power structures acting upon them in prison.

4.6.6 Manifestations of Resistance: A Role for Complaints and Litigation

While prison riots do occur, they are rare especially in European prisons, and given the nature of the environment, it is rather the mundane balance and surprising order which needs explanation (Sparks et al. 1996). The absence of riots, however, does not mean that there is an absence of resistance. Despite the unequal distribution of power in prison, the constraints of the environment and limited autonomy, prisoners do find ways to resist in prisons and this can manifest in a broad variety of ways. One form, explored by Ugelvik (2011) in his study of a Norwegian prison, is through the breaking of rules to alter prison food or to make food themselves. As discussed by Ugelvik (2011: 54), the decision to eat what and when you want is a normal decision for the average adult male which is often stripped away during imprisonment. Prison food was a persistent source of complaint in his study and prisoners would often be unaware of the food they were eating until they opened the container. It could serve as a constant reminder of the absence of loved ones to share meals with and the types of food they would choose themselves on the outside. Prison food was therefore seen as an attack on the prisoners' identity. In Ugelvik's (2011) study, prisoners discussed various ways around adherence to the prison diet, some of which broke prison rules and could if discovered led to harsh penalties for those involved. The fact the prison officers in some instances knew of these practices but chose not to strictly adhere to prison rules demonstrates the relationship between power and resistance which is continuously being negotiated in the minute details of everyday life in the prison. The alternative form of resistance in relation to diet would be to engage in a hunger strike but such resistance necessitates moving the resistance into the public arena and prompt the prison service to act. Therefore, more subtle forms of resistance have the benefit of allowing prisoners to regain a sense of identity and autonomy for an extended period rather than the potentially swift ending of a more overt form such as a hunger strike. As discussed elsewhere, prisoners generally seek to keep their head down and do their time and engaging in public forms of resistance is more likely to impact on access to visitations, or potentially increase their prison sentence through being excluded from remissions or receiving additional penalties.

This provides an example of the ways in which prisoners have developed methods of resistance in an otherwise significantly constrained environment. Use of the complaints system or bringing a case against the prison service, or even speaking to an inspector, could in some cases be perceived as a form of resistance. Complaints, as demonstrated by Calavita and Jenness (2015), are filed on a broad range of issues. In an environment where they are otherwise removed from the decision-making process regarding their daily lives, the complaint mechanism offers a legitimate avenue to voice their protest. It also allows for external bodies to examine the decision-making steps taken by the prison service. This allows prisoners to attempt to regain a degree of control over their lives. Bringing cases against the prison service can create public awareness of an otherwise closed off environment. This legitimate form of resistance would not have the same consequences as a hunger strike, as bringing complaints or cases against the service are subject to strike non-retaliation clauses in the governing legislation. Although the eventual finding may not be in favour of the prison or necessarily prompt change, the process can empower the prison and temporarily shift the power balance within the prison. Rather than simply submitting to the prison environment, the prisoner asserts through a legitimate means their protest and adds their voice to the prison setting.

As outlined above, power dynamics in prisons are present in every interaction in prison between members of staff but also between prisoners. This can lead to prisoners burying emotions for fear of exposing vulnerabilities that could be exploited and being cautious in their engagement with staff due to staff input in fundamental decision making. The overarching power concerns can make it difficult for meaningful, unguarded interactions to take place, further magnifying the pains of imprisonment by limiting access to support.

Oversight mechanisms such as complaints, litigation and even speaking to the inspector can be viewed as forms of resistance by prisoners to the established power structure. These mechanisms can serve as a legitimate means of challenging the power of officers and ensuring that their voices are heard. This can go some way towards ensuring prisoners reassert their autonomy and self-worth in an otherwise challenging environment.

4.7 Conclusion

As shown in this chapter, there has been limited analysis of prisoner' rights and rights' consciousness to date. This chapter advances the field through drawing on concepts of legal and penal consciousness, legal mobilisation, Rechtsburger and prison life dynamics to illustrate the contextual challenges and motivators to engaging with oversight in prison. As outlined in this chapter, providing for prisoners' rights is only one part of protecting those rights. As discussed by Kelk, legal citizenship or what he considers 'Rechtsburgerschap' of prisoners is made up of three elements consisting of material rights, procedural rights and information about both kinds of rights in order for a prisoner to be a legal citizen. This means that material rights must be supported by procedural remedies to both assert and protect those rights. In addition to this, research on experiences of imprisonment highlight key features which can act as barriers to seeking out rights protection. Low trust environments may mean those in prison struggle to place faith in others (Liebling 2004; Hawley 2012). Furthermore they may have little or no awareness of their own rights, or, as indicated by Sexton (2015), low expectations of what prison should be like, thus accepting subpar treatment as the norm. Additionally, the prison environment is one with an inherent power imbalance and prisoners may view as futile any effort to assert ones rights. Therefore, prisoners need to feel empowered to assert rights even after they become aware of those rights. Awareness of rights without feeling empowered to assert them can lead to feelings of embitterment and further undermine the work of the prison service.

Through exploring these areas, key questions about the role of rights consciousness and the impact it has on understandings of rights protection are developed. The literature on different aspects of life in prison highlights the potentially damaging nature of the prison environment on the self-worth and self-esteem of prisoners, which can restrain prisoners' capacity to seek out rights protection. Ensuring that rights mobility is still encouraged is important for the maintenance of effective mechanisms for oversight in relation to prisoners' rights. The next chapters discuss the lived experience of human rights protection in prison and consider the differences between the ideals of rights protection and the reality.

Notes

1 See further Alison Liebling, David Price and Guy Shafer, *The Prison Officer* (Leyhill: Prison Service and Waterside Press 2011).
2 See, for example, Prison Rules 2007 S.I. 252/2007, s. 5.

References

Sarah Armstrong, 'Securing Prison through Human Rights: Unanticipated Implications of Rights-Based Penal Governance' (2018) 57 (3) *The Howard Journal of Crime and Justice* 401.
Cormac Behan, *Citizen Convict: Prisoners, Politics and the Vote* (Manchester University Press 2016).
Cormac Behan and Richard Kirkham, 'Monitoring, Inspection and Complaints Adjudication in Prison: The Limits of Prison Accountability Frameworks' (2016) 55(4) *The Howard Journal of Crime and Justice* 432.
Karin A Beijersbergen, Anja JE Dirkzwager, Veroni I Eichelsheim, Peter H Van der Laan and Paul Nieuwbeerta, 'Procedural Justice, Anger, and Prisoners' Misconduct: A Longitudinal Study' (2015) 42 *Criminal Justice and Behavior* 196.
David Bierie, 'Procedural Justice and Prison Violence: Examining Complaints Among Federal Inmates (2000–2007)' (2013) 19(1) *Psychology, Public Policy, and Law* 15.
Miranda Boone and Mieke Kox, 'Neutrality as an Element of Perceived Justice in Prison: Consistency Versus Individualization' (2014) 10 *Utrecht Law Review* 118.
Kristin Bumiller, 'Victims in the Shadow of the Law' (1987) 12(3) *Signs: Journal of Women in Culture and Society* 421.
Michelle Butler, 'Prisoners and Prison life' in Deirdre Healy, Claire Hamilton, Yvonne Daly, and Michelle Butler (eds) *The Routledge Handbook of Irish Criminology* (Routledge 2016).
Michelle Butler and Shadd Maruna, 'Rethinking Prison Disciplinary Processes: A Potential Future for Restorative Justice' (2016) 11(1) *Victims & Offenders* 126.
Kitty Calavita and Valerie Jenness, *Appealing to Justice: Prisoner Grievances, Rights and Carceral Logic* (University of California Press 2015).
Eamonn Carrabine, *Power, Discourse, and Resistance: A Genealogy of the Strangeways Prison Riot* (Ashgate 2004).
Eamonn Carrabine, 'Prison Riots, Social Order and the Problem of Legitimacy' (2005) 45(6) *British Journal of Criminology* 896.
Ben Crewe, *The Prisoner Society: Power, Adaptation and Social Life in an English Prison* (Oxford University Press 2009).

Ben Crewe, 'Soft Power in Prison: Implications for Staff-Prisoner Relationships, Liberty and Legitimacy' (2011) 8(6) *European Journal of Criminology* 455.
Ben Crewe, 'The Prisoner Culture and the Prisoner Society' in Ben Crewe and Jamie Bennett (eds) *The Prisoner* (Routledge 2012).
Ben Crewe, Jason Warr, Peter Bennett and Alan Smith, 'The Emotional Geography of Prison Life' (2014) 18(1) *Theoretical Criminology* 56.
Manuela Cunha, 'The Ethnography of Prisons and Penal Confinement' (2014) 43 *Annual Review of Anthropology* 217.
Lauren B Edelman, *Working Law: Courts, Corporations, and Symbolic Civil Rights* (University of Chicago Press 2016).
David M Engel, 'Vertical and Horizontal Perspectives on Rights Consciousness' (2012) 19 *Indiana Journal of Global Legal Studies* 423.
Patricia Ewick and Susan S Silbey, *The Common Place of Law: Stories From Everyday Life* (University of Chicago 1998).
Didier Fassin, *Prisons Worlds: An Ethnography of the Carceral Condition* (John Wiley & Sons 2016).
Michel Foucault, *Discipline and Punish: The Birth of the Prison* (Vintage 2012).
Derrick Franke, David Biere and Doris MacKenzie, 'Legitimacy in Corrections: A Randomized Experiment Comparing a Boot Camp With a Prison' (2010) 9(1) *Criminology and Public Policy* 89.
Erving Goffman, *Frame Analysis: An Essay on the Organization of Experience* (Northeastern University Press 1986).
Russell Hardin, *Trust and Trustworthiness* (Russell Sage Foundation 2002).
Katerine Hawley, *Trust: A Very Short Introduction* (Oxford University Press 2012).
Kathleen Hull, 'Legal Consciousness in Marginalized Groups: The Case of LGBT People' (2016) 41(3) *Law & Social Inquiry* 551.
Marie Hutton, 'Visiting Time: A Tale of Two Prisons' (2016) 63(3) *Probation Journal* 347.
Yvonne Jewkes, 'Men Behind Bars: "Doing" Masculinity as an Adaptation to Imprisonment' (2005) 8(1) *Men and Masculinities* 44.
Anastasia Karamalidou, *Embedding Human Rights in Prison: English and Dutch Perspectives* (Palgrave Macmillan UK 2017).
Constantijn Kelk, *Recht voor Gedetineerde: een onderzoek naar die beginselen van het gevangenisrecht* (Samson, 1978).
Tom Kemp and Philippa Tomczak, 'The Cruel Optimism of International Prison Regulation: Prison Ontologies and Carceral Harms' (2024) 49(3) *Law & Social Inquiry*.
Alison Liebling assisted by Helen Arnold, *Prisons and Their Moral Performance: A Study of Values, Quality, and Prison Life* (Oxford University Press 2004).
Alison Liebling, 'Incentives and Earned Privileges Revisited: Fairness, Discretion, and the Quality of Prison Life' (2008) 9(1) *Journal of Scandinavian Studies in Criminology and Crime Prevention* 25.
Alison Liebling, 'Distinctions and Distinctiveness in the Work of Prison Officers; Legitimacy and Authority Revisited' (2011) 8(6) *European Journal of Criminology* 484.
Alison Liebling, David Price and Charles Elliott, 'Appreciative Inquiry and Relationships in Prison' (1999) 71(1) *Punishment and Society* 71.

Lucien Lombardo, 'Group Dynamics and the Prison Guard Subculture: Is the Subculture an Impediment to Helping Inmates?' (1985) 29(1) *International Journal of Offender Therapy and Criminology* 79–90.
George I. Lovell, 'The Myth of the Myth of Rights' (2012) 59 *Studies in Law, Politics, and Society* 1.
Robert J MacCoun, 'Voice, Control and Belonging: The Double-Edged Sword of Procedural Fairness' (2005) 1 *Annual Review of Law and Social Science* 171.
Anna-Marie Marshall, 'Idle Rights: Employees' Rights Consciousness and the Construction of Sexual Harassment Policies' (2005) 39(1) *Law & Society Review* 83.
Thomas Mathiesen, *The Defences of the Weak: A Sociological Study of a Norwegian Correctional Institution* (Tavistock 1965).
Sally Engle Merry, 'Concepts of Law and Justice Among Working-Class Americans: Ideology as Culture' (1985) 9(1) *Legal Studies Forum* 59.
Sally Engle Merry, Peggy Levitt, Mihaela Serban Rosen, Mihaela and Diana H Yoon, 'Law From Below: Women's Human Rights and Social Movements in New York City' (2010) 44 *Law & Society Review* 101.
Bronwyn Naylor, 'Human Rights and Respect in Prisons: The Prisoners' Perspective' (2014) 31 *Law Context: A Socio-Legal Journal* 84.
Barbara Owen, *The Reproduction of Social Control: A Study of Prison Workers at San Quentin* (Praeger 1988).
Nicola Padfield, 'Monitoring Prisons in England and Wales: Who Ensures the Fair Treatment of Prison-ers?' (2018) 70 *Crime, Law and Social Change* 57.
Laura Piacentini and Elena Katz, 'Carceral Framing of Human Rights in Russian Prisons' (2017) 19(2) *Punishment and Society* 221.
Prisons and Probation Ombudsman, *Learning from PPO Investigations: Why do Women and Young People in Custody not Make Formal Complaints*? (Prisons and Probation Ombudsman 2015). Available at: https://ppo.gov.uk/learning_research/learning-lessons-bulletin-why-do-women-and-young-people-in-custody-not-make-formal-complaints/
Mary Rogan, 'Judicial Conception of Prisoners' Right in Ireland: An Emerging Field. Academy of European Law, 'Improving Conditions Related to Detention' (Council of Europe, Strasbourg, November 2014).
Abigail Rowe, 'Women Prisoners' in Ben Crewe and Jamie Bennett (eds) *The Prisoner* (Routledge 2012).
Austin Sarat, 'The Law Is All Over: Power, Resistance and the Legal Consciousness of the Welfare Poor' (1990) 2 *The Yale Journal of Law and the Humanities* 343.
Kevin D Sawyer, 'Jailhouse Lawyering From the Beginning' (2021) 68 *UCLA Law Review Discourse* 98.
Stuart A Scheingold, *The Politics of Rights: Lawyers, Public Policy, and Political Change* (University of Michigan Press 2010).
Lori Sexton, *Under the Penal Gaze: An Empirical Examination of Penal Consciousness Among Prison Inmates* (US Department of Justice 2012).
Lori Sexton, 'Penal Subjectivities: Developing a Theoretical Framework for Penal Consciousness' (2015) 17(1) *Punishment & Society* 114.
Susan Silbey, 'After Legal Consciousness' (2005) 1 *Annual Review of Law Social Science* 323.
Richard Sparks and Anthony E Bottoms, 'Legitimacy and Order in Prisons' (1995) 46(1) *British Journal of Sociology* 45–62.

Richard Sparks, Anthony E Bottoms and Will Hay, *Prisons and the Problem of Order* (Oxford University Press 1996).

Elizabeth Stanley, *Human Rights and Prisons: A Review to the Human Rights Commission* (Human Rights Commission Auckland 2011).

Walter Suntinger and Moritz Birk, *Systemic Thinking in Preventive Human Rights Monitoring: A Dossier for National Preventive Mechanisms* (Ludwig Boltzman Institute Fundamental and Human Rights 2021).

Gresham Sykes, *The Society of Captives: A Study of a Maximum Security Prison* (Princeton University Press 1958).

Gresham Sykes and Sheldon Messinger, 'The Inmate Social System' in Richard A. Cloward, Donald R. Cressey, George H. Grosser, Richard McCleery, Lloyd E. Ohlin, Gresham E. Sykes, Sheldon E. Messenger (eds) *Theoretical Studies in Social Organization of the Prison* (Cambridge University Press 1960).

Sarah Tait, 'Prison Officer Care for Prisoners in One Men's and One Women's Prison' (DPhil thesis, University of Cambridge 2008).

Sarah J Tracy, 'Locking Up Emotion: Moving Beyond Dissonance for Understanding Emotion Labor Discomfort' (2005) 72(3) *Communication Monographs* 261–283.

Thomas Ugelvik, 'The Hidden Food: Mealtime Resistance and Identity Work in a Norwegian Prison' (2011) 13(1) *Punishment and Society* 47.

Jon Vagg, *Prison Systems: A Comparative Study of Accountability in England, France, Germany, and the Netherlands* (Clarendon Press 1994).

Dirk van Zyl Smit and Sonja Snacken, *Principles of European Prison Law and Policy: Penology and Human Rights* (Oxford University Press 2009).

James B Waldram, 'Challenges of Prison Ethnography' (2009) 50 *Anthropology News* 4.

Jason Warr, *The Values and Perspectives of Forensic Psychologists* (Emerald Publishing Limited 2020).

Max Weber, *Economy and Society: An Outline of Interpretive Sociology* (Vol. 1, University of California Press 1978).

John Wooldredge and Benjamin Steiner, 'The Exercise of Power in Prison Organizations and Implications for Legitimacy' (2016) 106(1) *Journal of Criminal Law Criminal* 125.

Lynn Zimmer, *Women Guarding Men* (The University of Chicago Press Ltd 1986).

5 Prisoner Awareness of and Perceptions of Oversight Bodies

5.1 Introduction

This is the first chapter to engage with the empirical data gathered through semi-structured interviews and surveys with those in prison in Ireland and explores how prisoners experience oversight structures in Irish prisons; specifically prisoners' experiences and views of inspection and monitoring bodies, complaints-receiving bodies and judicial oversight of prisons. Prisoners' general awareness and perceptions of oversight bodies are identified in the qualitative research and explored quantitatively through the survey data. These themes are strongly linked together and a lack of awareness of the bodies as a whole or a clear understanding of the bodies can feed into prisoners' willingness to engage and the expectations they have of the bodies. Subsequent chapters address areas such as rights' consciousness and prison climate which can explain the different factors which may create challenges for oversight in prison. This chapter starts with addressing the awareness of inspection bodies and perceptions of these bodies, followed by a discussion on complaints and court experiences. The chapter concludes by drawing these together and identifying parallels in the experiences across the different forms of oversight.

5.2 Inspection and Monitoring in Irish Prisons

As set out in Chapter 3, there are a number of different bodies which carry out inspection and monitoring in Irish prisons. These bodies have different roles and mandates when it comes to how they operate. Domestically, the Inspector of Prisons (OiP) and the VCs carry out inspections in Irish prisons. Important to bear in mind is the role of the VCs in dealing with prisoner complaints and, as will be outlined further below, this can lead to confusion as to what exactly inspectors are doing in Irish prisons. As well as these domestic bodies, Ireland is visited by the European Committee for the Prevention of Torture, Inhuman and Degrading Treatment or Punishment (CPT). This chapter starts by discussing levels of awareness of the different bodies, followed by the experiences prisoners had of interacting with each of these bodies in turn. While experiences varied across bodies, there were also

DOI: 10.4324/9781003477471-5

commonalities with the different bodies. There was an absence of trust in the OiP and VCs to get things done, as well as role confusion around the specific mandates of the different bodies. Despite scepticism surrounding the current system, there was a sense that inspection and monitoring was important to have in prisons. It concludes by highlighting the different perceptions held of different inspection and monitoring bodies, while the implications and some of the reasons for these perceptions will be explored in the next chapter on rights consciousness and barriers to engagement in the prison environment.

5.2.1 Awareness

As part of the survey, participants were asked about their familiarity with three inspection and monitoring bodies which carry out inspections and monitoring of Irish prisons concerning the treatment of prisoners: the VCs, the OiP and the CPT. Specifically, they were asked to indicate whether they knew about the bodies, whether they had contacted them and whether they had personally met them. As can be seen in Figure 5.1, there were different degrees of awareness across the various oversight bodies, with low levels of awareness (less than 50%) for bodies such as the OiP and the CPT. Awareness of different bodies and their specific mandates are key to building trust in these bodies. As explored by Hardin (1996: 35), assessments of trust are built around knowledge and expectations of different actors. Without this basis of knowledge, reliance on other experiences, such as interactions with prison authorities and broader life experience can shape perceptions of unfamiliar interactions. Therefore, understanding prisoners' awareness of oversight bodies was an important starting point to understanding the basis upon which perceptions of oversight developed amongst prisoners.

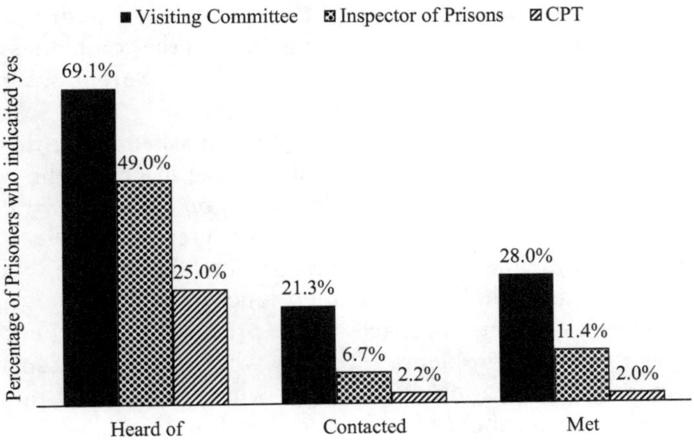

Figure 5.1 Familiarity with prison oversight bodies (n = 508).

As can be seen from Figure 5.1, VCs are the body with which prisoners were most familiar (69.1%), while the CPT (25%) was the body with the least familiarity, with three in four prisoners reporting not having heard of this body. There was a significant drop off between those who indicated that they knew about the bodies and those who had contacted or met them. Similarly in interviews participants frequently stated: *'I don't know anything about them'*. (Participant 20) or *'I have never heard about it'*. (Participant 39) or knowing vaguely about the existence of the body but never having *'met that kind* (rights protecting) *of inspector'* (Participant 41). This suggests that even when prisoners do know about the bodies, they are either choosing not to interact or are not provided with an opportunity to do so. This finding will be explored further in the next chapter.

Another finding in relation to awareness is the variability in terms of prisoner demographics across interview participants of those who were more likely to be aware of the various bodies and have interacted with them. In terms of awareness, interview participants serving a longer sentence, in particular, those serving ten years or more, were more likely to be aware and have interacted with the bodies, particularly the OiP. Those serving longer sentences may be more invested in learning about the different bodies in prison and have more opportunities to interact. Given that a significant number of Irish prisoners spend less than one year in prison, this finding raises concerns about access to rights protection for different groups in prison.[1] This lack of awareness could have implications for what makes it into the reports of the inspection and monitoring bodies. As outlined by Sexton (2015), the experience of imprisonment is a subjective experience and the perceived severity of imprisonment varies. Those serving shorter sentences may face different challenges to longer-sentenced prisoners, for example, access to services while in prison and opportunities to prepare for release. This finding is supported by a study conducted in Australian prisons by Naylor (2014), where it was determined that delays in the functioning of the complaints system resulted in short-term prisoners being less inclined to engage with the complaints process. This means that prisoners may not, due to a lack of awareness, seek to inform a rights-protecting body when given the opportunity.

Furthermore, as highlighted by Participant 24 when asked about the role of the inspector and setting out an example of an issue in prison, he noted *'I'm sure there's many more issues that I can't think of off the top of me head, you know'*. And returning to the point later in the interview *'some of the questions you've asked me there I'm sure there's a lot I could have said but I actually forgot'*. This quote indicates the importance of awareness of rights and oversight bodies, as prisons are spaces where prisoners may feel uncomfortable reflecting upon their problems, especially when operating in survival mode or as emphasised in Sexton's (2015) work where those in prison high expectations of what prison should be like and therefore may have differing standards of prison life to inspection and monitoring bodies.

In addition to the issue of awareness, analysis of findings raised concerns about participant knowledge of the various roles, functions and expectations prisoners have about the bodies. This next section sets out a deeper understanding of the degrees of awareness of the different bodies, as well as the perceptions of each of the bodies. A particular issue covered here is role confusion and the identification of different bodies in the prison. Sources of information for prisoners on what these bodies do are also discussed in brief within this section and further expanded on in Chapter 6.

5.2.2 Role Confusion and Knowing Who Is Who

A strong theme to emerge across the interviews was a high degree of confusion about not only the identity and existence of particular bodies or structures, but also their mandate. Participants discussed a variety of reasons for lacking information about oversight bodies. Some participants felt that they were not adequately informed by the authorities about their rights in prison and often relied on other prisoners to learn how things work in prison. Other participants suggested that the prison service did not want them to know about their rights and related bodies, demonstrating the low levels of trust which some prisoners had of the prison service.

A theme common across the data was that people in prison cannot rely on the prison institution to share information about human rights or to provide information about avenues for recourse and oversight. Rather, the onus is on people in prison to seek out this information for themselves, which can result in them being labelled a 'troublemaker'. Alternatively, some prisoners determined that seeking out such information would not result in any tangible assistance; deeming it a 'waste of time'. Similar views were expressed by participants in Behan's (2016) study concerning the OiP and VCs.

The prison was seen as a place with lots of different people coming and going, and where the opportunity to ask about people's roles was limited. As noted by one participant:

> *... if we see them, we might not know it's them, you know. That's the thing. Cos so many things happen like – people have probation officers, they have you know ... researchers, haha. They have – ISM, but ISM – you know by the uniform. But there's too many different things here ...*
>
> (Participant 25)

This participant felt that even if you saw an oversight body, identifying one as such and having an opportunity to engage in the moment would be quite difficult. It required the person near you to have the requisite knowledge. This was particularly pronounced in the case of foreign prisoners as gaining information was considerably more difficult if there was a language barrier and the prisoner relied on other prisoners for accessing information on rights. As noted by one participant:

> *...Like a lot of people get leaflets and don't understand what's on them so it goes back to the literacy issue, like some people just can't read or write like so. If you get a sheet, it would be useless to them. So, I think it is kind of a problem like and especially with the ... a lot of non-nationals coming in as well like, a few with poor English so it is hard to translate to them in all their languages as well like. I noticed especially over the last few months there, there is a lot of non-nationals coming in like, so. A lot of them with very poor English.... .*
>
> (Participant 30)

This highlights the additional challenges faced by those who do not speak the main language of the prison. These additional pains have been noted by Warr (2016) for foreign prisoners navigating bureaucracy while in prison, as well as in gaining information when prisoners do not speak the same language as the prison officers in the case of Boone and Kox's (2014) study on Belgian prisoners in a Dutch prison.

Obtaining information could also challenge for those with literacy issues, a significant problem for those in prison (Morgan and Kett 2003). Avenues to access information were more limited for this group. This also created challenges in engaging with inspection bodies and submitting complaints, as these groups had to rely on others for support in this regard. As previous research highlights, prisons are low trust environments and creating a relationship of dependence can have detrimental effects for a prisoner (Crewe 2009):

> *... . people that have difficulty writing and things like that. It would be difficult for them because if they make a complaint, if they can't read and write then they have to go to someone else and then that person could abuse them you know like putting down the wrong things and mix up the whole situation like. Get them further into trouble like.*
>
> (Participant 43)

This quote highlights the potential barriers to accessing accurate information and engaging with the complaints process for those with low literacy and who need to rely heavily on others.

In contrast to this, one of the participants (36) had a clear understanding of the inspection role and later sought out the inspection report. His view of the body was generally more positive. Having clarity as to the mandates of the various bodies was important in ensuring that the expectations of the prisoner were met and trust in the bodies was not damaged due to unrealistic expectations as to what bodies can do. As emphasised by Hawley (2012), placing trust in somebody requires an assessment of motives, capabilities and expertise. Therefore, building trust is dependent on clear expectations and knowledge surrounding the specific mandate of the various inspection and monitoring bodies. This is especially the case in prisons which tend to be low trust environments (Calavita and Jenness 2015) and as highlighted above, there is a heavy reliance on word of mouth in gathering information.

The point at which the information was provided was also important, as prisoners can experience shock upon entering the prison and may not take in all the information they were given. One participant only remembered the VCs existed when they were pointed out to him by another prisoner as he needed them due to a family member being banned from visiting:

> *... if I had of thought of them at the time like and she was barred over 7 months ... I would have seen them straight away. It's just when the other fella said it to me, then I thought of it and I said oh yeah, I forgot all about them, you know. I just wasn't thinking about them at all until I was told about them and that's when I asked for them...*
>
> (Participant 14)

This suggests that information needs to be provided at various stages so that prisoners can easily access it when necessary. It is unsurprising that rights-protecting bodies are not a primary concern on entry into prison as it is not an immediate need for prisoners. As noted by one prisoner, it often took him a period of time to realise he was in prison. There is a need to ensure that information is available at various stages throughout a prisoner's sentence in a clear and accessible manner so that it is available when they might need it or be able to take it in.

This section has provided an overview of the low awareness and clear understanding of different inspection and monitoring bodies mandates. The next sections outline the perceptions and experiences of the three inspection and monitoring bodies included in this study, to highlight the particularities of each and draw together the commonalities in prisoners' experiences with oversight bodies in prison.

5.2.3 Perceptions of Visiting Committees

As outlined above the VCs experienced high levels of awareness amongst participants in the study. The frequent visiting nature of the VCs and its longstanding nature contributed to the higher levels of awareness seen amongst respondents. However, higher levels of awareness did not mean that this body was immune to criticism, particularly in relation to the VC's lack of enforcement powers. As noted by one participant:

> *The Visiting Committee ... have the best intentions in the world, but no one takes them seriously ... including ... the management, the governors and stuff you know. I have met a lot of them and a lot of them are nice people.*
>
> (Participant 8)

This participant highlights a lack of faith in the ability of the VCs to actually change anything in prison and also acknowledges that this view is widespread across different levels in the prison of this body. This participant, along with others, elaborated by raising concerns about how VCs raise problems with prison management and the utility of having a body that essentially just repeats what has been said by the prisoner but is not taken seriously by the decision makers in the prison. Concerns about the utility of these bodies and similar bodies in the United Kingdom have been subject to criticism which was also reflected in the findings in this study (Behan 2016; Padfield 2018).

This section sets out the perception prisoners had of VCs, in particular participants' understanding of the role of the body, what they can achieve, experiences interacting with them and why some prisoners chose not to.

5.2.3.1 Focus on Complaint Mandate

As outlined above, VCs play a role in dealing with prisoner complaints and historically played a role in prisoner discipline. As discussed by Linos and Pegram (2017), the ability to deal with complaints in addition to having an inspection mandate, in the case of National Human Rights Institutions, can increase awareness and support for rights-protecting bodies. However, this can create challenges around understanding the purpose of the role when present in different capacities. Linked to this is the theme of role confusion and managing expectations as to what oversight bodies can actually do. In interviews, the complaint-handling role of the VCs was the main aspect of their role discussed by participants. This suggests that their understanding of the role may be incomplete, or the complaints function of these bodies is of greater relevance to prisoners. As noted by Participant 14:

> *Ah I always heard of them, but I never asked for them ... because it's ... I'm not one for trouble or that in the jail ... I'm quiet enough ... I've never had a problem with any of the officers or anything like that, do you know what I mean, or getting onto the Visiting Committee about this, that or the other but it's just me ma that time and she was barred for so long, I said here I have to see them and see what happens.*

This limitation in prisoners' understanding of the role may mean that their inspection role is overlooked or that when prisoners speak with them in their inspection capacity, they expect the VC to follow up on their specific issue which may lead to frustration or disappointment if this is not clear.

5.2.3.2 Ability to Make Changes

As outlined in Chapter 3, the VCs do not have formal powers to make decisions in the case of complaints brought to them or to grant a specific remedy, as is the case for similar bodies such as Supervisory Boards in the

Netherlands. Instead, VCs investigate the complaint and, based on this investigation, can recommend a course of action to the governor of the specific prison. Their lack of enforcement powers when it came to dealing with complaints had an impact on prisoners' views of the body. As highlighted above, some participants saw members of the VCs as people with good intentions but who were not taken seriously by the prison service and easily dismissed by those perceived to have power in the prison, such as governors. In some cases, this meant that prisoners did not see any point to speaking to a body which could not directly deal with their complaint and felt that it would be a pointless action that might draw unwanted attention to them.

5.2.3.3 Access and Approachability

Another key feature of oversight bodies is whether prisoners felt they could access them when needed and felt they were approachable. Rights-protecting bodies which are not readily available and accessible to those in prison fail in their mandate to provide for the prisoners' voice, a key component of procedural fairness (Behan and Kirkham 2016). As outlined in Figure 5.2, approximately three in ten respondents (31.1%) agreed or strongly agreed with the statement 'I can speak with the Visiting Committee in this prison if I need to'. However, a similar percentage of respondents showed disagreement (i.e., disagree and strongly disagree: 35.0%) or provided a neutral response (33.6%). Prisoners raised concerns about accessing the VCs in particular making a request to speak to a member of a VC usually involved giving your name to an officer and asking to see them as outlined by Participant 43: '*I went to the governor, and I said I was going to the Visiting Committee, and I was persuaded like you know not to kind of get them involved like*'. As noted above, this could result in officers directly or indirectly discouraging prisoners from seeking to see the VCs, as well as creating a sense amongst some participants that their name would not be passed on.

In addition to this, officers often asked for some information as to why the prisoner wanted to see the VC. While some officers may have had good intentions in doing so and wanted to resolve an issue without involving an external body or to simply pass this information onto the VC when making this request, this was not always the perception prisoners had of the interaction. Additionally, some felt that VCs were always accompanied by prison staff or guided by them when in the prison which made approaching them more difficult. This also suggested that to some prisoners, as also discussed in the UK context by Livingstone et al. (2008), that the VCs were perceived as close to the prison staff and lacked independence. As set out by Participant 30: '*They're all the same people, they're all ex-prison officers and they're all ex-probation officers*'. This perceived lack of independence served to undermine the perceived willingness of VCs to genuinely help prisoners.

Further to this, the backgrounds of VC members were important for some participants. As illustrated below, ordinary people were seen as relatable for prisoners and that they could bring an understanding to the role as they could draw on their own life experience.

> *But yeah, I think it's a great thing that the ordinary joe soap comes in and you can just talk to him on their level and say it is what it is.*
>
> (Participant 23)

While currently limited data is available on the constitution of VCs, similar bodies in the United Kingdom, IMBs, predominantly consist of older, middle-class individuals (Padfield 2018) and from speaking to prisoners and staff, as well as attending a training day for the VCs in Ireland, these characteristics are also prevalent amongst the Irish cohort. A diversity of membership of the VC is important for approachability and a sense that concerns raised by those in prison would be understood. Some participants were sceptical of professionals or people in suits who were removed from their life experiences.

As outlined above, some participants lacked information on who those specific people were when they came into the prison and may not know about their presence or only learn about it after the fact. Learning about bodies upon seeing them meant some prisoners were reliant on someone in their vicinity having the information about the body, which was not always the case, especially for those who did not speak English as a first language.

5.2.4 Perceptions of the Inspector of Prisons

As outlined in Chapter 3, the Office of the OiP has been a statutory body since 2007 with a non-statutory body in operation prior to this. However, as shown in Figure 5.1, slightly less than half of prisoners surveyed knew about the OiP with only 6.7% having contacted the office and 11.4% having met the Inspector. This suggests that even those who knew about the office either did not have an opportunity to meet the Inspector or had chosen not to engage. This section outlines key findings on prisoners' views and experiences of the OiP.

As can be seen from Figure 5.2, only a minority of respondents (14.8%) considered that the OiP makes things better in prisons. Slightly over half of the participants (52.4%) disagreed (i.e., disagreed or strongly disagreed) with this statement and nearly one-third provided a neutral response (32.8%). Despite this, participants did speak about the potential benefits of having external bodies coming into the prison more generally. The existing low awareness may have contributed to the relatively high level of neutral responding as prisoners simply did not know much about the office, which was also reflected in interview responses. As outlined above, awareness of oversight bodies was a significant issue amongst participants. Furthermore, gathering accurate information in the prison context itself presents challenges as asking too many questions has the potential to draw unwanted attention and make your prison life more difficult. As will be discussed further in the

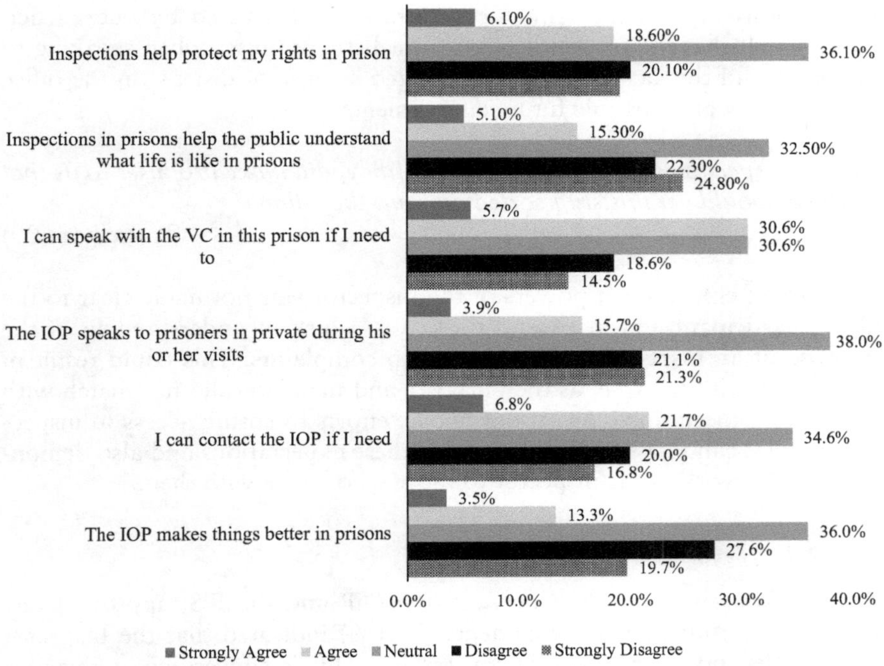

Figure 5.2 Views of inspection bodies in prisons (%).

next chapter, prison culture itself makes engaging with oversight bodies difficult. However, as highlighted by this quote, accessing bodies and a willingness to approach them is not easy for all prisoners:

> *And then like it's very hard for – some people aren't going to just go up and talk to them in front of a load of people because they would be like what were you saying to them.*
>
> (Participant 26)

Interacting with outside bodies may be perceived negatively by others in prison and the pervasive paranoia experienced by some prisoners, along with a lack of awareness about oversight means that the risk of engaging may not be worth it for some prisoners.

5.2.4.1 Role Confusion

Role confusion was evident in the case of the OiP. The OiP has no role in dealing with individual complaints but rather a general oversight role of the complaint system as set out in Chapter 3. This lack of clarity as to the powers of the Inspector could lead to dissatisfaction with the office due to expectations beyond the remit of the office. As discussed by one participant, he felt that the Inspector made unrealistic promises when speaking to prisoners and the lack of follow-up created a sense of distrust in the office more broadly and possible future engagements.

> *[The inspection body] made promises, [they] did make promises to us that [they] would get this stuff sorted out, but they didn't.*
>
> (Participant 09)

The lack of enforcement powers of the Inspector was not made clear to the above participant and in general there was a lack of understanding of the purpose of an inspector in comparison to complaints. This could result in frustration with the role, as the purposes and mandates did not match with prisoners' expectations. As set out above, efforts to ensure access to inspection reports can play a role in managing these expectations and also demonstrating the work of the inspector to those who spoke with them.

5.2.4.2 Independence

When asked about the link between the OiP and the IPS, approximately three out of four survey respondents (77.1%) indicated that the Inspector is not independent from the prison service. This is concerning as this was an important factor for those interviewed, who repeatedly highlighted the importance of someone independent being involved with the inspection of prisons. Additionally, almost 40% of those surveyed selected independence as a key feature of a good inspector. A lack of perceived independence could have repercussions for prisoners' willingness to engage with the inspector, as well as the information which prisoners were willing to share.

5.2.4.3 Fear of Reprisals

There was a perception amongst prisoners that engaging with oversight bodies could result in negative consequences in the prison. This was evident in discussions surrounding the OiP, as discussed by Participant (19):

> *... you would be worried that ... well I know I would be worried that if you start complaining about the prison to people and they start saying it back to the prison, the prison is going to say right, so you know, this lad is giving out about us to other people so I don't know.*

While he admitted that this might be a bit of paranoia on his part due to the nature of the prison environment, it was still something that he felt he could not help. This was noted by other prisoners, and they highlighted that the types of repercussions a prison could inflict might seem minor, such as unlocking a prisoner last or slamming doors, or may appear unrelated to actions such as complaining through repeated transfers, but they could impact heavily on someone's sentence and ability to do their time. This also highlighted concerns about a lack of confidentiality in prison interactions and the need to build trust with prisoners that information provided will not be shared back to prisons in an identifying manner.

5.2.4.4 Scepticism of Inspection Process

There was a lack of trust in the inspection process and the ability of the inspector to see the real prison. Many participants felt that they would be guided around the prison and only get to see certain parts. Additionally, they felt that the prison would keep inspectors away from those in prison or only allow a small number of trusted prisoners to engage with the inspector:

> *... there is kind of no interaction there ... so they are not getting ... exactly from a prisoners' point of view what problem there is or what kind of problems they are having, so that then they can have a look at that themselves and see if there is something that they can do to improve it ...*
>
> (Participant 13)

One participant stated his view that the inspection team '*always come when prisoners are locked up*' (Participant 01). This was echoed amongst other participants who stated: '*... they don't come around announcing that the Inspector's in the prison, or anything looking in, ... you know, if they are in, they do lock up bleeding up*' (Participant 11). Another said: '*[N]ah – you wouldn't see them like*' (Participant 20). These quotes illustrate the view shared amongst many participants that the inspector was largely absent from prison and missed seeing the 'real' prison even when present.

In addition to these feelings of scepticism, there was a perception that prisoners had a limited opportunity to engage freely with the inspector. Various issues were mentioned such as visibility of inspection bodies when in the prison as highlighted in the above quotes, as well as a sense that prisoners' voices were not always valued. This was linked to a feeling of not being trusted to tell the truth or an inability to get one's point across in a way that the inspection body would understand and take seriously:

> *.... if you wanted to write something stupid ... and ... it kind of goes back to everyone, it could be serious, but it is just the way some people write stuff as well like. It could be kind of stupid, you know.*
>
> (Participant 30)

This again highlights the need for greater transparency and for information to be provided to prisoners on what inspection bodies are doing in prisons and how they pick people to speak to.

Another point in relation to the scepticism around the inspection process was the feeling amongst some prisoners that their input would not be valued by the inspector:

> *I suppose you could get a prisoner to do it yeah, but I wouldn't have nothing to do with it cuz they wouldn't listen to me. That's the truth.*
>
> (Participant 21)

As can be seen from the above quote, some participants felt like their voice would not be trusted by an outside body due to their prisoner status. As highlighted by Hawley's (2012) research, those who experience distrust may struggle to place trust in others. Based on this, the participant did not see any point in speaking with the body as it would be a waste of time for him. This raises questions about the ways in which prisoners interact with bodies such as the inspector and the role of rights language in framing these discussions, as discussed by Calavita and Jenness (2015). Another participant made the point that the inspector should speak to groups such as those involved with the Red Cross in prison or those serving a life sentence as they would have informed views of the prison system and may be perceived as more legitimate than others in prison. This distinction between who felt listened to or who would be listened to by an outside body raises questions about how prisoners see themselves as someone worthy of rights and rights protection, as well as the value placed on their input. Given the important role of the voice of prisoners in experiences of procedural justice (Tyler 2010), the fact that some participants did not feel that their voices would be valued by rights-protecting bodies raises questions regarding who is given a voice in prison. Given the importance of diversity of views in inspection reports, as well as feeling listened to as a key component of self-worth, this concern could undermine the overall legitimacy of the process, as well as create a division between prisoners perceived as 'worthy' and those perceived as 'unworthy'.

5.2.4.5 Professional Gap

In addition to a scepticism of the process, some participants were sceptical of professionals more broadly and their ability to understand the environment and having a genuine interest in helping prisoners. As indicated by Participant 23: '*I don't trust professional people*'. This was further expanded on by other participants who felt that professionals or those in suits would not be able to understand the challenges those in prison faced and were too far removed from life in prison. This scepticism meant that prisoners were not willing to interact with bodies who would not be able or willing to help them. While some were willing to give the inspector a chance to prove himself, this was not always the case and the sense that he was not present in the prison deepened this mistrust.

There was a sense that some people who came into the prison such as professionals were focused on speaking rather than actually enacting change as noted by Participant 5:

> *I think if someone came into prison to seriously do something about it and to help the prisoners themselves, yeah to take some action. Action speaks louder than words that's the way I look at it.*

For some participants seeing change was more important than having an opportunity to speak with someone and there was a sense that inspection bodies need to prove themselves to a certain extent to gain prisoners' trust. This is unsurprising given the low trust nature of the environment, where gaining trust can be difficult (Liebling 2004), and underlines the importance of including prisoners throughout the inspection cycle so the work of the inspector, in particular, as well as all oversight bodies can be seen.

5.2.5 European Committee for the Prevention of Torture and Inhuman or Degrading Treatment or Punishment

As set out in Chapter 3, Ireland is also subject to visits by the CPT. At the time of the research, the prison service was due a visit by the CPT, which took place in September 2019. As outlined above, awareness amongst prisoners of the CPT is the lowest of all inspection and monitoring bodies, with 25% of 508 prisoners surveyed in three medium-security prisons having heard of the CPT. Perhaps unsurprisingly given the infrequent nature of visits by the CPT, only 2% had ever met or contacted the CPT. Interviews with people in prison revealed a similarly low level of familiarity with the CPT.

When the concept of the CPT and its work was described to participants, some concern was expressed about its ability to effect change. Some participants were concerned about the frequency of visits, with one participant (03), who, despite having extensive experience of prison, had not heard of the CPT, noting '[e]*very 4 to 5 years? That's a bit long ain't it … Anything could happen in 5 days in this place never mind 5 years*'. Others expressed concern about talking to an outside body, a feeling which related not only to the CPT, but monitoring bodies more generally. Participant 38 reflected on the prison culture of keeping your head down, stating: '*I wouldn't draw attention to anyone like that*'. But felt that '*[i]f it was confidential yeah … but I don't want them [the prison officers] to know what I have to say about this place*'. The small number of participants who were aware of the CPT, however, referred to the CPT's criticism of 'slopping out' and the use of padded cells, with one participant attributing the phasing out of slopping out to the CPT, and another noting: *they are against all this punishment in prison, so they don't like inhumane treatment of prisoners which is all about … it's about lock ups and stuff like*'.

It was also evident that people in prison valued the concept of an outside body, in particular one outside of the Irish system, coming to assess conditions and treatment. Cliquennois and Snacken's (2018: 16) contention that '[w]hen practiced routinely monitoring creates conditions that make extreme turns in penal policy less likely and protect human rights in prisons when populist pressures do build', seemed to be shared by many of the study's participants. One participant noted the importance of an impartial outside observer, saying: '*all these people that are non-biased or whatever are really the ones that can make the difference*' (Participant 22). Views on this were, however, mixed, with scepticism also evident about the likelihood of any positive change happening in prison. Participant 23 summed up this feeling well, describing the CPT as '*waffle*' and '*just another thing that just happens for a second*', suggesting that visits were quickly forgotten about and not taken seriously.

The relevance of the 'Europeanness' of the CPT was also explored with participants. Some participants felt that being a European body was an advantage, and that its work could be a way of sharing ideas about prison practices from different European countries and using them to improve the Irish system. However, others felt that the differing standards across prisons in Europe meant that CPT members might not see the Irish system as especially poor, and could even be viewed favourably compared to other prisons; as stated by Participant 33, '*there's some jails in Europe that have it a lot of worse or have it a lot better*'; with Participant 24 saying that CPT members might think '*sure that's only a hotel, compared to theirs*'. For some, the CPT was a body with greater authority and credibility than domestic bodies because of its European nature, and that it had more chance of being listened to by the government as a result. The distance of the CPT from Irish monitoring bodies and the Irish system generally was perceived as a positive by some.

These findings suggest that participants placed some value on the concept, at least, of an independent, neutral body visiting prisons in Europe, and that its European nature is something of particular merit. Notably, however, it cannot be said that people in prison in the current study considered European supervision of prisons to be a strong influence on Irish prison practice, or were even especially aware of it. This suggests that more work needs to be done at the national and European level to raise awareness of European-derived rights and protections amongst people in prison.

5.2.6 What Does a Good Oversight Body Look Like?

As highlighted by the above sections, participants' experiences of oversight in prisons varied widely across the different bodies in terms of awareness and understandings of the different bodies' roles, as well as interactions, or decisions not to interact. It also highlighted the challenges of placing and developing trust in the different bodies, as well as accessing them. Despite this, participants remained positive, overall, as regards the need for oversight bodies. Participants referred to oversight as driving *'change'* in prison as well a way of keeping *'staff motivated'* (Participant 34), as well as the potential for an inspectorate body to have an *'unbiased towards peoples' convictions and kind of just see them as another part of society that needs looking after like'* (Participant 36). This section draws together participants' views on what makes a good inspector, highlighting the core principles which were of importance to those in prison.

5.2.6.1 What Makes for a Good Inspector?

Both survey and interview participants were asked about reforming the inspection process in prison. This section outlines some of the suggestions made, which will be further discussed in the recommendation section in Chapter 8.

Survey respondents were asked to indicate which three features, drawn from the international criteria for inspection bodies such as the CPT standards, they considered the most important for a good inspector. As can be seen from Figure 5.3, over half of respondents felt that surprise visits were important to a good inspector, followed by confidentiality, unlimited access to the prisons, follow-up on report recommendations and being independent. These criteria were also highlighted by interview participants. Unfortunately, these criteria are in direct conflict with the experiences and perceptions of the inspection process in Ireland as outlined previously in this section, with a significant number of prisoners not viewing the inspector as independent and the prison service playing a role in guiding which areas of the prison were inspected and who got to speak to the inspector.

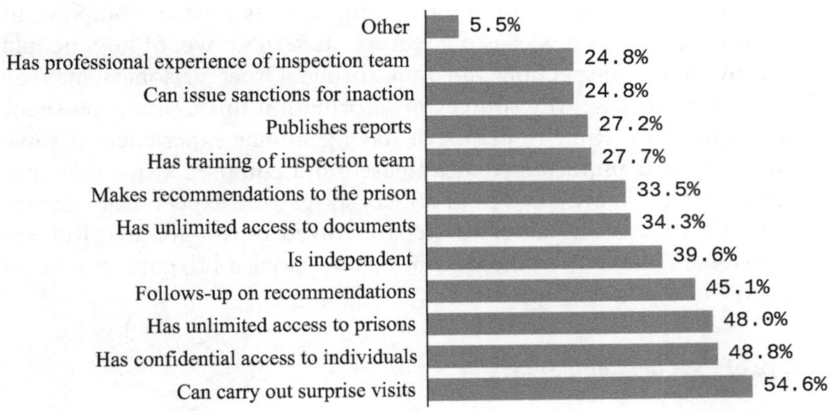

Figure 5.3 In your opinion what makes for a good inspector?

5.3 Complaints

This section outlines the views held by participants in relation to the complaint system in Irish prisons. Key themes arising in relation to the system include concern about reprisals for speaking up, lack of independence and delays within the system, and a lack of understanding about the system as a whole. This section starts by outlining general awareness and how those in prison learned about the system. This will be followed by key aspects around views, as well as experiences of the system. Next, the reasons why participants did or did not use the complaint system will be explored, in particular other ways in which complaints were resolved in prison. Finally, the section concludes by highlighting the features which prisoners identified as important for a good complaint system and their discussions around reforming the system.

5.3.1 Awareness and Gaining Knowledge of the Complaint System

While prisoners were often aware that the complaint system existed, of those who responded to the question 'Have you ever heard of the prisoner complaint system?', 76.9% responded that they had heard of the system, the specifics of how the system worked tended to be less clear in interviews. Participants were not aware of who handled different complaints, or the timelines for receiving a response. In some cases, this was due to a lack of experience with needing to use the system and therefore no need to learn how it worked.

Knowledge as to how the system was meant to and did work in practice can be impacted by who is informing prisoners about the system, therefore, it is important to reflect on how participants learnt about the system. As can be seen from Figure 5.4, a significant number of respondents (67%) referred to other prisoners as their source of information for learning about the complaint system. These are followed by the booklet (29%) and staff members (18.1%).

Relying on other prisoners for information, such as how to complain in prison, is unsurprising, and was also a feature, as seen above, of how people came to know about inspection and monitoring. Other prisoners may be perceived as more trustworthy sources of information through having spent a significant amount of time in prison or having similar experiences (Crewe 2009). However, it is important that unbiased and comprehensive information on these systems is provided to prisoners so realistic expectations can be set and prisoners know the different steps involved in the process. Relying on other prisoners may create misconceptions or may lead to gaps in what is known about the complaint system.

5.3.2 Usage of the Complaint System

Slightly over one in five respondents (22.41%) reported having used the complaint system in the prison where they were housed at the time of data

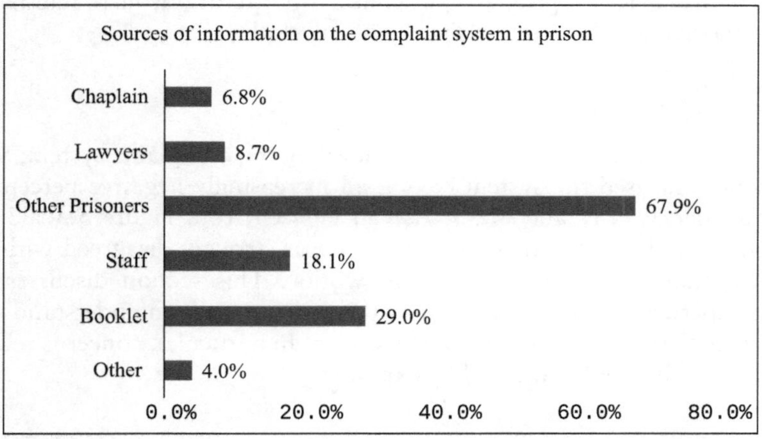

Figure 5.4 Sources of information on the complaint system in prison.

collection. Seneviratne (2005: 121) highlights the limitation of statistics when discussing complaint systems. Low numbers may be an indication of 'insurmountable barriers to complaining' rather than a 'sign of bureaucratic health'. While these figures give a general overview of usage of the system, it is important to further investigate experiences of the system and in particular barriers to accessing the system itself. These will be discussed further in Section 5.3.3. As discussed by Mathieson (1965) in relation to censoriousness, the additional rules and restrictions in prison were used by some prisoners to seek to hold staff to a similar code of conduct and adherence to their own rules. In the current study, some participants referred to the prison rules as standards which both staff and prisoners could be held up to.

From the interviews it was clear that those serving longer sentences were more likely to use the complaint system – of the nine participants who had submitted a complaint during their sentence, six were serving sentences of ten years or more. This is in line with other research in the area such as Morgan and Liebling (2007) and Naylor's (2014) work in the United Kingdom and Australia. In the case of Naylor's (2014) study, this was attributed to delays in the processing of complaints, which meant that those serving a shorter sentence may not hear back during their sentence. This was also a concern highlighted by participants in our study and noted by the OiP in his report on the complaint system. Participants repeatedly referred issues such as *'no response from any complaints with an answer'* (Respondent 47) or *'no reply, ignoring* [complaint]' (Respondent 38). Those serving longer sentences may also have a greater interest in resolving an issue in prison, while shorter-sentenced prisoners may be able tolerate or deal with an issue. This was highlighted by longer-term prisoners who complained about issues such as access to school or loss of jobs which could impact on progression, while shorter-term prisoners referred to more immediate needs such as visits or missing clothes.

5.3.3 Views of the Complaint System

Overall, those in prison had negative views of the complaint system, with those who had used the system having an increasingly negative perception of it (van der Valk et al., 2022). As can be seen from Figure 5.5, 63.8% of respondents indicated that they disagreed or strongly disagreed with the statement that 'The complaint system works'. This section discusses the various experiences and views noted by those in the study to understand why prisoners held this negative view of the system. In particular, concerns related to procedural justice factors will be explored.

5.3.3.1 Feeling Heard

As discussed in Chapter 3, poor experiences of procedural justice in prison can give rise to negative outcomes, including violence, anger, misconduct, and feelings that their imprisonment is not legitimate (Bierie 2013; Beijersbergen et al. 2015), findings reflected in the Woolf (1991) report into riots in Strangeways prison in the United Kingdom. A key component of procedural justice is having a voice and feeling heard (Tyler 1984). As reflected in Figure 5.6, a significant number of prisoners did not feel that 'Using the complaint system gave [them] a voice in prison', with 59% of respondents disagreeing or strongly disagreeing with the statement and only 15.3% agreeing or strongly agreeing.

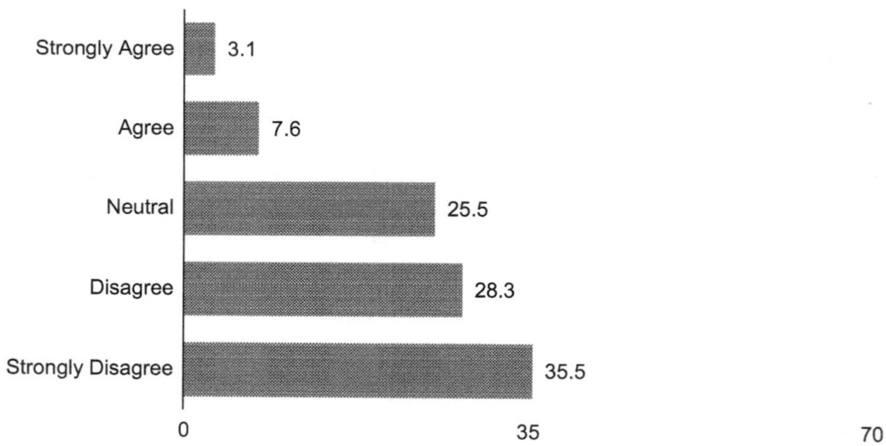

Figure 5.5 Responses to 'The complaint system works' (%).

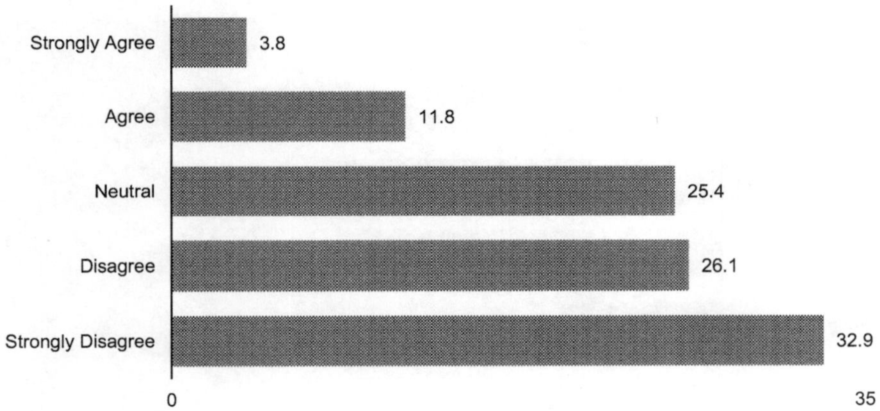

Figure 5.6 Responses to 'Using the complaint system gives me a voice in prison' (%).

This suggests that prisoners currently feel excluded from the complaint system and, as indicated by interview participants, some felt that complaints were forgotten about or not taken seriously by the prison service or those investigating them. Some participants went so far as to suggest that complaints were thrown in the bin. In addition to this, participants spoke about staff sticking together and therefore putting in a complaint would not result in their voice being heard. This resulted in feelings of pointlessness and futility in using the complaint system as a legitimate means to resolve complaints.

5.3.3.2 Access

Bordt and Muschano (1988) raise the issue that bureaucratic procedures can heighten 'the likelihood of [complaint procedures] becoming dominated by professionals or paraprofessionals'. Figure 5.7 shows that not all participants felt that they were able to make a complaint in the prison with 41.9% disagreeing or strongly disagreeing with the statement.

The interviews and surveys identified four main reasons as to why some participants did not feel able to make a complaint; access to forms, knowledge as to how the system worked, literacy/language barriers and concerns about submitting a complaint. Currently the complaint mechanism in Ireland, as outlined in Chapter 3, entails a prisoner submitting a written form outlining what happened, where it happened, when it happened and whether there were any witnesses to the incident. The IPS policy states that these forms are available on each wing of the prison next to a dedicated post box for completed forms. While this means that all prisoners should be able to pick up a form easily, this was not always the case as indicated by participants who noted that forms were not readily available, and they had to request

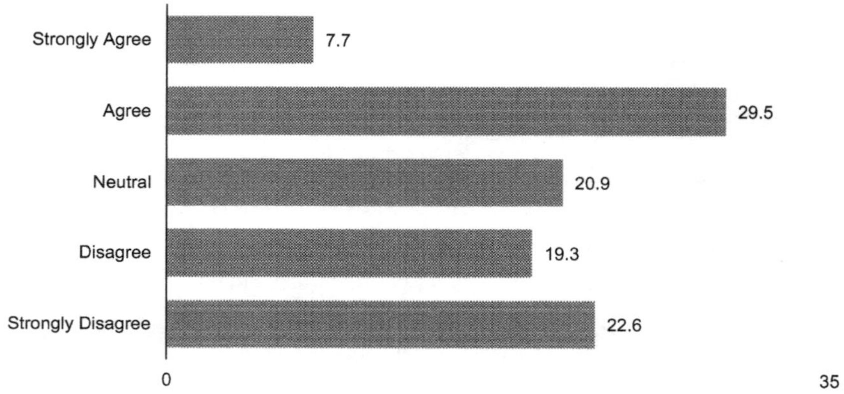

Figure 5.7 Responses to 'I feel able to make a complaint in this prison' (%).

forms from officers. Drawing attention to the fact that he wanted to complain eventually discouraged the below participant due to officer comments:

> *First of all, when I was going up to get the form like, do you know. I was getting it off the officer ... and he was kind of saying it to another officer then when I was leaving. 'Do you know, he is looking for a complaint form.' There's no complaint form there. I was three days looking for the form so there was a lot of people knew I was going to put in a complaint before I even got the form like so I didn't bother then.*
>
> (Participant 43)

This visibility around accessing the complaint form can act as a barrier and discourage prisoners who do not want to expose potential vulnerabilities or, in some cases, complaining was seen as the equivalent of siding with prison staff or telling on another prisoner which could result in inter-prisoner conflicts due to suspicions around the nature of the complaint.

Other participants spoke about the challenges of completing a written form due to literacy issues and feeling that they could not express themselves clearly on paper:

> *[P]eople that have difficulty writing and things like that. It would be difficult for them because if they make a complaint, if they can't read and write then they have to go to someone else and then that person could abuse them you know like putting down the wrong things and mix up the whole situation like. Get them further into trouble.*
>
> (Participant 43)

Currently, there are no formal supports for those who are not able to complete the form themselves and, as outlined by the participant above, asking another prisoner to help with this could cause problems through exposing vulnerabilities or the possibility that another prisoner might write the complaint differently than the complainant intended. This formalisation of the complaint process through a written form creates accessibility issues for some prisoners, while bureaucratising the system may be discouraging for those who already hold pre-existing negative views of complaining.

5.3.3.3 Delays

As outlined in Section 5.3.2, those serving longer sentences of ten years or more were more likely to have used the complaint system. One of the reasons put forward for this and evident in other research was delays in dealing with complaints Naylor (2014). As can be seen from Figure 5.8, 61.9% of respondents disagreed or strongly disagreed with the statement that 'Complaints made are dealt with quickly'.

This concern was also evident in discussions with interview participants who felt that complaints were often forgotten about *'[m]aybe they would listen to you but when they walk away it's like the conversation never happened'* (Participant 34); *'You're waiting eight weeks for it to come back and three to four months, you know? Not going to be happy with that'* (Participant 25).

The issue of delays can serve to dissuade prisoners from complaining as responses are not received before the prisoner leaves the prison or when an issue such as a complaint over, for example, a family visit does not receive a

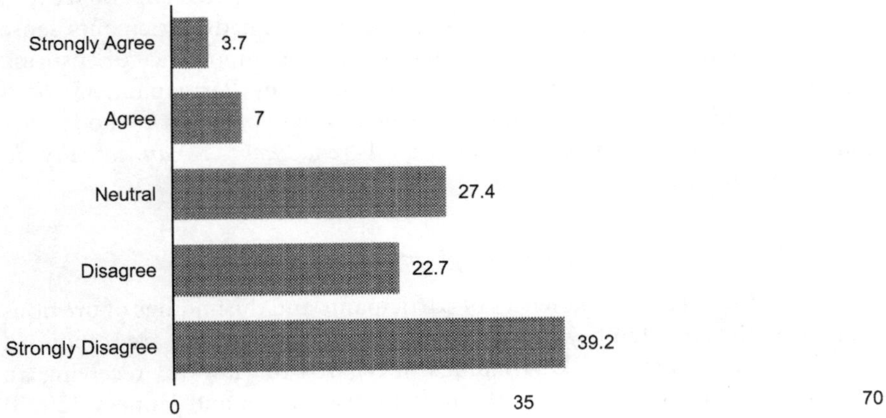

Figure 5.8 Responses to 'Complaints made are dealt with quickly' (%).

response until after the visit was supposed to have taken place. This created a sense of futility and pointlessness to bringing a complaint as illustrated by Participant 35: *'listen, do you think they'd be reading them [complaint forms]? Nah. They wouldn't'*. However, participants were clear to highlight that efficiency should not be viewed in isolation and that in some cases they understood that more time was needed to carry out a proper investigation and receiving a response too fast suggested that these steps may not have been taken. In cases such as these what was important to prisoners was being kept informed that something was happening. Delays in dealing with complaints or never getting back to prisoners on complaints was seen as disrespectful and showed a lack of concern for the well-being of the prisoner. It communicated an attitude of disinterest in resolving issues in prison and minimising the problems experienced by those in custody. This can further engrain the overall perception of lack of worth to prisoners, as the system which is supposed to help protect their rights instead also does not recognise their concerns.

5.3.3.4 Independence and Confidentiality

Both independence in dealing with prisoner complaints and confidentiality of the complaints process were considered important for participants, though confidentiality was perhaps less of a critical issue than might have been expected. However, participants raised concerns about these being present in the current system. Some participants felt that officers on the landing were accessing complaints submitted by prisoners and in some cases discarding complaints or approaching those who filed a complaint to try and resolve it personally or suggest it be withdrawn, as illustrated by Participant 37's experience: *'I put my complaint in the box like and it was kind of handled internally like you know and I felt like you know kind of the whole experience was kind of futile you know'*. These experiences undermined participants sense that the system was confidential and highlighted the importance of ensuring independence in the complaint process. As noted by Participant. 35: *'if it went to an independent professional person, it would be better'*, who further emphasised that independent people would *'read them … can actually do something about them'*.

5.3.3.5 Reasons for Decisions and Complaint Outcome

As outlined above, the experiences of participants and the findings of previous reports on the complaint system reveal that not all complaints are responded to. This section discusses key findings in regards to views of receiving an outcome for a complaint, especially in light of Calavita and Jenness' (2018) finding that in the prison context the outcome of the complaint can take on additional significance due to the high-stakes environment of the prison. Providing reasons for a decision is seen as a key component of procedural justice and, as outlined by Tyler (2017), providing reasons can help the complainant accept a decision even when it is not in their favour. Jenness and Calavita (2018) have argued that procedural justice theory breaks down in the context of incarceration. Drawing on the work of Berrey et al. (2012), they noted that in high-stakes and highly hierarchical environments involving deeply embedded power imbalances and historical disadvantage, outcomes matter a great deal, a finding which holds true across racial groups (Calavita and Jenness 2018). Figure 5.9 shows that similar to Jenness and Calavita's study respondents placed an increased importance on the outcome of a complaint in the prison setting; however, the result was very close to the neutral point of the scale (3.4 on a scale of 1 to 5 where 3 reflects neither agree nor disagree).

This finding suggests that while outcomes may take on a slightly higher significance in the prison context, the full extent of this needs to be further explored and other aspects of procedural justice are still important such as voice and independence, discussed above.

Another important element of the procedural justice literature is the need for reasoned decisions. This involves letting the complainant know why a certain decision has been made. As can be seen from Figure 5.10, respondents to the survey saw this as important with 58.5% responding agree or strongly agree to the statement 'Being given a reason helps me understand rejected complaints and accept the decision'. Providing a reason for a decision helps to show that the decision maker has put time and effort into considering the complainant's problem and communicates concern for the person.

However, the interviews provided nuance as to what being given a reason for a decision actually meant to participants. Some felt that resources or lack of staff was used as a catch all by the prison service for why certain activities

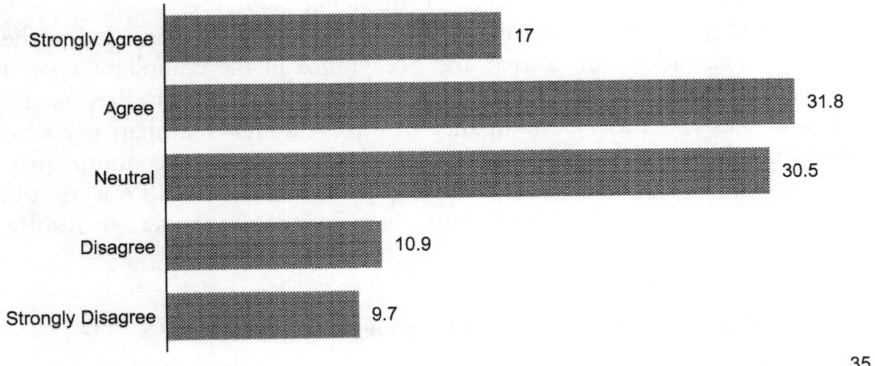

Figure 5.9 Responses to 'When making a complaint, it is the outcome that matters not the process' (%).

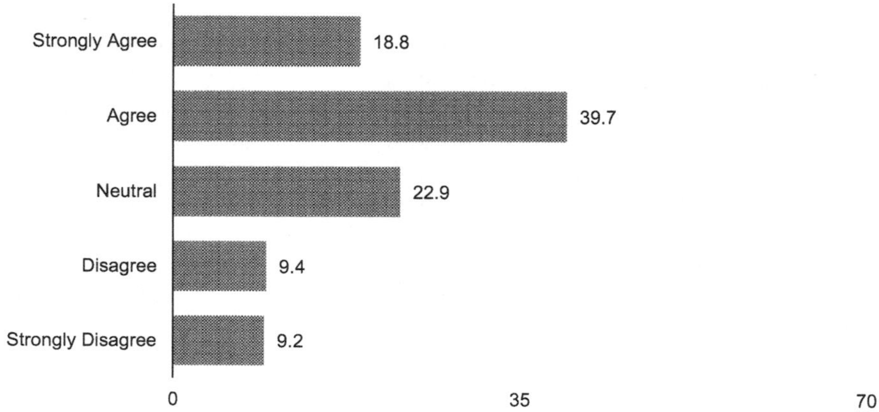

Figure 5.10 Responses to 'Being given a reason helps me understand rejected complaints and accept the decision' (%).

or requests could or could not be accommodated. While prisoners were understanding of the limitations of the prison environment and resources, the response felt generic and automated. This suggests that more specific detail might be needed to fulfil the requirement of a reasoned decision. The desire for a reason was also communicated by those who preferred to speak directly with a person about a complaint such as a member of staff, VC member or the governor as illustrated by Participant 25: *'I wouldn't fill out any forms at all I'd just go in and complain and say look Governor, I have a problem'.* They felt that by speaking to someone directly about their complaint they could ask follow-up questions, whereas written responses were sometimes delivered to prisoners by a member of staff who had not dealt with the complaint itself and was simply acting as the messenger.

These findings highlight the importance of procedural justice within the prison context and building trust and acceptance in the complaint system as a legitimate way of handling complaints in prison. As emphasised by Tyler and Bies (2015: 77), the quality of interpersonal treatment plays an important role in people's assessment of their treatment as procedurally just. The next section explores the reasons why prisoners did or did not use the complaint system and alternative routes used by some prisoners to resolve their complaints.

5.3.4 Why Participants Did or Did Not Use Complaint System

As highlighted above roughly one in four (22%) of participants had at some stage in their current sentence made use of the complaint system. This section outlines the reasons prisoners provided for using or not using the complaint system. Prisoners gave a wide range of reasons.

Some participants who complained emphasised a sense of having no choice but to complain and a general disdain for having to take these steps. Others spoke about the benefits of having evidence written down and linked complaining to potential court cases in the future. Another finding to emphasise here is the different ways of complaining referred to by prisoners. While the study focused on the formal complaint system, participants in the interviews referred to speaking to staff or seeking to speak to the Governor to submit a complaint. Some participants preferred oral complaints due to literacy issues but also the immediacy in receiving a response in dealing with a person. They felt that it would be more difficult to brush a person off as compared with submitting a written form and that it offered a greater opportunity to explain their case.

The high visibility of everyday life in prison also played a role in prisoners' perceptions of complaining in prison. As emphasised by participant 23, being seen to put something in the complaint box could have serious implications:

> *If you're seen in the prison putting an envelope into that fucking box, you'll lose your friends very fast… .. people will look at you and say what the fuck is he doing like? What's the big secret, you know? You wouldn't be trusted, do you know. So yeah that's the core of it there now.*
>
> (Participant 23)

There was a sense amongst some participants that they would be viewed as untrustworthy by other prisoners through complaining due to the perceived secrecy of putting in a complaint. In prison, there is a need to maintain an appearance, and this could be damaged by complaining. This finding is linked to the prisoners' discussions of ratting in prison and a sense that complaining could be about other prisoners. The heightened atmosphere of distrust and paranoia in prison meant that some prisoners would presume the worst.

When discussing interacting with oversight bodies and raising your voice in prison, one participant noted:

> *I don't know whether to voice that opinion either, whether it will work or not.*
>
> (Participant 17)

This example highlights the risk/benefit analysis carried out by prisoners when considering whether to interact with an inspection or monitoring body or raise a complaint. The participant concerned was speaking about the weekly allowance granted to prisoners and the cost of buying tobacco, an issue which prisoners spoke about together and whether speaking up about this issue would be worth the risk as he was unsure of the potential difference it would make. This relates back to issues around awareness of the bodies themselves but also the work they have done. In deciding whether to speak up about an issue in a high-stakes environment, such as a prison, where reprisals could have significant consequences on your daily life, there is a heightened need for accurate information. This could be information about the possibility of success, i.e. how have previous complaints been dealt with, how the system works, or a perception that you will be listened to. Such information helps build trust in bodies and encourages prisoners to speak up when they have an issue.

5.3.4.1 Reprisals

Reprisals were a concern for almost half of the survey respondents with 45.4% agreeing or strongly agreeing with the statement that 'prisoners who make complaints are punished by staff' as shown in Figure 5.11. This is an important finding as the risk of reprisals can act as a strong deterrent for those making a complaint, especially in light of other concerns such as the feeling amongst prisoners that the complaint does not work, discussed above, and the finding reflected in Figure 5.12, in response to the statement 'Prisoners who complain get what they want in prison', where 76.3% of respondents disagreed or strongly disagreed with this statement.

In the prison context, reprisals can take a wide variety of forms as highlighted by participants in the interviews. While some discussed issues such as being transferred to a different prison, potentially far away from their family, due to complaining, others spoke about losing privileges or being the last to be unlocked each morning. In prison, these more subtle forms of reprisals could take on added significance as prisoners may lose out on precious out of cell time or there may be knock on effects of being perceived as a troublemaker.

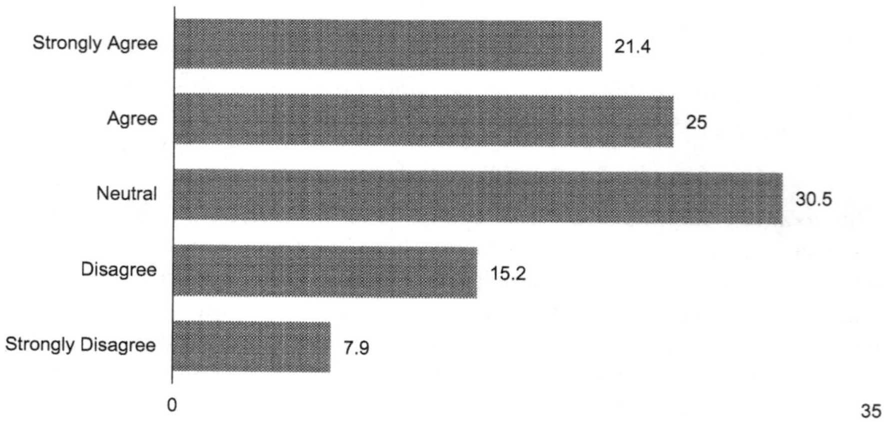

Figure 5.11 Responses to 'Prisoners who make complaints are punished by staff' (%).

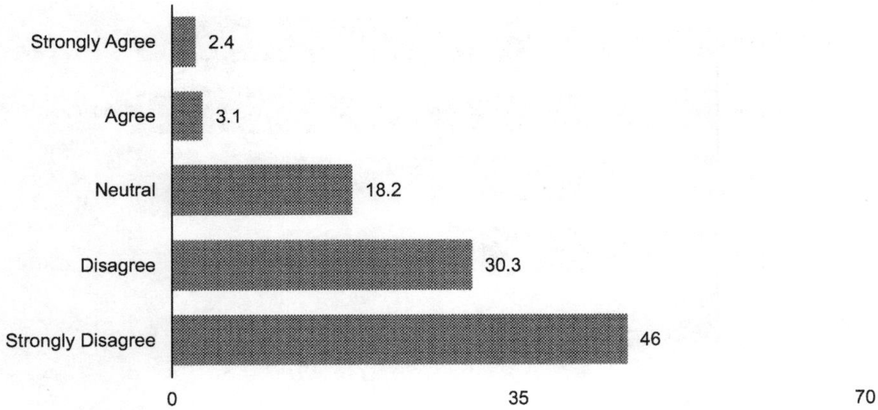

Figure 5.12 Response to 'Prisoners who make complaints get what they want in prison' (%).

The fact that respondents did not think those who made complaints got what they wanted in prison shows an overall lack of faith in the complaint system for resolving prisoner complaints and suggests that using the complaint system might actually work against the prisoner.

5.3.5 Resolving Problems in Prison

When asked how they would resolve a problem in prison, a majority of respondents referred to speaking to a trusted officer or a governor with a discussion of the complaint system itself frequently only arising when promoted. This can be seen in the case of Participant 24 who stated that: *'I think I'd actually just write out what I had to write out and bring it into the governor… I wouldn't fill out any forms at all I'd just go in and complain'*. This is also reflected in the survey findings. As demonstrated by Figure 5.13, almost 60% of respondents either strongly agreed or agreed with the statement 'I prefer to solve issues myself rather than through the complaints system'. This further emphasises the concerns raised above that prisoners do not trust the system or see the benefits of its use.

5.3.6 What Makes for a Good Complaint System?

As part of the study, participants were asked about features of a good system as well as possible reforms for the system. This section outlines the key features which were important to participants.

As can be seen in Figure 5.14, dealing with complaints quickly, independence and providing reasons were identified as the most important features by

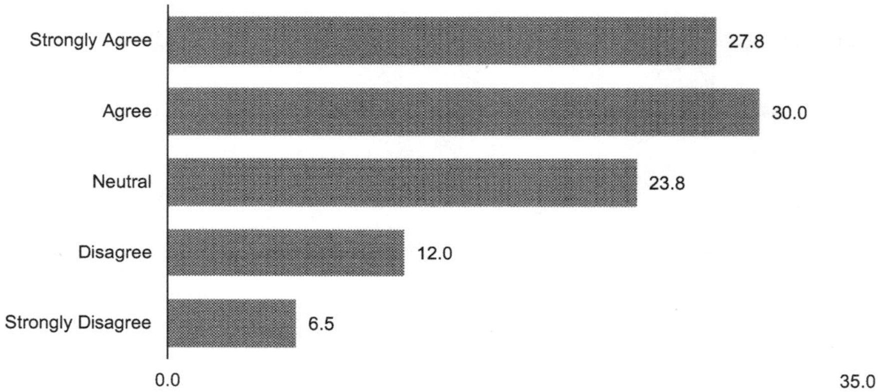

Figure 5.13 Responses to 'I prefer to solve issues myself rather than through the complaints system' (%).

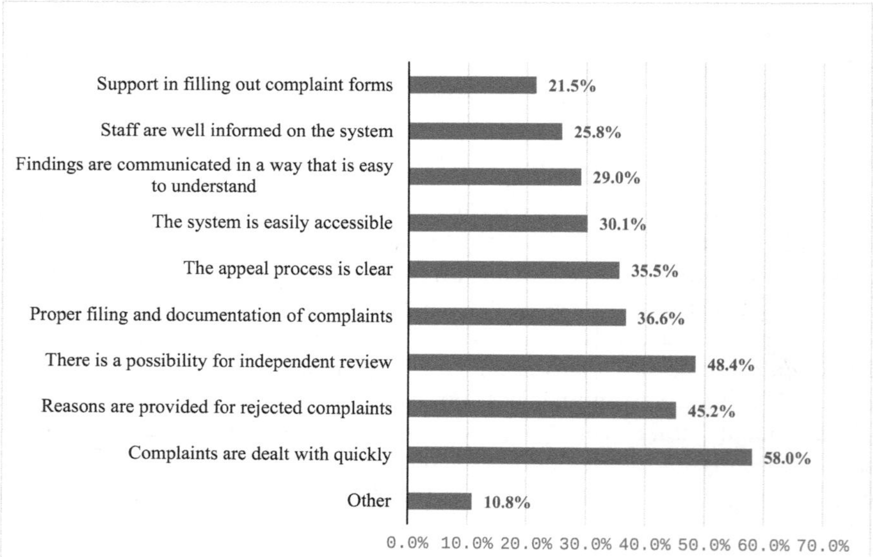

Figure 5.14 Responses to 'What makes for a good complaints system?' (%).

those in prison. Similarly in interviews, participants referred to the importance of receiving a response in a timely manner and the possibility of an independent body handling the complaint. Participants spoke about a lack of independence in the current system, which resulted in a hesitancy to use the system as they felt it would not be dealt with properly. Additionally, a proper response was perceived as a sign of respect and taking prisoners' issues seriously rather than brushing them off.

5.4 Courts

This section outlines participants' experience of the courts and access to justice in relation to prison conditions and rights violations. As outlined in Chapter 3, prisoner litigation in Ireland is still in its infancy (Rogan 2014). However, it is gradually expanding, and this section gives important insights into how participants feel about the courts as accessible arenas to uphold their rights. A number of key themes outlined in this section will be returned to in later chapters, in particular a sense that judges understand problems in prison or see prisoners' as worthy of rights, the risk of reprisals for speaking up about an issue and potential implications for prisoners, as well as the ways in which issues are resolved in prison.

5.4.1 Experiences of Bringing a Case

In line with the low number of prison cases in Ireland, very few participants had experiences of bringing a case in relation to prison conditions and treatment while in prison. Despite this, a significant number of interview participants and survey respondents did say they would bring a case if they had to, as indicated in Figure 5.15 in response to the statement 'I would consider suing the prison service if I had an issue in prison'. 40.4% of respondents agreed or strongly agreed with this statement. However, this drops significantly when asked to respond to the statement 'I think it is worth it to sue the prison service' which only 23.7% of respondents agreed with. This reflects a sentiment

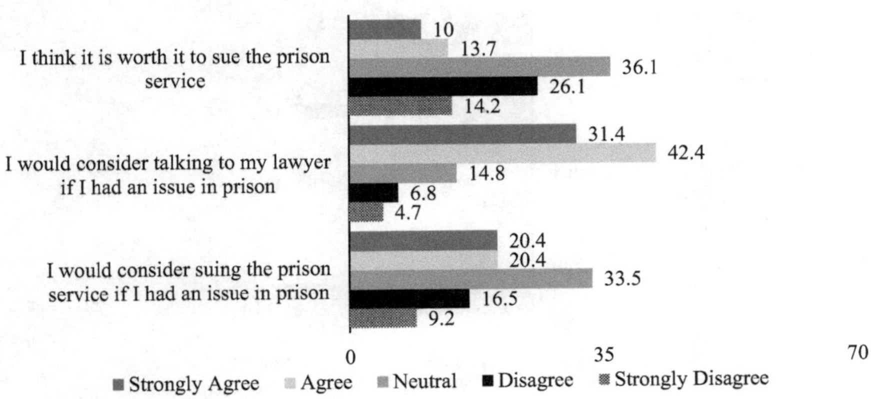

Figure 5.15 Responses to statements on views on bringing a case (%).

discussed above amongst participants that the system will always win in some way and that affecting change in prison is difficult. As highlighted by Participant 44:

> *Before I used be putting in applications to the High Court and this and that but I kind of stopped that, you know. It doesn't get you anywhere like.*

This sentiment was reflected by a number of participants, a sense that bringing issues to the attention of the authorities only served to make life more challenging for oneself and would not resolve the problem.

Figure 5.15 also shows that a much higher number of respondents would seek legal advice if an issue arose in prison, with only a minority (11.5%) saying that they disagreed or strongly disagreed with the statement 'I would consider talking to my lawyer if I had an issue in prison'. In discussions with interview participants this was seen as a way of getting things done in prison, as they prison service were more likely to respond and take action to a letter from a solicitor than a complaint by a prisoner. This suggests that external bodies, in particular the threat of legal action from a solicitor's letter, may be perceived as more legitimate and something which could develop into a court case, which should be avoided by the prison service. Interestingly, some participants, who had spent longer periods of time in prison or had a history of imprisonment, spoke of cases in the past but felt that they were less likely to arise in newer prisons.

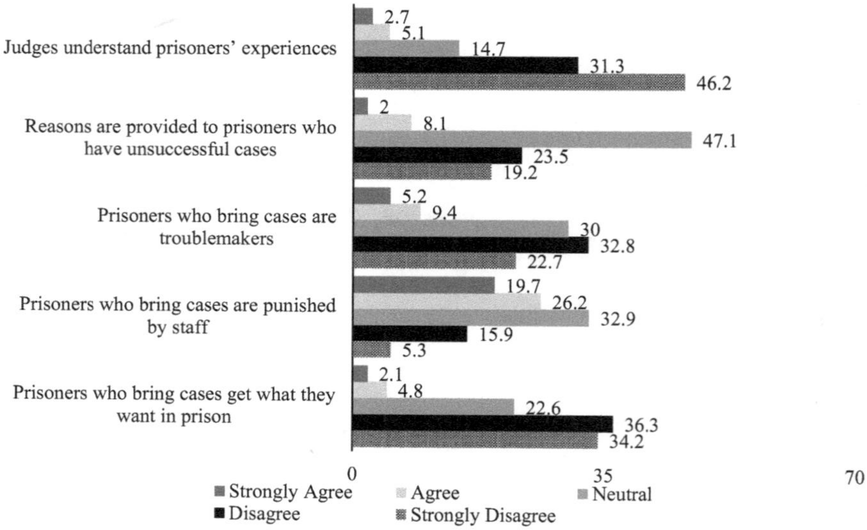

Figure 5.16 Views of litigation in prison (%).

I have heard of people from old prisons doing it or wherever, but I haven't heard much now.

(Participant 34)

In this participant's case, it was seen as a reflection of improvements in prison conditions where prisoners were treated better overall and renovations had taken place across the prison campus. As will be discussed further in the next chapter, while these improvements are a welcome change to life in prison, this may reflect prison expectations and prisoners setting a low bar on acceptable prison treatment.

However, as can be seen in Figure 5.16, prisoners had mixed feelings about how the litigation and the potential outcomes. Some participants spoke about waiting until after they had finished their sentence to bring a case due to fears of reprisals while in prison. However, there was a distinction drawn between different kinds of cases with participants seeing some cases as more personal and would be seen poorly by staff and others more systematic and not directly affecting the staff they interacted with most often. This is reflected in Calavita and Jenness' (2015) research and the language of complaining. Bringing complaints or cases which could be perceived as a personal attack should be avoided or rephrased as a system issue concerning the institution.

As discussed above, respondents felt that for the most part judges would not understand prisoners' experiences, and this could make it challenging to portray the significance of an issue in the prison context. Some participants felt that being seen as a prisoner by the court would make them view you definitely to someone who was bringing a case from the general population. In particular, one participant referred to preferring to bring a case once released so he could dress appropriately for court and not arrive escorted by prison officers. This highlights the implications of being seen as a prisoner on one's sense of self and how prisoners felt they would be viewed by others.

5.5 Conclusion

This chapter has highlighted different views and perceptions of oversight bodies in Irish prisons and suggest that the ambitions of rights-protecting bodies are not in line with the experiences of those in prison. The study found a significant lack of awareness of the existence of some of the inspection and monitoring bodies in Irish prisons and participants at times unwilling or unable to engage with those bodies. Participants demonstrated a lack of trust and faith in both the inspection and monitoring bodies, as well as the complaint system in achieving their goals and helping prisoners. Participants also expressed concerns around reprisals for interacting with inspection and monitoring bodies, or for filing a complaint or bringing a case. The pervasiveness of the prison system, as discussed by Foucault (2012), meant that the range of reprisals which prisoners might experience was quite broad but could have significant implications for surviving prison life. Participants also spoke about a severity threshold in raising an issue either through inspection and monitoring or complaining through the existing system or the courts, which may create a disconnect between the standards of these different bodies and prisoners' expectations of what they are entitled to while in prison or what is worth speaking up about. As discussed by Sexton (2015), prisoners' experiences and expectations are shaped by their concept of what prison can and should be like, this therefore can have implications for how they interact with oversight bodies. These findings are concerning given that these bodies are intended to protect the rights of those in custody and while some participants had positive experiences, this was not always the case. Despite these findings, prisoners, as in the case of those in Calavita and Jenness' study (2015), maintained a belief in the need for and the potential of oversight bodies in prison. This suggests that despite their low expectations and experiences of oversight, prisoners retain hope in the possibility of the prison system to change and a recognition of their inherent human rights. The next chapter outlines key findings regarding prison culture and rights consciousness to explain factors which play a role in shaping the views outlined above.

Note

1 Of the 4,812 committals in 2018, 3,559 were sentenced to less than a year in prison. Irish Prison Service, Annual Report 2018. Available at: www.irishprisons.ie/wp-content/uploads/documents_pdf/Annual-Report-2018.pdf (Accessed 14 May 2020).

References

Cormac Behan, *Citizen Convict: Prisoners, Politics and the Vote* (Manchester University Press 2016).

Cormac Behan and Richard Kirkham, 'Monitoring, Inspection and Complaints Adjudication in Prison: The Limits of Prison Accountability Frameworks' (2016) 55(4) *The Howard Journal of Crime and Justice* 432.

Karin A Beijersbergen, Anja JE Dirkzwager, Veroni I Eichelsheim, Peter H Van der Laan and Paul Nieuwbeerta, 'Procedural Justice, Anger, and Prisoners' Misconduct: A Longitudinal Study' (2015) 42 *Criminal Justice and Behavior* 196.

Ellen Berrey, Steve G. Hoffman and Laura Beth Nielsen, 'Situated Justice: A Contextual Analysis of Fairness and inequality in Employment Discrimination Litigation' (2012) 46(1) *Law & Society Review* 1.

David Bierie, 'Procedural Justice and Prison Violence: Examining Complaints Among Federal Inmates (2000–2007)' (2013) 19(1) *Psychology, Public Policy, and Law* 15.

Miranda Boone and Mieke Kox, 'Neutrality as an Element of Perceived Justice in Prison: Consistency Versus Individualization' (2014) 10 *Utrecht Law Review* 118.

Rebecca L. Bordt and Micheal C. Musheno, 'Bureaucratic Co-optation of Informal Dispute Processing: Social Control as an Effect of Inmate Grievance policy' (1988) 25(1) *Journal of Research in Crime and Delinquency* 7.

Kitty Calavita and Valerie Jenness, *Appealing to Justice: Prisoner Grievances, Rights and Carceral Logic* (University of California Press 2015).

Kitty Calavita and Valerie Jenness, 'Race, Grievance Systems and Prisoners Perceptions of Justice in three California Prisons' (2018) 15(1) *Du Bois Review: Social Science Research on Race* 153.

Gaëtan Cliquennois and Sonja Snacken, 'European and United Nations Monitoring of Penal and Prison Policies as a Source of an Inverted Panopticon?' (2018) 70(1) *Crime, Law and Social Change* 1.

Ben Crewe, *The Prisoner Society: Power, Adaptation and Social Life in an English Prison* (Oxford University Press 2009).

Michel Foucault, *Discipline and Punish: The Birth of the Prison* (Vintage 2012).

Russell Hardin, 'Trustworthiness' (1996) 107(1) *Ethics* 26.

Katerine Hawley, *Trust: A Very Short Introduction* (Oxford University Press 2012).

Valerie Jenness and Kitty Calavita, '"It Depends on the Outcome": Prisoners, Grievances, and Perceptions of Justice' (2018) 52(1) *Law & Society Review* 41.

Alison Liebling assisted by Helen Arnold, *Prisons and Their Moral Performance: A Study of Values, Quality, and Prison Life* (Oxford University Press 2004).

Katerina Linos and Tom Pegram, 'What Works in Human Rights Institutions?' (2017) 111 *American Journal of International Law* 628.

Stephan Livingstone, Tim Owen, Alison Macdonald, Blinne Ní Ghrálaigh and Helen Law, *Prison Law* (Oxford University Press on Demand 2008).

Thomas Mathiesen, *The Defences of the Weak: A Sociological Study of a Norwegian Correctional Institution* (Tavistock 1965).

Mark Morgan and Mary Kett, *The Prison Adult Literacy Survey: Results and Implications* (Irish Prison Service 2003).

Rod Morgan and Alison Liebling, 'Imprisonment: An Expanding Scene' in Rod Morgan, Mike Maguire, and Robert Reiner (eds) *The Oxford Handbook of Criminology* (Oxford University Press 2007).

Bronwyn Naylor, 'Human Rights and Respect in Prisons: The Prisoners' Perspective' (2014) 31 *Law Context: A Socio-Legal Journal* 84.

Nicola Padfield, 'Monitoring Prisons in England and Wales: Who Ensures the Fair Treatment of Prison-ers?' (2018) 70 *Crime, Law and Social Change* 57.

Mary Rogan, 'Judicial Conception of Prisoners' Right in Ireland: An Emerging Field. Academy of European Law, 'Improving Conditions Related to Detention' (Council of Europe, Strasbourg, November 2014).

Mary Senevirante, 'Researching Ombudsmen' in Reza Banakar and Max Traver, *Theory and Method in Socio-legal Research* (Bloomsbury Publishing 2005).

Lori Sexton, 'Penal Subjectivities: Developing a Theoretical Framework for Penal Consciousness' (2015) 17(1) *Punishment & Society* 114.

Tom R Tyler, 'The Role of Perceived Injustice in Defendants' Evaluations of Their Courtroom Experience' (1984) 18(1) *Law and Society Review* 51.

Tom R Tyler, 'Legitimacy in Corrections' (2010) 9(1) *Criminology & Public Policy* 127.

Tom R Tyler, 'Procedural Justice and Policing: A Rush to Judgment?' (2017) 13 *Annual Review of Law and Social Science* 29.

Tom R Tyler and Robert J Bies, 'Beyond Formal Procedures: The Interpersonal Context of Procedural Justice' in John S Carroll (ed) *Applied social Psychology and Organizational Settings* (Psychology Press 2015).

Sophie van der Valk, Eva Aizpurua, and Mary Rogan. '"[Y] ou are better off talking to af****** wall": The Perceptions and Experiences of Grievance Procedures Among Incarcerated People in Ireland'. *Law & Society Review* (2022) 56(2) 261–285.

Jason Warr, 'The Deprivation of Certitude, Legitimacy and Hope: Foreign National Prisoners and the Pains of Imprisonment' (2016) 16 *Criminology & Criminal Justice* 301.

Harry Woolf, *The Woolf Report: A Summary of the Main Findings and Recommendations of the Inquiry Into Prison Disturbances* (Prison Reform Trust 1991).

6 Barriers to Engagement

6.1 Introduction

As highlighted in the previous chapter, participants in this study had various degrees of awareness of the existence of oversight bodies and the specifics of their roles, with a considerable portion unaware that such bodies existed. Additionally, their experiences and perceptions of the bodies varied widely, though some important common themes emerged. This chapter explores some of the factors which shaped prisoners' awareness and expectations of these bodies, as well as the experiences they had with them. Specifically, it identifies barriers to engaging with oversight bodies due to factors inherent to the prison environment, such as prison culture and rights consciousness. In particular, relationships and trust building in prison, as well as rights and penal consciousness amongst the prisoner population will be explored. As outlined by Merry (2009: 1), 'in order for human rights to be effective … they need to be translated into local terms and situated within local contexts of power and meaning'. This chapter sets out the context in which human rights protecting in prison operates. This chapter explores the factors which can create barriers to accessing and awareness of rights-protecting bodies amongst prisoners. The increasing bureaucracy of oversight bodies can act as a barrier to those who have had negative past experiences with authorities or who may not be able to engage due to literacy issues (Hood et al 1999; Crewe 2011). Key to this chapter is the idea that oversight bodies for prisoners should be designed with those who they are intended to protect in mind.

6.2 Barriers to Engagement

The prison environment and penal culture can create barriers to engaging with oversight, whether such oversight is carried out through inspection bodies or complaints. Research conducted with prisoners in Ireland on voting rights highlights the challenges in accessing rights while in prison (Behan 2016). Behan (2016) highlighted the difference between circumstantial and voluntary abstentionism in relation to exercising the right to vote by people in prison. While some prisoners were unaware of the specifics of how to

DOI: 10.4324/9781003477471-6

exercise their right and the bureaucracy around voting, others actively choose not to vote due to their own feelings towards Irish politics and for some a sense of alienation from the outside world through imprisonment (Behan 2016). This distinction can also be seen in this research between oversight in prisons and prisoners' views of oversight. While some deliberately choose not to engage with oversight mechanisms, due to the fact that at times they were viewed as another arm of the prison service or a layer of bureaucracy to prevent prisoners from accessing decision makers, others were simply not aware of the existence of bodies to protect their rights, or what their rights even were. This section starts by discussing prisoners' views of their rights while in prison, followed by their expectations in prison drawing on Sexton's work on penal consciousness discussed in Chapter 4. This will be followed by barriers created by the prisoner code and aspects of the penal culture, such as reliance on key relationships which can hinder prisoners seeking to inform or access rights protection. Finally, the concept of trust (or lack thereof) in the prison context will be discussed and how low trust environments, combined with low awareness of the existence and activities of oversight bodies, can in turn limit the opportunities to engage with those bodies.

6.2.1 Rights Consciousness in Prison

This section examines the interaction between rights consciousness and participants' views of oversight bodies, including those topics which people in prison were most willing and motivated to raise as issues. As outlined in Chapters 3 and 4, under law, prisoners formally retain their rights while in custody other than the right liberty – however, there is scant literature on the lived experience of rights while in prison and rights awareness amongst prisoners. One notable exception is the work by Piacentini with Russian prisoners where she explores rights awareness and consciousness amongst prisoners. Her research demonstrated that, despite penal reform incorporating a human rights framework, this mindset did not necessarily filter down throughout the institution (Piacentini and Katz 2017). This highlights the importance of moving beyond the formal statements of an institution and engaging with the lived experiences of actors themselves to understand the reality of rights and rights protection in prison. This section considers the role of prisoners' rights and rights consciousness in understanding prisoner perspectives of oversight bodies. A key consideration is the level of rights consciousness amongst prisoners. As outlined in Chapter 4, rights consciousness is shaped at an early age and prisoners enter the prison system with preconceptions about what a prison should look like and expectations of their rights in prison. This can have significant implications for how they view rights and engage with oversight bodies. This chapter shows that in the current study participants had low expectations of their rights, tied into low expectations of prison conditions and in some cases a low sense of being worthy of rights. This will be followed by an overview of what matters to those in prison and what triggers prisoners to seek help or speak up about rights in prison. In the current study, being proactive was found to be an important part of learning and accessing rights in prison, which went against the prison culture of 'keeping your head down' and 'getting on with your time'. Prison culture and the norms and values amongst prisoner such as through the prisoner code encourages stoicism and getting on with your time as central to surviving prison, with some prisoners willing to hide their feelings to avoid looking weak (Jewkes 2005). However, as will be discussed below, certain issues – in particular contact with family – can result in prisoners seeking recourse to other mechanisms and therefore problems with family visit and contact can be a trigger point to break from the silence of bearing pains of imprisonment. This narrow understanding of what rights mean in prison has implications for engaging with the bodies, as those in prison may simply not identify issues in the same way or see certain aspects of prison life as worth speaking up about but rather something to be tolerated and survived.

In prison, while the concept of rights may be visible in the legal framework and official guidelines of the organisation, the permeability of these concepts into the everyday life of both staff and prisoners may differ. In Ireland, as outlined in Chapter 3, prisoners' rights have been discussed before the courts, as well as contained within the Prison Act 2007 and the Prison Rules 2007. However, as was clear in the current study, the scope of rights and right protection in prison was limited amongst the majority of participants.

6.2.1.1 *Being Informed*

As discussed in Chapter 4, Kelk (1978) developed the concept of Rechtsburgerschap (legal citizenship) which consists of three elements for an effective legal position regarding the protection of prisoners' rights – those are material rights, procedural rights and information about both types of rights. Therefore, the component regarding information about rights themselves and structures to protect them is a key consideration linked to rights consciousness amongst prisoners. Respondents to the survey in the current study were asked about their rights in prison and whether they felt informed, able to assert and knew where to find information about their rights, as well as whether they felt their rights were respected in prison. Figure 6.1 illustrates the lack of rights awareness and information prisoners' felt was available to them in prison.

As can be seen from Figure 6.1, 45.3% of participants agreed or strongly agreed with the statement 'I don't know where to find out about my rights'. 51.5% of participants disagreed or strongly disagreed with the statement 'I feel that rights are respected in prison'. 49.5% of participants disagreed or strongly disagreed with the statement 'I feel informed about my rights', while 49.6% of participants disagreed or strongly disagreed with the statement 'I feel able to assert my rights in prison'. This suggests that prisoners do not know what their rights are or where to get information about their rights.

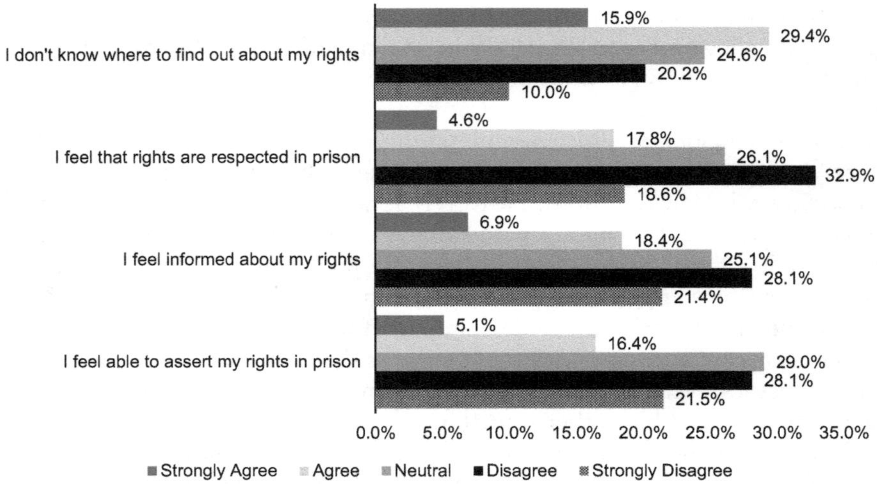

Figure 6.1 Views on rights in prison (%).

Additionally, rights are not perceived as respected in prison and asserting rights in prison is not something they feel able to do. This suggests that rights awareness amongst prisoners is low and there can be challenges in speaking about rights when that information is lacking. This finding is supported in the interviews where participants spoke about a sense of having no rights and some participants felt that the prison service deliberately limited the information given to prisoners.

6.2.1.2 Sources of Information

As discussed in Chapter 5, prisoners were sometimes confused about the specific roles of different bodies or lacked information about the bodies and their rights more broadly. Some felt that the institution was unwilling to share information about rights and rights-protecting bodies and that looking for information on these from staff was a waste of time and could draw unwanted attention. Reliance on other prisoners for information was evident throughout the research, as can be seen in Figure 6.2, where other prisoners were the most frequent source of information on rights in prison with half of the respondents learning about their rights from other prisoners. Similarly in interviews, participants referred to other prisoners as the main source of information on life in prison and what they were entitled to.

This is unsurprising in an environment with low levels of literacy, as oral communication is increasingly important. As noted above, 28.3% of

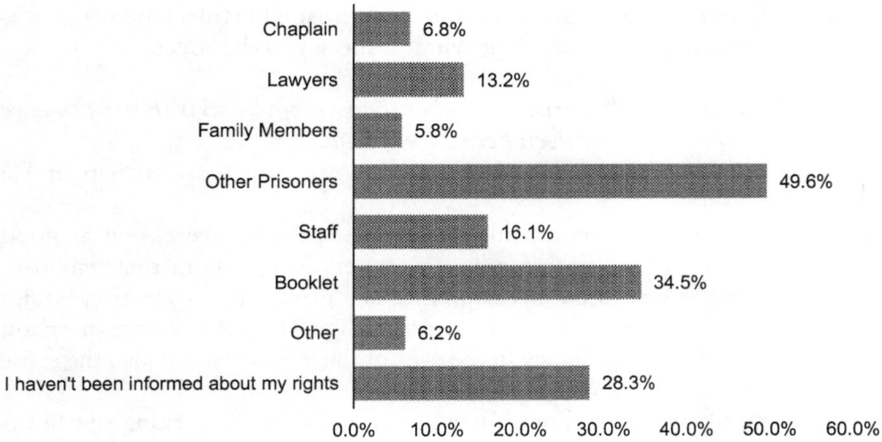

Figure 6.2 Sources of information on rights in prison (%).

respondents indicated that they had not been informed about their rights. Given the wide range of rights impacted by imprisonment, this figure is indicative of the lack of rights language within the prison and potentially vulnerable groups having even less information about their rights.

As discussed by Ugelvik (2017) and Warr (2016), foreigners can face additional challenges in prison such as practical difficulties around understanding the culture and dealing with the administrative and bureaucratic requirements of an unfamiliar system. This can arise due to the existence of languages barriers between prisoners and staff, as well as the majority of the prison population. There has been a growth in the number of foreign nationals across Western European prison systems in recent years. In the case of Ireland, committals of non-Irish prisoners increased 50% between 2015 and 2018.[1] While the current study did not oversample from this group, there was some indication from the interviews that those who did not speak English were particularly reliant on other prisoners to gain information on prison life and on who was present in the prison. This can result in gaps in knowledge or delayed learning about who is present in the prison. As noted by one participant, who did not speak English as his first language, he relied extensively on others to ask questions about prison life. Therefore, if someone who spoke the same language was not around when an inspector was in the prison, he could not ask for information or interact with the inspector. In combination with the lack of awareness of oversight bodies amongst prisoners outlined in Chapter 5, this meant that some prisoners could miss out on the opportunity to learn about these bodies.

Another issue discussed by those in prison was the importance of relationships in relying on other prisoners for information on rights in prison and the information they had on rights in prison. As this quote illustrates, prisoners frequently referred to learning about prison life through experiences or someone taking you under their wing to show you the ropes.

> *... I'd take advice off a prisoner rather than an officer to be honest in here like, the ones that have been here a long time.*
>
> (Participant 41)

In particular, prisoners with a lot of prison experience were seen as good sources of information, both for how prisoners learnt about their environment but also, as discussed in Chapter 5, as a group that inspection bodies should talk to in order to learn about prison life. Their experience in prison gave them a sense of legitimacy in the eyes of the prisoners and also the sense that they would be believed by outside bodies.

Prisoners often spoke about a need to be proactive in seeking out information, but also relied on other prisoners and their own observations and experience to learn how things worked. For example, when asked about how he learnt about his rights in prison, this participant explained:

> *... [P]risoners more so really than anything else. They kind of tell you how things work like do you know and when you get food do you know and when you get banged up and everything like that, do you know.*
>
> (Participant 30)

This highlights a gradual learning curve in prison. Prisoners learnt about rights and services in prison as a need arose, such as a complaint. In addition to this, prisoners learnt about things that were perceived as important, in this case the routine of prison life, as this was a first-time offender with no prior engagement with the criminal justice system. It also highlights who prisoners trust in prison, in terms of learning about prison life and who prisoners turn to when they have questions. This is particularly striking considering that the prisoner had no prior engagement with the prison service. It highlights that those entering prison may bring in preconceptions from the outside regarding who they can turn to for information, as well as who they have access to with their questions.

A reoccurring point noted by prisoners was the need to be proactive in order to find out about your rights or to access certain rights. Many prisoners felt that the prison would not simply provide you with the information or inform you of your rights unless you went looking. As emphasised by this extract from an interview:

> *The simple fact is there's a European book on prisoners' rights and all, you don't get that.*
>
> ***Okay. So, you don't get to know what your rights are?***

Even if you get one of those books, it could be half the stuff does be ripped out. Because apparently, you're not entitled to everything that you are entitled to.

(Participant 33)

As the above extract highlights, getting information on rights in prison was not always straightforward and prisoners were reliant on the prison service to gain access to this, which he felt they tampered with.

Seeking out information and asserting your rights was considered by many participants to be antithetical to the prison culture of keeping your head down and getting on with your sentence as noted by Participant 17:

I don't really ask [the prison staff] *for anything. I just get on with my jail, that's it like. I wouldn't ask them for much in here.*

This sense of getting on with your time in prison, which will be discussed further below in relation to prison culture, was seen by participants as a way of surviving in prison and speaking up was seen by some as risky and drawing attention to yourself. Some felt that speaking up was pointless, while others perceived it as resulting in repercussions for themselves.

Despite this, there were certain rights and situations which prompted even those who presented as tough or stoic prisoners to speak out. These trigger points show a significant shift in the behaviour of prisoners to protect their loved ones or access to healthcare, especially if it was likely to have a long-term impact on release. In the case of Participant 28, it took getting a letter from a solicitor for his healthcare concerns to be taken seriously, as highlighted by this quote:

Yeah, so it is terrible having to do something, but it was the only way that I could do it myself ... a letter from the solicitor worked wonders because that got the ball moving along.

The need to contact a solicitor was not something that the participant wanted to do but felt it was the only way to get the prison service to listen to his needs.

Similarly, Participant 06 noted the need to speak to a Governor if you needed to find out about anything but that even when you did this action was unlikely to be taken:

You don't find out nothing, you just go to the Governor I suppose, and you are still told they do this and they do that but they do nothing. The only time they do anything for you here is to bring you to hospital. Do you know and even that is hard.

As he noted, it was hard to convince staff that action needed to be taken at times and there was a sense that prisoners were not taken seriously. This lack of faith in the prison to assist a prisoner, even in serious situations, has implications for people speaking up as it may feel pointless.

Moreover, prison culture can mean that some prisoners may be hesitant to seek out others or ask questions about their rights. As illustrated by this quote, the participant felt that he did not want to be a source of information for too many prisoners.

> *Now I wouldn't advise everyone of this, but I really felt for this guy like ... But I say I wouldn't talk to every Tom, Dick and Harry. I'm not a counsellor. It's not my job you know but sometimes you can be forgotten about in the Irish prison system as well.*
>
> (Participant 06)

This participant, a person at a later stage in his life sentence, also spoke about the fact that he was not responsible for providing other prisoners with information about life in prison and while he was willing to chat with some, given his vast experience, relying on others to inform and empower others resulted in varying views of rights. This participant also spoke about the majority of rights as privileges, rather than something which prisoners are entitled to. As someone who prisoners relied on for information, his perception could therefore shape others' views of their rights and the bodies that protect those rights. As illustrated by this quote from another participant, asking too many questions could lead to being perceived as a troublemaker:

> *No, I'd never really questioned anything, like I'd be afraid, do you know, if you question too far into something you might be known as a troublemaker and then things could get worse for you, do you know that sort of way.*
>
> (Participant 19)

Multiple participants spoke about the risk of speaking up too much and drawing attention to oneself. This runs antithetical to much of the prisoner code and key tactics for surviving prison which will be discussed further below. Speaking to someone who you did not know much about or about an issue that one perceived as minor could be felt as a waste of the limited agency retained by prisoners while in prison. Prisoners may not want to waste an opportunity to speak up, when the benefit is unclear and especially in light of the risk to relationships and other forms of retaliation discussed in Chapter 5. These concerns are also evident in literature, as noted by Stanley (2011: 26), 'rights are ... about relationships with people'. This was evident in the current research from discussions with prisoners who learnt whom to approach for help or had certain officers they avoided asking for anything. Relationships with other prisoners and staff in prison were seen as key to accessing rights and receiving information on rights.

6.2.2 No Rights in Prison

Prisoners in the current study often felt they had no rights in prison: '*No rights, I haven't got any rights*'. (Participant 07), while others had a very limited view: '*You have a right to your hour of exercise, that's all you have really*' (Participant 06). There was also a sense that rights could be easily taken away and were seen as privileges which the prison had full control over, as illustrated by Participant 06:

> *[T]he only thing they can't take off you is your hour exercise and your meals. Everything else they can. You can get everything but then everything can be taken away from you and the only thing they can't take away from you is the food and your hour of exercise basically, so you kind of have to work from basic up to enhanced.*

This sense of having no rights or the ability of the prison to take away rights is a sharp contrast to the significant reform of prison policy and legislation concerning the treatment of prisoners which has taken place in recent years. Participant 18 asked the author about the legal status of the European Human Rights Act in Ireland and enforceability of rights in prison. Two other prisoners made reference to the EPRs. However, in general, and as with Karamalidou's (2017) research, prisoners did not see rights in prison as legally protected beyond a narrow conception such as an hour of exercise and the meeting of basic needs such as food and hygiene.

Furthermore, one participant (45) highlighted that '*in prison they only give you things to take them off you, that's always the way*'. This quote portrays the sense that rights are not protected in prison and that additional benefits are simply an extension of staff/prison control over the prisoner and their life. This lack of control over one's own circumstances and what one receives while in custody can build a sense of frustration, which may contribute to fatalism or create division between prisoners as they see others receiving things they do not have nor know how to gain in prison. This feeling is exemplified by the following quote:

> *No rights, I haven't got any rights… . I don't even look at anything like that I just … I just do what do be asked of me, it is better that way, you know what I mean. If you are having problems, it is better than roaring and shouting at them yeah or snapping or … sometimes you feel like doing it but there is no point in it, you are not going to get anywhere doing that, you know.*
>
> (Participant 7).

As will be discussed further below, this participant highlights some of the concerns prisoners had about speaking up and being vocal about your rights. In addition to this, he felt uninformed about what rights he had while in prison and a sense that the best approach to managing imprisonment was to keep your head down and do your time. This was reiterated by Participant 29, as seen from the quote below, who felt that keeping his head down was the best way to manage completing his sentence.

> *There are certain times you would say to yourself this is wrong or like you feel like (complaining), but I haven't done it, you know. … . You could make trouble for yourself in here and to me the quietest way is the best normally.*
>
> (Participant 29)

Additionally, there was a lack of clarity about rights in prison amongst participants and, in the case of the participant above, he relied more on a sense that something 'felt wrong', rather than having concrete information on his rights. He also noted that he did not *'want to get too deep into it'*, which suggests that reflecting on what goes wrong in prison can be difficult for a prisoner to deal with, especially when there is no hope of changes being made or being successful in resolving problems. This corresponds with Jewkes (2005) and Maguire's (2021) research, which explore the hyper masculinity of the prison environments where surviving prison is about having a tough front. Being asked to lift this front, even temporarily, to reflect on your experiences and identify issues can be a difficult task and may have longer implications for when the prisoner re-enters the general prison space.

6.2.3 Rights That Mattered

Prison inherently involves infringement on a vast range of rights beyond loss of liberty due to the interdependent nature of many rights. As noted by one participant, the range of rights which are impacted by imprisonment is beyond many people's imagination until they experience it:

> *I suppose only in relation to what I was saying if you have never been in prison before you would have no reason to ever have those thoughts or to even imagine what it is like really become aware of how your rights can just be completely taken away and you know that kind of way.*
>
> (Participant 01)

As demonstrated by this quote, many rights are taken for granted on the outside which come into sharp focus in prison, where a prisoner is heavily reliant on staff for daily needs and has little control over basic decision making such as contacting family members or even, in the case of prisons without in-cell showers, when to go for a shower. This sense of reliance and sharp deprivation of rights upon imprisonment is emphasised in international research (Crewe 2009) and was experienced by many prisoners in this study. As will be discussed below, this can lead to infantilisation of prisoners as decisions they may have been making for years are taken out of their hands and can have an impact on their sense of self. The degree to which prisoners accepted those decisions varied and some prisoners outrightly resisted prison control over their decision making, while others took small actions to exercise agency over their daily lives, such as closing their own door a few minutes before evening lock up. Other participants spoke about collectively complaining about issues or being persistent in speaking up to staff members about their needs.

The legal protection model, which oversight bodies rely on, is based on the presumption that actors have a degree of awareness of their rights, recognise injurious situations and have the resources to act upon them (Bumiller 1987: 422). As will be outlined in this section, these presumptions are not straightforward and at times are significantly called into question in the prison context. This has implications for the degree of protection oversight mechanisms can offer in a penal setting and the extent to which prisoners feel that their rights are protected. Learning about rights, as discussed by Merry et al (2010), requires legal expertise, resources and networks, which are not readily available to marginalised groups. As noted in Section 6.2.1.2, prisoners were often reliant on each other to learn about how prisons worked and what rights they had. While many prisoners in this study spoke about rights in the court room, rights once convicted were not often framed in the rights language or seen as protected. This section highlights the findings in relation to prisoners' expectations of the prison environment, as well as which rights triggered prisoners to take action and engage with the legal protections available to them.

In discussing rights in prison, it is also important to consider expectations of those in prison of the treatment they should be receiving. When speaking about the question of rights, many placed a high threshold on what constituted a rights breach, at times referring to torture as something that did not happen in the prison. As outlined in Chapter 5 in relation to the CPT, this created a sense amongst some prisoners that they were unnecessary in modern Irish prisons, as conditions were not that bad in Ireland, frequently referring to the torture aspect of the CPT mandate rather than other forms of treatment falling under Article 3 of the ECHR. Despite the high tolerance of prison conditions displayed by prisoners in the current study and low expectations of rights, certain situations did give rise to a need to act.

As with Naylor's (2014) research in Australia, prisoners did not use rights rhetoric when speaking about their experiences and problems in prison. However, they did refer to situations which *'felt wrong'* and issues which they were willing to speak up about. Naylor (2014: 93) noted that when asked about their rights in prison a significant portion of participants 'identified particular treatment and conditions in prison as of concern, rather than referring to breaches of abstract human rights'. A range of rights were referred to by prisoners during the interviews; however, as discussed above, a number felt that they had no rights in prison and that everything could be taken away by staff. Those prisoners viewed their rights as limited to fundamental basics such as food and exercise, and access to a toilet. Despite this limited view of rights held by some participants, three areas in particular were reoccurring across the interviews – contact with families and related rights, access to medical care and being treated with dignity and respect. The last of these is an overarching aspect of prison policy and manifests itself through everyday interactions in the prison. A key finding in relation to family rights and healthcare was the sense that these impacted areas of life which went beyond the prison walls. Family life involved those who were not deserving of punishment, as unlike the prisoner themselves they had not been sentenced, while healthcare could impact on life outside of the prison such as working in a chosen profession. Therefore, the findings in this section suggest that while prisoners are willing, in most cases, to accept the conditions of imprisonment, when prisons interfere in certain aspects of their life beyond the perceived boundaries of the prison, prisoners are more likely to feel a sense of injustice and a need to take action such as complain.

6.2.3.1 Family

As already mentioned, one area which promoted prisoners to take action was around contact with family and visits. Even those prisoners who presented a tough persona of tolerance about the majority of prison issues, drew a line under treating family members badly and interfering with family visits by prison staff. One participant who spoke about never having complained, despite having served a number of sentences, and 'ratting', was much more vocal when discussing the issue of family visits:

> *I have never complained to anyone or ratted on anyone in jail or anything like that or complained about anyone or anything. I have never once put anything in them boxes.*
>
> (Participant 31)

There was a sense of pride in not being a complainer in prison, which was in sharp contrast to the frustration and upset at the violation of family life when speaking about complaining about issues around visits and the exposure to prison procedures of his partner and young child: *'the only complaint I have … I ever had is my visits'*. This was despite outlining other problems in prison which could have been the source of a complaint.

Previous research, such as Hutton's (2016), highlights the important role of families in prisoners' lives, especially in coping with time. Support from family is a key survival tool for those in prison and this was emphasised by participants in the current study. While many participants felt they deserved to be punished and tolerated prison conditions, they felt that their family had done nothing wrong and should not be made to feel as if they had. As with Behan's study (2016), there was an acceptance that their rights could be taken away and impacted but families were different. Access to families served as a reminder of life after prison and a connection to the outside world (Hutton 2016). Focus on life after prison and the reminder of other roles besides being a prisoner was a key component of contact with family and friends. As noted by one survey respondent *'[visits] is all we have'*. Family visits were also the subject of several complaints raised with the VCs. Participants referred to a range of issues around family visits and contact. This included the use of discretion during visits, banning and screening procedures and delays in adding members to visits and call lists. In addition to this, participants referred to the number of visitors allowed on visit lists as and the impact of transfers on family contact, as the burden on family members of travelling to the prisons could be quite time consuming.

When discussing the issues around family rights while in prison, a key theme was that family members had not committed an offence and the treatment they were receiving, whether it was particularly invasive searches on visits or being on screen visits due to suspicions around drugs, was a punishment which they did not deserve. The prison was interring with someone who was free from blame and the prisoner stigma and deserved to be treated as such. This created a feeling amongst prisoners who might otherwise tolerate disrespectful treatment themselves to speak up and push back. As discussed by Participant 8: *'So, I was stuck there for Christmas. Lost my Christmas after I was telling my children and my mother that I would be coming home ... you wouldn't do it to a dog like'*.

As illustrated by this quote, through failing to respond to his request and eventually denying it, he felt that the prison service extended the punishment and power of the prison into his private and family life. They caused unnecessary upset for those perceived as undeserving of punishment and, as will be discussed further below, this experience was seen as disrespectful and dehumanising for the prisoner.

This section highlights the strong feelings associated with family life and contact amongst prisoners and the sense that families should be protected from the harsh realities of prison, which some were willing to tolerate themselves. As highlighted by Sexton's (2015) work on penal consciousness, injustices associated with family contact are experienced as particularly harsh and this was also clear amongst the findings illustrated here.

6.2.3.2 Healthcare Access

Participants also spoke frequently about healthcare and in particular access to healthcare while in prison. Those in Irish prisons are entitled to equivalent healthcare to those on medical cards in the community. This entitles the holder to public healthcare such as medical treatment, hospital visits and certain dental procedures. Several participants raised concerns around the right to healthcare while in prison. Unlike for those in the community, prisoners' access to healthcare is controlled by the prison service. While in custody it is not possible to ring the doctor and make an appointment or to present oneself at the hospital, instead prisoners must submit a request to a staff member to put their name down on the appointment list to see the doctor.

Participants discussed various issues in relation to the provision of healthcare in prison. Key issues which arose concerning healthcare in prison related to injuries while in prison which could impact on a prisoner's ability to work in their chosen profession upon release and their ability to earn a living once released from prison. Participants spoke about the challenges in being taken seriously by staff when seeking to receive treatment or make an appointment with a medical professional. Prison staff acted as gatekeepers to accessing treatment and some participants felt that this resulted in delays or that some staff felt prisoners were exaggerating their need to see a doctor. Participants also spoke about delays due to long lists to see the doctor and concerns about the quality of healthcare in prison. The scale of delays in accessing treatment is highlighted by Participant 16 below:

> *So if you have a hole in your tooth like, your tooth is gone like because you're not going to be able to get it filled because you have to be doing over 16 months, which is ridiculous.*

Currently access to dental care is limited to those serving longer sentences; however, those serving shorter sentences do not have access to an alternative outside of prison while serving their sentence. As noted by the above participant this leads to a paradox where those on shorter sentences, particularly repeat offenders, are falling through the gaps and may result in long-term damage.

Participants felt that their concerns were dealt with differently than they would have been in the wider community. In some cases, there was a tendency to give out tablets rather than provide physiotherapy, which would provide a long-term solution to ongoing issues, while tablets were a quick fix and could result in more damage. This feeling is emphasised by this quote:

> *That was it, you know what I mean. In here, they just keep giving me tablets after tablets, I mean sure what good are they going to do on the liver.*
>
> (Participant 17)

For this participant, this approach of constantly prescribing painkillers communicated a lack of care for his long-term well-being and a disregard for the impact of his injury on his life outside of prison.

Due to the structuring of healthcare, some participants spoke about a lack of follow-up care from doctors, or constantly dealing with different doctors, and participants spoke about prescriptions being renewed without being assessed as to whether a particular medication was still necessary. Participants spoke about not being able to receive outside treatment and pick a doctor they knew and trusted. The ability to make decisions about one's physical health and healthcare was restricted by imprisonment. However, some participants spoke about contacting their doctor directly or via a solicitor to get support or request for care in prison. This established relationship of trust was important to participants and there was a sense that seeking support from outside of the prison gave legitimacy to the concerns of the prisoner.

Restrictions on the type of medication which can be prescribed to those in prison created a sense amongst some participants that their choice over their healthcare was being taken away and their own knowledge of their body and illness was being disregarded. These blanket policies can convey a message that the prisoner's experience in relation to their own health is not worth listening to and that their status as a 'risky' prisoner is more important than their well-being. Participants also spoke about access to mental health services while in prison and the high prevalence amongst the prison population. While those who had accessed the service valued it, some spoke about limited resources being available and, as with other areas, long waiting lists to access them. This was a particular concern for those serving longer sentences for violent crimes, where accessing such services for the purpose of reports could impact on progression through the system and the prospect of early release. Challenges in accessing such services could communicate a disregard for the mental health of those in prison but also remove the hope of accessing early release for those on long sentences.

These issues were linked to longer-term impacts on prisoners of not receiving adequate care, as well as to a sense that staff did not care how they were treated or presumed they were playing up their issues. For participants who spoke about healthcare in prison, as with the issue of family rights discussed above, the focus was on the impact of healthcare on their life post release and also on quality of life overall.

6.2.3.3 Dignity and Respect

As noted by McCall-Smith (2016: 1180), the consistent thread throughout the Mandela Rules 'is that human dignity must be at the core of all considerations' when it comes to the treatment of those in prison. This desire was also reflected throughout the interactions with people in prison during the study. The desire to be treated with dignity and respect was a clear cornerstone of prison experiences. While many issues discussed were unlikely to give rise to a rights violation, the everyday reminders that they were prisoners and staff had power over almost every aspect of their life pervaded the conversations which took place. As discussed by Crewe (2009), the small things matter in prison and these small things were where interactions and actions could give rise to feelings of disrespect and indifference. One example of the small things in prison and the manifestation of respect between an officer and a prisoner was given by Participant 23. He had an evening ritual of closing the door himself in the evenings, rather than having the officer close it in. This gave him back some control over his routine, an important aspect of life in prison, where prisoners have limited control over their life in custody. This was his moment to shut himself off from the rest of the prison and he actively chooses to do it before a staff member came around.

It was a rare moment in prison life, where routines are highly structured, and staff have the power to open your door at any time. This was a routine he had developed with the officers on his landing and showed respect to the participant in ending his day, as he pleased:

> *I like to close my door, I always close it myself, before time. I love that. My day is done ... That's it now and no one come in that door till 8 o'clock in the morning and that's my time and I like that.*
>
> (Participant 27)

These gestures, which may seem minor in the outside world, take on additional significance in the prison, especially given the prevalence of doors in the prison and the distinct sound of slamming which pervades throughout the prison.

Another aspect of being treated with dignity discussed by participants was being seen as human. As one participant wrote on his survey *'we are human, we're not dogs'*. Treating those in prison with respect was seen as a recognition that prisoners were seen as humans. The reference to being perceived as a dog or less than a dog was referred to by several participants when describing situations in which staff treated them as inferior or animals. Other participants spoke about being seen only as a number while in prison and that their plans while in prison were overlooked by logistical imperatives. This impacted on prisoners' view of staff while in prison, as well as on the prison system as a whole. This theme has been explored by other studies on prisoners' experiences and corresponds with Sexton's (2015) research, where these interactions and experiences were viewed as a deeply ingrained symptom of a system which does not view those in custody as humans.

This stripping away of personhood and humanity can also play a role in how prisoners perceive of themselves. Although individuals in prison occupy a range of roles in the outside world, while in prison these roles are taken over by the prison service and the prisoner identity becomes the dominant role. Dignity and respect are key to encouraging self-worth and embedding the sense that rights are attainable within the prison. As noted by Karamalidou (2017: 131) 'infantilisation accentuate[s] prisoners' feelings of insecurity, helplessness, loneliness, dependence and abandonment, which imprisonment so naturally gives rise to, [and] also attacks with force the core of their being, that is, their individuality'. Through the removal of key roles in the prisoners' life and a lack of dignity and respect in interactions, prisoners' feelings of desperation and abandonment while in prison are further compounded. As outlined by Simon (2011), dignity in imprisonment is central to the ban on inhuman and degrading treatment in prisons.

This stripping away of dignity was furthermore perceived as depersonalisation for participants and moves prisoners from active participants to passive observers of their former selves as agency is stripped away by prison life such as decision making by staff and identification through prison numbers (Karamalidou 2017: 132). This deadening effect impacts on self-confidence and the assertiveness of prisoners, along with experiences of fatalism. As will be discussed in Chapter 7, this can have implications for recognition of harms of imprisonment, sense of worth and ability to speak up when a perceived injustice occurs.

6.2.4 Expectations of the Prison and Prior Experiences

Sexton's (2015) work on penal consciousness highlights how our expectations of a specific environment can shape our experience in terms of the severity of our experiences. In the penal context, this means that those who have low expectations of what prison should be like, such as the expectation that prison should be tough or that certain treatment was acceptable in prison, can lead to some prisoners seeing poor treatment as in line with their expectation of prison and therefore not see issues with their treatment or conditions.

There was a feeling amongst some prisoners in the study that prison is quite good due to low expectations about the quality of prison life and poor past experience in relation to their rights. Many participants, and prisoners in general, come from backgrounds where they may not have experienced full rights, and this shapes how they view prison and their treatment, as demonstrated by Participant 5:

> *At the moment, I think prison is okay at the moment. The way it is like the prisons in general today. There are no more stabbings in prison like there used to be. If there are problems today it is just people get a hiding that would be it. Getting stabbed the way they used, like the last time I was here there was 3 or 4 stabbings a day ... every day nearly. Prison is grand these days, I think.*

This participant highlights the level of violence which he accepted as part of the prison experience. This sets a low threshold for an acceptable prison environment and brings into sharp focus the expectations of those in custody. The idea of what was good in prison was relative to prison experience and how prisons had changed over time. In the Irish context, this was particularly clear when it came to discussing 'slopping out'. Slopping out is the practice of using buckets for relieving yourself and emptying the buckets at a communal area on the landing. This practice was widespread in Irish prisons until recently and is still carried out by a small number of prisoners.[2] This practice was frequently used by prisoners in interviews as an example of how things had gotten better in recent years and that there was less to complain about as a result. This visible change in prison conditions was seen as a significant improvement and therefore prisons were 'good' now. The impact expectations can have on prisoners' perceptions of the prison environment has been explored in Sexton's (2015) work on penal consciousness and is also evident in the current study. In her study, she found that punishment was a subjective experience and that prisoners' expectations of the prison environment played a role in how they perceived their punishment. As discussed by Sexton (2015), the punishment gap between expectations and reality of prison life played a significant role in how prisoners perceived their experience. In applying penal consciousness to the context of oversight in prisons, when it came to identifying problems in prison and interacting with oversight bodies, these low expectations of prison life create a disconnect between the standards set by oversight bodies and human rights frameworks and how prisoners perceive the prison environment.

Additionally, participants spoke about the reality of what prisons could be expected to do. Participant 33 noted that

> ...you kind of accept, you know, some circumstances whether that it is down to prison staff that you know ... you kind of accept ... there are some things that you can't get that you may be entitled to because of other reasons.

This participant felt that over time you learn that prisons simply do not have the resources to give prisoners everything they may be entitled to. This understanding of the limitations on staff and prisons was a reoccurring theme across the interviews, with prisoners relating to staff and the difficulties they faced in doing their job at times.

Another point relevant to the discussion on expectations is related to those who are institutionalised to the point where prison becomes their idea of 'home'. Participant 7 in particular spoke about the prison in this way and this coloured his experience of punishment and also hampered his desire to fight back when something was an issue. The participant spoke about staff members as the people who cared about him and that his basic needs were more likely to be met in the prison than outside. He had a long history with institutional settings, having being placed in care at an early age and he described his experience of incarceration as:

> *I do be out for a few weeks and then I come back in. On purpose kinda I do, because I feel better, I feel more comfortable here, I feel more relaxed too... Like I don't have a home outside, I have nothing outside, so I try to come here because I am well looked after, I get my meals here, there are staff here, they are alright like, do you know what I mean, they look after me well, they are harmless, they are nice people, you know.*

Unlike other participants in the study, he did not know the details of his release date or speak about prospects of early release. When asked if he was close to finishing his sentence, he stated *'It could be yeah, I don't bother asking them, you know'*. This institutionalisation and close relationships with staff member impacted on his expectations for prison and his experience of prison. Prison as a source of comfort for institutionalised individuals clearly shapes and impacts on their expectations of the environment. It also creates an additional power dynamic, as while the relationships within prison are important, the external support which play a key role in exiting the prison system is absent. This in turn plays a role in motivating prisoners to change their behaviour and want better for themselves. This theme features in other studies, as discussed by Symkovych (2020) adjusting to prison life is dependent on personal circumstances, and in the case of those who are in survival mode and want to maintain a familiar environment, causing tension through seeking out rights information could disrupt established relationships.

In discussing the topic of voting in prisons with participants in his study, Behan (2012: 24) found that many had 'resigned themselves to the denial of some rights'. As highlighted by Stanley (2011: 9) '[p]risoners tend to be those who have *not previously enjoyed secure access to human rights*'. These expectations of an inherent lack of rights can impact on the possibility of prisoners asserting their rights. It is important, therefore, that prisoners are promptly informed of their rights and that the language of rights is not lost within the prison. Fostering a culture, which embeds rights is a challenge in many penal systems, as the prison does not exist in isolation. Prisoners bring with them preconceptions about rights and prisons from the outside and prior prison experience, which shape their interactions with other prisoners, staff and the institution itself. As has been outlined above, some prisoners are particularly vulnerable due to their difficult background and their conceptions of rights and ability to assert them can be significantly lower than prisoners with different life experiences.

Drawing on this, prisoners' own expectations may therefore create a barrier to seeking to engage and communicating with oversight bodies. Prisoners may perceive situations as good, due to their own perceptions of what prison can and should be like, as well as their understanding of their rights in custody. This has implications for the topics which prisoners may perceive as necessary to bring to the attention of oversight bodies. In addition to this, those who perceive prison as their home may be unwilling to jeopardise their sense of a self-place for matters which may be perceived as minor or too risky to draw attention to.

Participant 5 referred to above also spoke about how an inspector was for more vulnerable prisoners such as those with disabilities or mental health problems, as for the general population there were not really any complaints. This study also shows that the expectations prisoners have of prison can impact on what information they feel is necessary to share with an inspector or what they might see as worth complaining about, as emphasised by Participant 40:

> *I think prisons is meant to be bad like, so you won't come back... I think this is the best we are ever going to get, you know, we have a toilet now like. I remember when we were in the old jail everyone was urinating and faeces into a bucket, yeah and cleaning it out like that was bad like and that was only a few year ago. Now we have toilet, shower, like we are allowed X-boxes if you are on the enhanced wing.* ***What more can you get like. I don't think you can get anymore; you know what I mean.***

As is evident from the final line of the quote above, and in line with Sexton's (2015) research on penal consciousness, prisoners' expectations are based on prior experience and prisoners' perceptions of what prison should be like. Meeting the basic needs of those in prison was seen by this participant and others as all that could be achieved in prison. The wider rehabilitative mandate of prisons evident in the international and domestic frameworks, as well as the standards of the inspection and monitoring bodies, was not reflected in all participants' mindsets of what they expected of prison. As emphasised by Sexton (2015), prisoners' expectations are shaped by subjective experiences and thus their identification of issues in prison are shaped by those expectations. These minimal expectations of what prison was supposed to be like, could limit the interactions between prisoners and oversight bodies. This could in turn have implications for what oversight bodies identified as problems in prisons, given the key role of prisoner engagement in shaping reports and submitting complaints.

6.2.5 Prison Culture

Prison culture was a reoccurring theme in the interviews, with prison culture itself at times acting as a barrier to oversight in prisons in terms of prisoners' attitudes to oversight and potential concerns about consequences of speaking up. As Sykes (1958: 134) stated in his seminal work on prisons, when an individual enters prison, it is into a 'complex social system with its own norms, values, and methods of control'. As will be discussed in this section, prison culture by its nature places constraints on individuals' agency and ability to build trust and social capital which are key to engaging with rights and rights protection.

6.2.5.1 *Low Trust Environments*

Previous research highlights prisons as low trust environments (Crewe 2009). This can make it difficult for prisoners to build relationships and they may also be less likely to risk engaging with authorities or oversight bodies, especially when they know little about them. Hawley (2012: 19) notes that:

> [p]eople who are rarely trusted do not have the opportunity to develop trustworthiness, and cannot be expected to respond with alacrity when

> trust is offered to them. This is one of the damaging elements of suffering from long-term distrust: in such an environment, it makes little sense to develop traits of trustworthiness, if these will go unrecognized. This in turn makes the habitually distrusted harder to trust, and the downward spiral continues.

As highlighted by Participant 21:

> *I suppose you could get a prisoner to do it [speak to inspection bodies] yeah but I wouldn't have nothing to do with it cuz they wouldn't listen to me. That's the truth.*

His prison experiences made him feel that speaking to an inspection body would not be worthwhile, as he would not be believed. While this participant did not feel as though he would be perceived as worth listening to, other participants suggested groups of prisoners, such as those serving life sentences who would have a lot to say and be perceived as legitimate. This demonstrated a sense that some prisoners were perceived as more worthy of voicing their experiences than others.

Participants in the current study spoke about the lack of trust they had in prison, whether as a result of prior experiences or their experience with authorities more broadly. As noted by Participant 20: *'I wouldn't trust anyone in here to be honest'*. Another participant noted the importance of clear independence in building trust and the fundamental need to trust a body when providing them with sensitive information such as a complaint:

> *It's very hard to trust people now in a prison system … because this fella could be all nice but then you know he's going back to this person and you know things could be [*said differently*]. I don't know like, you want to be able to trust someone you know like, people in prison don't really trust, you know what I mean. It's very hard to trust someone you know that kind of way like because you have seen it all before like, people charging this fella and sending him to a different jail, you know things like that, it's very hard.*
>
> (Participant 45)

A lack of trust can create a barrier to speaking to external bodies, especially with limited information on them or, as in the case of some of the bodies, they are not perceived as independent from the prison service itself. Despite this, some participants were willing to engage with bodies, even where they knew little about them but had limited expectations about what the bodies could actually achieve. The cost-benefit analysis of the risk involved in seeking out and choosing to engage with these bodies was altered in this case and some may be willing, on a one off basis at least, to forego the knowledge usually necessary to make this assessment, especially if a pressing issue was concerned. For example, Participant 21, despite a delay in hearing back on his request to meet the VC, felt that he would be willing to meet them and ask for their help:

> *If they can help, they can help, if they can't I can't do anything about it.*
> (Participant 21)

In line with Hawley's (2012) observations, in order to build trust there is a need for the trust which this prisoner extended in engaging with the VC to be reciprocated either through helping the prisoner resolve the issue or providing an explanation as to why the body he requested to meet, the VC in this instance, could not help with the issue. This would allow the prisoner to see that he had been listened to and that the body had taken steps as a result of his disclosure. This closing of the feedback loop is key to building trust and promoting future engagement with these bodies.

6.2.5.2 Relationships in Prison

Linked to relationships in prison was a key feature of the prisoner code of not telling on other prisoners, referred to as 'ratting' by some participants. Given the heavy reliance on relationships in prison and the complications that may arise from damaging a relationship, it is unsurprising that seeking out information on and engaging with oversight bodies is low on the list of priorities for prisoners. Carrabine (2005: 897), in describing imprisonment, states that prison consists of a situation where 'prisoners are confined against their will, with people they would normally not choose to be with, in circumstances they can do little to change and are governed by custodians who police practically every aspect of their daily life'. This feeling of powerless and reliance is clearly evident in the prison culture and the willingness to seek out information. A willingness to seek out information and to complain depended on what was at stake, with family visits as outlined in the previous chapter and above frequently mentioned as a trigger for when action needed to be taken.

As discussed in relation to complaints in Chapter 5, a number of prisoners spoke about 'ratting' when asked about the prisoner complaint system. There was a view amongst some prisoners that using the complaint system was equivalent to 'ratting' on either prisoners or staff and this went against the prisoner code:

> *I just think complaint forms anyway are for little weasel people like … . I wouldn't do that like.*
> (Participant 38)

In addition to relationships with staff, prisoners are reliant on one another to survive prison life and relationships with other prisoners can mediate some of 'the pains of imprisonment' (Sykes 1958). Speaking to external bodies or lodging a complaint was viewed by some participants as suspicious behaviour that might make other prisoners distrust you or think that the complaint was about them and could bring trouble. Given the importance of these relationships, prisoners may take this into account when considering engaging with oversight bodies. Is the risk of engaging worth damaging a vital prison relationship? As demonstrated by Participant 38 above, those who used the complaint system were not always viewed kindly by other prisoners and some may be suspicious of what a prisoner is complaining about.

In addition to prisoner/staff and prisoner/prisoner relationships, the relationships between staff and the prison officer code acted as a barrier to some prisoners complaining.

> *… . I don't think it works to be honest the complaint, all it is is a complaint form. What's the point in putting that in, sure they all agree with each other, … one officer is not going to disagree with another officer, they are going to agree. They are all best of mates for the best part. There are probably one or two who don't like each other but … they won't go against one another … That's the way I look at it.*
>
> (Participant 14)

As demonstrated by this quote and discussed by Liebling et al. (2011), a key feature of the prison officer code is not to disagree with another member of staff, especially in front of a prisoner. This led prisoners, such as Participant 14, to see complaining and speaking up as futile, as a prisoner would never be believed over a staff member and that staff would stick up for one another. This was further exacerbated in the Irish context due to the lack of an independent appeals mechanism and the sense that all complaints were dealt with by prison staff.

6.2.5.3 Survival Tactics

Previous prison research, such as that conducted by Jewkes (2005), discusses how prisoners adapt to the prison environment to survive and some of these adaptation techniques can act as barriers to engaging with rights and rights-protecting bodies. This theme was also present in the current research. For example, Participant 13 explained that:

> *… .in prison you have to have your wires around you like, you know, you have to … . watch what you are saying.*

As highlighted by this participant, he survived prison by avoiding disclosing information about himself, especially to those he did not trust. This protection may be difficult to dismantle to disclose vulnerabilities to oversight bodies.

Another survival tactic in prison was keeping your head down. As discussed, keeping your head down was seen by the majority of participants as the best way to do your time. This idea of keeping your head down was also found in Behan's (2016) research and his discussions with prisoners on engaging with oversight bodies. As discussed by Behan (2016: 173), prison and prison structures were about creating 'compliant prisoners' rather than active citizens, through encouraging obedience, conforming to norms and patterns of behaviour. Prisons were focused on achieving compliance 'where individuals do not act or do as they felt', and 'choices suppressed or pacified lead only to organisationally determined identities; one becomes what the environment dictates' (Behan 2016: 173). For participants in the current study, by limiting interactions they were engaging in self-preservation strategies to protect themselves from unwanted attention and avoiding unintentionally aggravating staff, for example, as highlighted by Participant 39 *'Just get a job, keep the head down and keep doing what you're doing'*.

6.2.6 Bureaucracy

The inspection process and complaints procedures in Ireland have been subject to significant reforms in recent years. This has led to a focus on a formal complaints procedure where prisoners complete a written complaint. However, for some prisoners resolving complaints via a formal system was not the way of doing things, as emphasised by one respondent to the survey:

> *The system takes too long and delays mean that issue may already be dealt with or punishment in the case was already mostly served. The Visiting Committees provide an opportunity to explain position and actually listen to you.*
>
> (R223)

In this case, the respondent had attempted to resolve the complaint formally and noted that he had *'[w]rote a letter to the Governor with the help of another prisoner. Didn't receive any response to letter so requested to meeting with Visiting Committees after that. Complaint was not dealt with'*. This demonstrates that complaints in prison were about receiving a response rather than using the proscribed system.

Speaking to people and being able to get your point across verbally through accessing someone was a recurring theme for a number of prisoners. For some prisoners, this was related to perceptions of who held power in the prison, with prisoners noting the governor was someone they wanted to access as he would be able to a decide quickly. The complaint system was viewed by some as a barrier to accessing those with the ability to make decisions and a way of dismissing prisoners' complaints. As Crewe's (2009: 67) research demonstrates, the written complaint system was sometimes used by staff as a way of avoiding directly dealing with prisoners, in particular when they were understaffed, and this was felt as disengagement from prisoners. Similarly in the current study, at times the shift to paper-based approaches was perceived as an unwillingness by the prison to deal directly with prisoners or resolve their problems. Written complaints could be lost or ignored, and some felt that they would be better placed to receive a response or communicate their complaint orally.

Giddens (1984: 16) developed the concept of the 'dialectic of control' which encompasses a range of possible modes or dimensions of influencing other agents in a social system. Sparks et al. (1996: 84) see this as being of fundamental importance as it can influence a prisoner's choice of action when confronted with an issue. The use of formal channels over an outright show of resistance is 'likely to depend at least in part upon the prospect of obtaining some degree of success via the "legitimate" avenues'. Currently, the complaint system and the inspection bodies in Irish prisons are not widely regarded positively by those in prison. In the case of the complaint system, this increases in the case of those who have used the system (van der Valk et al. 2022). Therefore, prisoners may seek different modes or resolving problems or simply tolerate prison conditions. As highlighted by the findings set out in this chapter, various factors influenced prisoners' decisions to engage with inspection and monitoring and complaints systems while in prison.

Some participants spoke about how they would prefer to resolve issues themselves with other prisoners rather than resort to the complaint system, especially when this could result in additional charges for the prisoner involved. Additionally, prisoners spoke about keeping their head down as a way of managing prison and maintaining relationships with staff members. As noted by one participant: *'They do their thing, I do mine'* (Participant 7) when he was asked whether he would engage with the inspector if he came into the prison. This participant spoke about not being the kind of person to use complaint mechanisms or to sue the prison service, preferring to deal with staff where problems did arise or for the most part to leave things as they were.

The challenge in being heard and getting your point across is evident in other areas of research, including a study conducted by Crewe (2009), who notes that issues in prison may be seen as small things outside of the prison context. The delay often experienced by prisoners when dealing with complaints and inspection bodies can cause smaller issues to build up, but it is also important for oversight bodies to understand the significant restrictions placed on those in custody and the symbolism of more minor incidences. In the current study, privacy and door banging was referred to by some participants as a way of staff to either show respect or to aggravate those they had issues with. This struggle to get their point across in a manner which will be understood by those outside of the prison is also evident in Calavita and Jenness' (2015) study of the Californian prison complaints system, where prisoners spoke about getting the complaint 'right' and writing the 'perfect complaint'. Prisoners in their study made frequent references to Title 15, the rules and regulations for Californian prisons, in framing their complaints as a way of ensuring that the prison heard and understood their complaints. Prisoners lacked the same reference point for framing complaints in Irish prisons.

Despite limited awareness and personal interactions with the bodies, participants were sceptical of the inspection process and how inspections were carried out. There was also a sense amongst participants that limited changes were possible in the Irish Prison Service and that the service was unwilling to act on recommendations, especially in the absence of enforcement powers.

6.2.7 Human Rights Protection and Rights as an Abstract Concept

Despite the growing push for oversight in prisons, the practical benefits to participants were not always clear. Some questioned the utility of a body who could not assist with individual cases, or lacked enforcement powers to make changes. The discussions about inspection in prisons were at times far removed from the reality of prison life and the need for immediate action for individuals in their experiences is not reflected in the timelines evidenced in inspection reports. As will be expanded on in the following chapter, prisoners are unlikely to speak about rights as a collective experience or in the terms discussed in rights rhetoric, instead they use examples of experiences of where they that felt wronged. The impact this has on how they would engage or bring issues to the attention of an oversight body needs to be considered.

Some felt that inspection was a fruitless exercise which would result in limited changes within the prison, or at least changes that would be long lasting and have a deep impact on the system. Painting the walls and sweeping the floors were described as a quick facelift but one unlikely to deal with the longer-term concerns' prisoners faced. As emphasised by Participant 31 physical repairs were not necessarily the problems prisoners were concerned with:

> *Well they can listen to them but sure who is going to complain about a broken window. When someone comes in, when them windows are closed, them cells are like saunas. So you would want a hole in your window.*

There was a sense amongst some prisoners that inspection bodies would not be able to understand the environment and issues which prisoners may have. As highlighted above, broken windows, which may on the surface seem like something that needs to be fixed, was actually something that some prisoners welcomed. Including the voice of the prisoners in recommendations to get a full understanding of the environment is important to ensure recommendations are something that will benefit those in custody and not negatively impact those in prison. As noted by one participant (38) in response to the question as to whether inspections could make prisons better:

> *They probably could yeah. They could probably make them worse than as well.*
>
> ***Researcher:*** *Okay, why do you think that?*
>
> *I don't know, just they could change something that no one wants changed, do you get me.*

This participant was sceptical of the inspection process and whether the changes would be something that would actually benefit the prison. This is linked to the findings previously discussed that professionals might not actually understand the prison and the problems which prisoners face in prison due to their lack of lived experience and distance from the prison.

6.3 Conclusion

As discussed in the previous chapter, awareness of the existence of oversight bodies and a clear understanding of what they can do is important in encouraging constructive engagement with the bodies. However, the prison environment itself presents additional challenges for engagement. Barriers to engagement such as prisons being low trust environments, with significant power dynamics at play can prevent prisoners from learning about or engaging with rights-protecting bodies. Prisoners spoke about staff interfering in the process and not feeling heard by a system where their voice is not trusted or valued. This is concerning in a system focused on rehabilitation and in the context of rights-protecting bodies in a coercive environment.

It was clear that prisoners' experiences of oversight bodies was inextricably linked with their experiences of punishment generally, penal culture, their views of rights and themselves as rights holders. Rights and rights protections were removed from the prisoner experience for the majority of participants. A lack of rights language and a narrow concept of rights were evident amongst the participants. Overall, participants felt uninformed about their rights and the avenues to seek redress. There was also a sense that they had to or preferred to rely on other prisoners for information due to a lack of trust in the prison service and a sense that they would not willingly provide information on rights.

Despite this, certain areas did give rise to a willingness to take action, in particular issues of family contact and healthcare. This suggests that the perceived injustice of interference in this area creates motivation which overcomes the barriers to engaging otherwise found in this chapter. However, areas which triggered action were the exception rather than the rule. In general prisoners had low expectations about what prison should or would be like. Similar to findings from Sexton's (2015) study, this study confirms that penal consciousness shaped prisoners' experiences of imprisonment and prison conditions, in certain incidents, were perceived as not that severe as it met their existing low expectations of prison life. In addition to this, prison culture is infused with an attitude of tolerance, where prisoners feel that speaking up will draw unwanted negative attention and is pointless due to their relative powerlessness within the prison hierarchy. There was a sense amongst participants that they were not worthy of rights while in prison; however, there was a desire amongst participants to be treated with dignity in their interactions with staff and by the prison service.

This chapter brings together key aspects related to rights, which impact upon prisoners' views and engagement with oversight bodies. Drawing on right consciousness literature, the expectations of prisoners of the prison itself and their treatment was explored, followed by identifiable rights which triggered prisoners to speak up. This narrow perception of rights impacts upon prisoners' abilities to address these issues and to seek better treatment. Prison culture, in Ireland, focuses on keeping your head down and doing your time, which required prisoners to go against the norm in seeking to assert their rights (Behan 2016). As discussed by Karamalidou (2017: 142):

> [w]hen combined with prisoners' uncertainty about their human rights and lack of knowledge of their legal status, the need of raising prisoner awareness as much of their human rights as of their human responsibilities becomes evident, with implications for prisoner education.

The next chapter draws together these findings to highlight the challenges faced by oversight bodies in the prison context, as well as further situate these findings within the literature on rights consciousness, rights protection and procedural justice.

Notes

1 Irish Prison Service, *Nationality Group of Persons Committed by Year* (Irish Prison Service 2020). Available at: www.irishprisons.ie/wp-content/uploads/documents_pdf/NATIONALITY-GROUP-Year-2007-to-Year-2019.pdf (Accessed 18 February 2021).

2 Irish Penal Reform Trust, 'As of October 2023, there are 7 people in prison slopping out, without in-cell sanitation.' Available at: www.iprt.ie/prison-facts/9-there-are-68-people-in-prison-slopping-out-without-in-cell-sanitation-april-2019/ (Accessed 30 December 2024).

References

Cormac Behan, 'Still Entitled to Our Say': Prisoners' Perspectives on Politics' (2012) 51(1) The Howard Journal of Criminal Justice 16.

Cormac Behan, *Citizen Convict: Prisoners, Politics and the Vote* (Manchester University Press 2016).

Kristin Bumiller, 'Victims in the Shadow of the Law' (1987) 12(3) *Signs: Journal of Women in Culture and Society* 421.

Kitty Calavita and Valerie Jenness, *Appealing to Justice: Prisoner Grievances, Rights and Carceral Logic* (University of California Press 2015).

Eamonn Carrabine, 'Prison Riots, Social Order and the Problem of Legitimacy' (2005) 45(6) *British Journal of Criminology* 896.

Ben Crewe, *The Prisoner Society: Power, Adaptation and Social Life in an English Prison* (Oxford University Press 2009).

Ben Crewe, 'Depth, Weight, Tightness: Revisiting the Pains of Imprisonment' (2011) 13(5) *Punishment & Society* 509.

Anthony Giddens, *The Constitution of Society: Outline of the Theory of Structuration* (University of California Press 1984).

Katerine Hawley, *Trust: A Very Short Introduction* (Oxford University Press 2012).

Christopher Hood, Oliver James, George Jones, Colin Scott and Tony Travers, *Regulation Inside Government: Waste Watchers, Quality Police, and Sleaze-busters* (Oxford University Press 1999).

Marie Hutton, 'Visiting Time: A Tale of Two Prisons' (2016) 63(3) *Probation Journal* 347.

Yvonne Jewkes, 'Men Behind Bars: "Doing" Masculinity as an Adaptation to Imprisonment' (2005) 8(1) *Men and Masculinities* 44.

Anastasia Karamalidou, *Embedding Human Rights in Prison: English and Dutch Perspectives* (Palgrave Macmillan UK 2017).

Constantijn Kelk, *Recht voor Gedetineerde: een onderzoek naar die beginselen van het gevangenisrecht* (Samson, 1978).

Alison Liebling, David Price and Guy Shafer, *The Prison Officer* (2nd edn, Willan Publishing 2011).

David Maguire, *Male, Failed, Jailed: Masculinities and 'Revolving Door' Imprisonment in the UK* (Springer Nature 2021).

Kasey McCall-Smith. 'United Nations Standard Minimum Rules for the Treatment of Prisoners (Nelson Mandela Rules)' (2016) 55(6) *International Legal Materials* 1180.

Sally Engle Merry, *Human Rights and Gender Violence: Translating International Law Into Local Justice* (University of Chicago Press 2009).

Sally Engle Merry, Peggy Levitt, Mihaela Serban Rosen, Mihaela and Diana H Yoon, 'Law From Below: Women's Human Rights and Social Movements in New York City' (2010) 44 *Law & Society Review* 101.

Bronwyn Naylor, 'Human Rights and Respect in Prisons: The Prisoners' Perspective' (2014) 31 *Law Context: A Socio-Legal Journal* 84.

Laura Piacentini and Elena Katz, 'Carceral Framing of Human Rights in Russian Prisons' (2017) 19(2) *Punishment and Society* 221.

Lori Sexton, 'Penal Subjectivities: Developing a Theoretical Framework for Penal Consciousness' (2015) 17(1) *Punishment & Society* 114.

Jonathan Simon, 'Mass Incarceration on Trial' (2011) 13(3) *Punishment & Society* 251.

Richard Sparks, Anthony E Bottoms and Will Hay, *Prisons and the Problem of Order* (Oxford University Press 1996).

Elizabeth Stanley, *Human Rights and Prisons: A Review to the Human Rights Commission* (Human Rights Commission Auckland 2011).

Gresham Sykes, *The Society of Captives: A Study of a Maximum Security Prison* (Princeton University Press 1958).

Anton Symkovych, 'Negative Visibility and 'the Defences of the Weak': The Interplay of a Managerial Culture and Prisoner Resistance' (2020) 24(2) *Theoretical Criminology* 202.

Thomas Ugelvik, 'The Incarceration of Foreigners in European Prisons' in Sharon Pickering and Julie Ham (eds) *The Routledge Handbook on Crime and International Migration* (Routledge 2017).

Sophie van der Valk, Eva Aizpurua, and Mary Rogan. '"[Y] ou are better off talking to af****** wall": The Perceptions and Experiences of Grievance Procedures Among Incarcerated People in Ireland.' *Law & Society Review* (2022) 56(2) 261–285.

Jason Warr, 'The Deprivation of Certitude, Legitimacy and Hope: Foreign National Prisoners and the Pains of Imprisonment' (2016) 16 *Criminology & Criminal Justice* 301.

7 Protecting Human Rights in Prison

7.1 Introduction

This chapter builds on the previous chapters but exploring their implications for oversight and effective rights protection. It has two main aims: first, to examine the factors which contribute to and shape the perceptions and experiences of prisoners with oversight structures, and, second, to assess the challenges which oversight structures face in engaging with people in prison. The chapter starts by analysing the findings previously outlined under three primary categories: the relationship between rights consciousness and experiences and views of oversight structures amongst prisoners; the interaction of 'trust', including perceptions of being worthy of trust and the context of a low trust environment, with experiences of oversight; and, finally, the misalignment between the design and/or activities of oversight structures and lived experiences of prison. In doing so, it draws together the findings arising out of experiences of the three oversight structures explored in this research: complaints, inspection and monitoring and the courts, contextualises them within existing scholarship, particularly that concerning legal mobilisation, rights consciousness, trust and relationships in prison and assesses the scholarly implications of this study. While this book has settled on the term 'oversight structures' to describe inspection and monitoring, complaints structures and access to legal remedies, for reasons outlined in Chapters 1 and 2, these mechanisms are also grounded in human rights standards and, as such, this chapter places a good deal of emphasis on the interactions of these structures and experiences of rights.

Participants' accounts highlight a lack of awareness of oversight bodies, sometimes, due to difficulties in accessing information, or, more deeply, a result of tolerance or stoicism towards poor treatment or conditions (Crewe 2009; Calavita and Jenness 2015), and a strong lack of belief in the ability of the prison environment to change. As well as low levels of awareness, this study also found limited trust in the activities of oversight structures and their power to make changes. This lack of trust was found to be shaped by the general low levels of trust in prison, but also the low expectations prisoners held of prison and a feeling that nobody cared about prisons or people in

DOI: 10.4324/9781003477471-7

prisons, with such bodies also viewed in this way. As Sexton (2015: 133) describes, a person's experience of imprisonment is deeply connected to their expectations for prison and '[n]o single prisoner's punishment is identical to another's, because each will have her own lived experiences and expectations' of punishment. This study adds to Sexton's work on penal consciousness by exploring how experiences of human rights-protecting structures are also shaped by pre-existing conceptions of the value with which prisoners are held, a feeling intimately connected with their rights consciousness. Moreover, this endemic and corrosive lack of trust combined with feelings of being unworthy led to a strong belief that oversight bodies could never 'see' participants' experiences or fully understand their lived reality. Despite this, some participants, as with those in Calavita and Jenness' (2015) study, maintained a latent hope that, somehow, the prison system could change. When viewed together, these findings indicate that the domestic and international law's 'imaginary' (Girling 2006) concerning oversight bodies often does not align with the experiences of those in prison, people whom these bodies are designed to protect. These key themes form the basis for the recommendations put forward in the final chapter.

7.2 The Relationship between Rights Consciousness and Experiences of Oversight Bodies amongst Prisoners

As set out in Chapter 2 and explored through the findings set out in Chapter 5, those in prison are not always aware of their rights or feel worthy of rights protection. This section analyses this study's findings in relation to awareness of oversight bodies, examining them in the context of people's expectations of prison and of oversight bodies. In doing so, it highlights the relationship between the rights consciousness of those in prisons and their resources and tools to learn about and engage with oversight bodies. Previous research such as that by Merry (1985) demonstrates the importance of understanding the law from the position of the ordinary citizen or the intended beneficiary in order to gain an insight into how it is perceived and operates at different levels. This book adds to the existing literature through exploring the perspectives of people in prison of their rights and rights protection, specifically through an analysis of three human rights-protecting mechanisms which are grounded in international prison standards.

7.2.1 Rights Consciousness: The Context for Encounters with Oversight Bodies in Prison

Merry (2009: 3) notes the importance of rights consciousness at all levels in her research stating that 'if human rights ideas are to have an impact, they need to become part of the consciousness of ordinary people around the world'. In the context of prisons, this means moving beyond rights in policy documents and embedding them in penal practice so that prisoners recognise their rights as being attainable and protected. As set out by Karamalidou (2017), it is through embedding the positive developments in human rights legislation in everyday prison life that the full benefits of human rights will be achieved. However, as discussed by Engel (2012), there is a distinction between the vertical and horizontal experiences of rights consciousness which was very evident in this study. Engel (2012: 428) highlights how the high-level concept of rights developed at a policy or managerial level may not filter down to the horizontal level. He notes that:

> [R]ights consciousness refers to the ways in which individuals draw upon, resist or simply do not consider formal, rights–based legal elements, whether consciously or unconsciously in their perceptions and behaviour.

Participants referred to having no rights or discussed a narrow construct of rights limited to access to food, hygiene facilities and fresh air. They often lacked information on rights, either through a sense that this information was not provided to them or that they were not entitled to more. Though limited, existing research specifically within prisons aligns with this finding that prisoners' awareness of their rights can be minimal. Karamalidou (2017: 120), in her study of Dutch and UK prisons, found that there was uncertainty amongst UK prisoners of their entitlements to rights and a lack of official information on their human rights. In contrast to this, in Calavita and Jenness' (2015: 48) study in the context of California, prisoners were driven to complain by their strong belief in a legal right to certain entitlements in prison and the existence of a grievance procedure, in fact, fuelled their rights consciousness, shaping their identity as rights-bearing subjects.

As will be expanded upon further below, awareness of rights was also found to be low in the present study, but more profoundly, there was evidence of a view that a right was something provided by the prison authorities or state, rather than a product of participants' inherent dignity as humans. This position was clearly reflected also in awareness of oversight bodies, through this varied between the structures, with complaints procedures being relatively well known, but enjoying low levels of trust, and some inspection and monitoring bodies being poorly known. As set out in Chapter 5, levels of awareness of inspection and monitoring bodies varied, with local Visiting Committees being the most well-known, and the European Committee for the Prevention of Torture (CPT) the least well-known of the three inspection and monitoring bodies in Ireland. This can be partially explained by the backgrounds of many people in prison, who are often serving short sentences and have limited time to learn about and meet these bodies, especially if the bodies are only present in the prison on an irregular basis. It was clear from interviews that those serving longer sentences, in particular life sentences, had greater knowledge of these bodies. However, for those serving shorter sentences, it was very often the case that the OiP or the CPT was not familiar to the participant. As noted by Dâmboeanu et al. (2021), those serving longer sentences have time to build resources to utilise the complaints procedures in prison, as well as growing dissatisfaction with conditions when imprisoned for longer periods.

Legal mobilisation literature highlights the importance of skills and resources in utilising systems such as the complaint system and by extension accessing inspection and monitoring bodies (Calavita and Jenness 2015: 2). These tools are not always readily available to those in prison and, as evidenced by the variance in awareness and depth of knowledge about the different mechanisms in this study, the legal mobilisation literature surrounding the challenges faced by vulnerable and marginalised groups in accessing rights-protecting bodies are also applicable in the prison context. In particular, participants' knowledge of the rights they had was limited, and so acting on breaches of rights was unlikely. There was also evidence of a lack of awareness of how to activate procedures if they had a problem, key aspects of the lack of resources spoken of in that literature. A basic precondition for vindicating rights was not present.

Prior research has found awareness of rights to be low amongst people in prison and this was also evident in the current study. This study furthers our knowledge through drawing attention to the low awareness of many rights-protecting bodies amongst prisoners in Ireland, posing fundamental questions about how those in prison gain information about their rights and rights-protecting bodies and the retention of information on them. This suggests that low awareness of rights and low awareness of oversight structures are interconnected and, as set out here, there is a generalised lack of knowledge about mechanisms to protect human rights.

Participants in the current study rarely used rights language when discussing problems in prison. This finding differs from participants in Calavita and Jenness' (2015) study where prisoners relied heavily on rights language in discussing their rights in prison and complaints in prison. As noted by Calavita and Jenness (2015: 54), however, 'the presence of grievable problems ... is not in itself sufficient to explain the recognition of injury, much less the launching of a grievance, particularly in a context of vulnerability, self-blame, stigma and a commitment to "hanging tough" '. For participants in the current study, most had not made the leap to identify their problems as actionable issues.

This finding is unsurprising given the histories of disenfranchisement and marginalisation amongst prison populations as outlined by Behan (2016) in the Irish context. In contrast to the United States, Ireland has a relatively recent history of prison law cases and prisoners serve shorter sentences (Rogan 2018). As will be set out below, prison culture is infused with stoicism and this, in conjunction with shorter sentences, can partially explain why participants were not interested in seeking out information on oversight bodies or file a complaint. As noted by Behan and Kirkham (2016: 447), the 'function [of inspection and monitoring bodies] could be trumped by embedded cultural understandings as to what is required to maintain social order'. The present study indicates that prison culture itself can act as a barrier to prisoners' seeking out information on rights and rights protection and acting upon it, with features such as stoicism and tolerance of poor prison conditions evident amongst participants.

As set out in Chapters 5 and 6, other prisoners were a key source of information for prisoners in learning about oversight bodies and rights in prison more broadly. While prisoner relationships are discussed by Sykes (1958) as important for alleviating the pains of imprisonment and for gaining insight into life in prison, this reliance can create a hierarchy and dependence amongst prisoners (Crewe 2009), as well as the potential for misinterpretation of the role of oversight bodies and subjective experiences when relying on information about the bodies. In addition to this, those who were relied on for information either through informing prisoners on their rights or assisting with complaints were concerned about being viewed negatively and potentially being subject to reprisals for this role. As discussed in a study by the UK Ombudsman those who helped others file complaints described being labelled as troublemakers (Prisons and Probation Ombudsman 2015: 12). This concern about being labelled a troublemaker was also evident in Behan's (2016: 164) study where participants felt that seeking to get involved in prison governance would earn this label and could have consequences. Similarly, Sawyer (2021: 120) in the United States described how 'guards and administrators have a standard practice of "singling out jailhouse lawyers" for discipline in retaliation for ... challenging the status quo' through helping other prisoners file complaints and appeals. In the current study, participants spoke about other prisoners as an invaluable resource in helping them to settle in and learn about the routine of the prison; however, those who were relied upon for information sometimes noted a reluctance to assist everyone with information on prison life as they would be seen as informing others on how to complain which could lead to being perceived as an informant or being relied upon by too many in prison.

The low level of rights consciousness in prison and awareness of oversight bodies has significant implications for how such bodies do their work, a point with most direct relevance to inspection and monitoring. As will be discussed further below, low awareness means that prisoners are asked to make a judgement as to whether to trust those working for oversight bodies in a very short period of time or fleeting encounter with potentially sensitive information. This study has found that this may result in some choosing not to engage in order to avoid making this assessment. In addition to this, low awareness also meant that some prisoners were not clear about the specific mandates of different bodies, and this could impact on their expectations of what the bodies could achieve, potentially leading to dissatisfaction or frustration when their understanding did not align with the body's actual powers or function. In particular, as outlined in Chapter 6 and below, prisoners sometimes struggled to understand the wider purpose of inspection and monitoring which was about long-term change in contrast to individualised complaints. A fundamental challenge in the prison environment for oversight bodies is the recognition of rights by those in prison and embedding rights consciousness in those in prison. As outlined by Calavita and Jenness (2015: 2), 'the ability and willingness to name a problem, blame someone for it, and lodge a claim is socially and culturally patterned, with a vulnerable or self-blaming populations facing daunting barriers' and rights consciousness forms the basis for identifying problems in prison, as well as the substantive content and experiences which prisoners bring to the attention of oversight bodies. While their study highlighted that in prison people can overcome these barriers, the current study suggest that these barriers still act as an impediment to naming and claiming. Additionally, as highlighted by Gilliom (2001: 91) 'institutional, structural, and social pressures push against the assertion of rights' especially for the most marginalised and disempowered in society such as prisoners. The current study demonstrates the role of penal culture and institutional barriers which made it difficult for prisoners to assert their rights through seeking out and engaging with rights protection bodies.

7.2.2 Being a Rights Holder

A further key finding of this study relates to prisoners' feelings of themselves as rights holders or of being worthy of rights. There were varying positions evident amongst participants. For most people, the term 'rights' was very infrequently understood or used, with what human rights norms would see as rights being translated into the language of 'entitlements', or privileges which were granted by the prison authorities. This meant that some participants spoke about entitlements in prison as part of the incentivised regime, which could be gained through compliance and engaging in prison activities rather than something they would receive automatically or inherent to them as human beings. Often, participants asked the researcher to clarify what was meant by 'rights' and spoke of particular instances where they felt they had not got an entitlement, such as a family visit, or they had been wronged in some way. This contrasts with rights literature such as that by van Zyl Smit and Snacken (2009: 69), who state that recognising prisoners as rights holders 'supposes an unprejudiced image of prisoners as human beings', where rights are inherent to the individual and not dependent on others to grant them or on the behaviour of the individual prior to or during incarceration. This perspective is one grounded in how rights are viewed from the perspective of legal standards, which did not chime with the lived experience of people in the current study.

Despite this, there was also a sense of a desire to be treated decently and humanely by staff and the prison service amongst participants. This appeal to humanity and wish to be seen as a person is evident in other prison research such as Sexton's work on penal consciousness. As noted by Sexton (2015: 123), '[l]oss of personhood renders prisoners subhuman, one of many faceless objects of punishment' and represented the most complete loss of freedom experienced by those in her study. Additionally as observed by Liebling (2011: 534):

> [t]he absence of respect and fairness is experienced as psychologically painful ... As vulnerable and dependent creatures, human beings depend on acknowledgment (recognition) and justice as a condition of human flourishing. Their opposite, disrespect and indifference, cause pain and damage.

The present study also found that participants felt that often their humanity was denied in prison, and they were treated as animals, with participants often using the term 'dogs' to refer to how they perceived their treatment by officers. This denial of their human dignity by staff was viewed by participants as the basis upon which they could be treated badly. For participants, respecting their humanity was about two main things. First, prison staff and authorities simply meeting basic needs such as providing food and shelter was seen as a very impoverished way to respect human dignity, and respect was much more than this. As discussed by Tait (2011: 449) in her study of care in prison, prisoners' description of care encompassed 'sociable and respectful relationships with staff, feeling understood and listened to, having requests for help followed through on and being given reassurance and encouragement'. As outlined in Chapter 6, similar examples were given by participants of incidents where they did not feel respected or were dehumanised by the prison or prison officers through indifference or unfair treatment. A desire to be treated with dignity was also manifested in participants' descriptions of language they found dehumanising. For example, a common description of the times when prisoners receive food in prison is called 'feeding' time by staff members, as observed by the researcher on numerous occasions and referred to by prisoners. This invokes animalistic imagery rather than human. Participants felt dehumanised and infantilised in prison and a failure to recognise prisoners as fully grown adults, who prior to imprisonment made daily decisions about their life such as when they would go to sleep, or what they would eat. As discussed by Karamalidou (2017: 131), this depersonalisation and infantilisation can arise both directly and indirectly in the treatment of those in prison and, through an indifference to the needs of those in prison and in combination with the power differentials in the prison environment, this can 'accentuate prisoners' feelings of insecurity, helplessness, loneliness, dependence and abandonment ... [and] also attacks with force the core of [prisoners] being, that is, their individuality'. This experience of being perceived as less than or unworthy of rights impacted on participants' sense of entitlement to rights and being a holder of rights.

While a sense of lack of respect and denial of humanity in prison in general was evident in this study, it was also experienced in how complaints were dealt with. Having no answer to a complaint or no response to a concern was felt as being totally in limbo, and a denial of a recognition of being a human worthy of the respect of a response. As highlighted by Naylor's (2014: 112) research, being listened to and taken seriously by staff was referred to by participants as a sign of respect. Therefore, the lack of respect and voicelessness felt in the prison environment itself expanded into the tools through which prisoners were given to resolve problems in prison adding an additional layer of silence to their needs and sense of worth.

7.2.3 Asserting Rights

Another key finding from this study in relation to being a rights holder was that certain rights in particular did give rise to people seeking to speak up and take steps where the otherwise might not, despite the inherent barriers to rights assertion in the prison environment. As outlined in Chapter 6, prisoners frequently spoke about having no rights in prison. This finding differs from that of Calavita and Jenness (2015), where prisoners, in writing and speaking about complaints, spoke about their rights and used the language of rights. Instead, the findings in the current study, reflect those of Naylor (2014), where when those in prison did speak about problems in prison it was based on needs and an appeal to being seen as human, rather than identifying specific rules and rights from the prison rule book. The current study also found certain rights were either referred to directly as 'rights' or described as something worth speaking up about as outlined in Chapter 6. Similar to Naylor's study (2014), family and contact with the outside world was discussed by prisoners when identifying rights in prison, as well as being a likely subject for complaints complaining, and further seen as an area in need of reform. Issues which affected family visits and contact were perceived as going beyond the bounds of the prison, impacting on those who, unlike the prisoner themselves, had not committed a crime and therefore should not be being punished by proxy. This reflects a mindset amongst some prisoners that while they as a prisoner had been sentenced and earned their punishment, their family members as non-prisoners did not deserve this treatment. This shows an interesting distinction drawn by prisoners themselves between deserving and underserving people. Also, important here is the feeling amongst participants that there was a symbolic message conveyed by the prison service and experienced by prisoners through the impact on family life, and a disregard at times for family contact. This deeper sense of injustice, also found by Sexton (2015: 126), increased the severity experienced when these rights were impacted. This greater sense of injustice and experience of punishment was also reflected in the emotive language used by participants in speaking about these experiences. As described by Sexton (2015: 128), incidents experienced as 'severe symbolic punishment created angry desperate individuals who either pushed against the system or found themselves being beaten down by it'. Family visits and contact were the main reason provided by participants for filing a complaint.

As well as family rights, healthcare and access to healthcare was seen as an area where prisoners needed to speak up, and akin to family life this was seen as something which could have a long-term impact such as on a prisoner's ability to work in their chosen profession after prison and on their quality of life. Finally, as dealt with above and in Chapter 6, those in prison spoke about dignity and being treated with respect as something which oversight bodies should aim to improve in prison. However, this right was more challenging to articulate and reflected a broad range of experiences in prison. This was also an area which those in prison saw as a problem but might not be willing to complain about directly as it could be a staff-specific complaint and may result in damage to a key relationship. As discussed by Ahmed (2021), certain complaints are by their nature more risky, specifically those which name and identify abuses of power and confront hierarchies and inequalities. As set out in Chapter 5, complaints about staff relationships and treatment were felt by some prisoners to be unsuitable for written complaints, especially in the current study where complaints were dealt with internally. Complaining was viewed as unlikely to improve the situation and could instead create additional conflict between the staff and the prisoner. Participants spoke instead about this being a concern but that they developed different ways of dealing with challenging staff relationships by avoiding a particular staff member as much as possible and only asking for things from other staff members.

7.2.4 Expectations of Prison and Oversight Bodies

Expectations played a role in experiences of oversight bodies in two distinct ways. First, prisoners' expectations of what oversight bodies could and should be able to do and second, prisoners' expectations of what prison should and would be. These expectations being met or not shaped prisoners' perceptions and interactions with the different mechanisms.

In relation to expectations of oversight bodies, as highlighted in Chapter 5 for inspection bodies in particular, participants did not always have a clear understanding of the specific mandate of each body and role confusion arose where some spoke about dealing with individual complaints within the context of the OiP or only focused on the complaint mandate of the VCs. This resulted in unrealistic expectations of what a particular body could achieve and associated feelings of frustration and disappointment when those expectations were not met. This in turn damaged the sense that a body could be trusted and impacted on the likelihood of future engagement, as some participants felt that it was not worthwhile, as the body did not help or meet their expectations in the previous interaction. Additionally, as set out in Chapter 6 and above, those in prison rely on other prisoners to learn about bodies and this can play a role in setting expectations and sharing experiences. Another finding in relation to expectations of oversight bodies was a feeling that these bodies could not really do much anyway, and some participants had low expectations about what oversight bodies could achieve in prisons.

While some prisoners might still interact and engage with them regardless of these feelings and give them a chance, this low bar meant that prisoners were not particularly hopeful about change in prison or a body being able to protect their rights. As discussed by Calavita and Jenness (2015), for some people in prison speaking up or filing a complaint was a way of retaining their dignity in prison and resisting the system's attempts to further victimise them through speaking up. Similarly, in this study people in prison had little faith in the system changing or that the complaint system would resolving their complaints, but speaking up about it meant that there was still a latent hope of being heard and they showed the system that they were still capable of speaking up.

The second facet of expectations in prisons was expectations of the prison itself, that is, how those in prison expected prison to be and how they should be treated. Chapter 6 explored how those in prison saw their prison treatment and how it aligned with their expectations (Sexton 2015). As argued by Sexton (2015), it is the punishment gap, the difference between the expectations of severity of punishment and the actual experience which impacts on the prisoners' penal consciousness and subsequent experience of punishment. This sense of prison expectations had a direct impact on how those in prison experienced the severity of punishment and in the case of the current study whether they felt that prison was or was not meeting their expectations. Sexton (2015: 115) states that it is important to remember that '[p]unishment is not just something that is done—it is something that is done to people and experienced by people'. This further highlights the importance of understanding the context and direct experiences of those in prison to broaden our perspectives of rights and rights protection. As discussed above, some prisoners did not feel worthy of rights and prison expectations shaped their views of what they were entitled to while in prison. In the case of the current study, this gap between expectations and experience of punishment played a role in identifying issues in prison which in turn those in prison brought to the attention of the various oversight bodies. However, as outlined in Chapter 6 those in prison often held low expectations of what their actual rights were in prison and also how they should be treated in prison. This meant that speaking up and identifying issues could be a challenge due to the sense that everything was acceptable based on their standard of expectations. The long history of slopping out in Irish prisons, detailed in Chapter 6, meant that having in-cell sanitation was a significant step in improving the experience of prison for many prisoners and therefore their expectations of prison were met by these improvements. As highlighted by Sexton (2015: 129):

> [e]xpectations of punishment can be based on vicarious knowledge of prison, prior first-hand experiences with punishment, and even expectations of what punishment should or ought to be in an ideal sense.

This was also the case for prisoners in the study, with some speaking about knowledge being passed down by family members or friends with prior experience or from those they met while in prison. Others spoke about prison as an environment which was supposed to be tough and that modern prisons made life too easy for prisoners, while others spoke about deserving to be punished and being a prisoner meant loss of liberty and all that entailed. Those serving their first sentence in prison referred to the shock of entering prison and the challenges in adjusting. Those serving longer sentences or with significant prison experience referred to their expectations of prison lowering over time due to their experience and an acceptance of the limitations of prison resources was referred to.

These findings add to the prison literature by applying the concept of penal consciousness and expectations to the context of oversight and highlighting the implications this can have for identifying and interacting with oversight bodies. By exploring the disconnect between prisoner expectations of prison life and oversight, these findings underline the role of expectations in engaging with oversight mechanisms.

7.2.5 Prison Culture and Breaking the Silence

The context in which oversight bodies operate are important in understanding views of rights and rights-protecting bodies. As emphasised by Merry (2009: 9), culture is important 'as a construct that defines the relationships and meanings and constructs the possibilities of action'. Additionally as highlighted by Scott (2015: 58), there are structural, systematic and institutional ways through which people are kept from the resources they need and in prisons 'autonomy and choices are severely curtailed; human well-being, potentials and development are undermined; feelings of safety and sense of security are weak; and human needs are systematically denied through the restrictive and inequitable distribution of resources'. This includes the resources and knowledge available to those in prison to access oversight bodies and file complaints, as well as a culture which creates barriers to speaking up and obtaining information. Additionally, Silbey (2005: 338) notes that 'perceptions [of the utility of the legal system in demanding rights] are cultural products learned, shaped and framed by interactions in specific locations'. As set out in Chapter 6, many participants reflected on prison culture as being infused with an attitude of keeping your head down and getting on with your time. This is similar to Calavita and Jenness' (2015: 66) finding where 'staying out of trouble was a persistent theme' in prisoners' narratives of surviving prison. However, this attitude is in direct conflict with interacting with oversight bodies where those in prison are asked about their experiences, in particular to identify challenges and instances in which the experiences of prison do not align with the rights of those in prison and the standards of treatment set out in domestic and international prison guidelines.

In addition to this, as highlighted by Jewkes' (2005) work on masculinity in prison, there are limited spaces where those in prison feel able to expose their vulnerabilities and this is particularly important when discussing engaging with oversight bodies, as prisons are hypervisible environments, where interactions are constantly observed, and misinterpretations of a specific interaction can have serious repercussions. As discussed by some participants, putting a complaint form into the box on landing could be perceived by some prisoners as telling on other prisoners due to heightened suspicions in prison. Additionally, in opening up about challenges in prison and speaking about vulnerabilities to oversight bodies those in prison may be delving deep into experiences that are difficult to reflect upon with little time to recompose themselves before returning to the prison environment. Prison culture for many is about tolerating conditions and presenting a stoic appearance to those around them. As outlined by Crewe (2009: 179), stoics were concerned with the negative aspects of prison and the possibility of losing privileges through non-compliance. In addition to this, Jewkes (2005) highlights the need to maintain a tough appearance to survive in prison.

Another aspect of prison life which impacted on oversight interactions was power in prison. Foucault (2012: 28) discusses the role of power in the production of knowledge, highlighting that power-knowledge relations are defined by 'the processes and struggles that traverse it and of which it is made up, [and which] determines the forms and possible domains of knowledge'. In the current study, participants spoke about feeling powerless in prison, particularly in relation to seeking information and speaking up. As noted above and in Chapter 6, they relied on other prisoners to gain information on life in prison and learn about the different bodies which had roles in oversight. Important to note here is that oversight bodies were not seen as something that prisoners needed to learn about right away and information retention on arrival could be impacted by 'entry shock' (Sykes 1958). The prison service and staff, however, ultimately held the key to the official information available to those in prison and as discussed by one participant in relation to the EPRs and accessing a copy in prison, there was a sense that they did not want prisoners to know about all their rights in prison. Staff and prisons shaped the information that prisoners could access and the skills necessary to acquire knowledge on rights and rights-protecting bodies. Knowledge is created in a specific environment and through relationships. This in turn defines the 'possible corpus of knowledge, and knowledge extends and reinforces the effects of this power' (Foucault 2012: 29). In closed environments, such as prisoners, gatekeepers exercise additional control over the information which is available to those in prison and in the absence of official knowledge misconceptions can arise such as role confusion in relation to the mandates and powers of the various bodies. This effect was reflected in the ways in which prisoners sought to complain, emphasising preferences for accessing the decision maker, such as the governor, so they could get a direct answer and they would not need to be concerned about a complaint form going missing or being thrown away. For those in prison, resolving complaints or problems more broadly was about finding the most effective way of dealing with it rather than the proscribed route. Having knowledge in prison on how things work and how to complain takes on increasing significance through the limitations placed on material resources and services. Foucault (2012: 147) also refers to a hierarchy of knowledge in prisons. This was reflected in how prisoners spoke about inspection and who the inspector should speak with. Those serving long sentences were seen as invaluable sources of information about life in prison and viewed as legitimate sources of knowledge by other prisoners, reflecting an imposed hierarchy by prisoners themselves on who would be perceived as worthy, as well as knowledgeable on prison life.

Another element of power reflected in the findings was the changing nature of power in prisons as discussed by Crewe (2009: 449). As outlined by Crewe (2009: 449), power in modern prisons has become deeper and heavier, creating 'new weights and burdens, particularly around issues of powerlessness, autonomy, insecurity and the meeting of personal needs'. This complexity of pains of imprisonment was reflected in how prisoners spoke about reprisals and the grip of imprisonment when it came to accessing services and progressing through the system. Staff discretion and control over the incentivised regime could be used as subtle forms of reprisals that have long-lasting impacts on both a prisoner's experience of imprisonment and potential release date. For some participants in the current study, this also resulted in scepticism around the potential for reform in prisons as an old form of familiar power was replaced with less obvious and penetrating forms of control under the guise of penal reform. Some of the participants in Crewe's (2009: 179) study spoke about suppressing their frustrations and complaints out of a sense that this was a more sensible approach to incarceration, and it would hasten their progress through the system. The ideal of release or having an 'easier' sentence therefore was more important to prisoners than in prison complaints.

Despite the challenges of speaking up due to aspects of the prison culture and power in prison, Calavita and Jenness (2015) discuss the hypervisibility of law in the prison environment and its impact on prisoners in seeking to hold staff to account. Similar to Mathieson's (1965: 23) concept of censoriousness, whereby those in power are held accountable for not adhering to their own rules, the additional rules in relation to prison life and constant reminders of the law resulted in prisoners who sought to use the rule book to hold staff to account based on their own standards. While some participants in the study made reference to the rule book and perceived unfairness when staff did not adhere to their own rules in decision making and interacting with prisoners, the comparatively lower level of formal complaints suggest that prisoners in the current study did not respond in the same way to perceived violations of the prison rules. However, as outlined in Chapter 6 and above, certain violations such as those around family contact and healthcare were referred to as issues worth speaking up about despite the perceived challenges.

These findings add to the existing literature through providing insight into the interaction between prison culture and accessing oversight mechanisms. Prison culture in Ireland and elsewhere is focused on survival in prison through keeping one's head down and managing yourself in prison. This impacts in turn on prisoners' decisions to seek out information on rights and rights protection, as well as on their willingness to speak up. In addition to this, power dynamics in prison hinders the information available to those in prison, as well as decisions in speaking up and the modern prison system with privilege regimes can influence prisoners' abilities to interact with oversight bodies. Overall, these findings highlight the importance of contextualising rights protection within the culture of a specific institution. As noted by Naylor and Winford (2019: 117), culture is 'not just legal compliance but also underlying attitudes'. Therefore, while prisons may appear to be complying and allowing inspection bodies into the prison and complaining by prisoners, the attitudes within the prison can create additional barriers to accessing these.

7.3 The Implications of Trust on the Experiences of Oversight

This section explores the implications the low trust nature of prisons discussed by participants in this study had on the operation of oversight bodies in prison. As highlighted by Crewe (2011: 459), '[p]risons are low trust environments, holding people who experiences of trust tend not to dispose them to faith in others'. In addition to this, as discussed by Hawley (2012: 18) for those who feel that they are deemed untrustworthy, there are additional challenges to building trust. Hawley (2012: 18) states that those who are in 'positions of privilege may find it easier to take a chance with trusting, simply because the risks and stakes are lower' for them. This section considers how low-trust environments and feeling untrustworthy can impact on interacting and assessing bodies through the lens of prison experience. Gaining trust is particularly important in prisons due to the heightened risks of trusting the wrong person. As will be seen, this phenomenon is particularly important for interactions with oversight bodies, especially when sharing potentially sensitive information about oneself.

7.3.1 Prison as a Low-Trust Environment

Prior research has highlighted the prison as a low-trust environment, where those in prison face challenges in placing trust in others (Crewe 2009). As highlighted by Liebling's (2011: 486) research, legitimacy plays an important role in prison life and the experiences of prisoners. It can improve information flow and allow trust to develop. As will be highlighted by the findings discussed in this section, the social world in which prisoners and oversight bodies interact has an impact on the trust prisoners place in these bodies. Relationships are central in shaping prison culture and as outlined by Liebling (2011), right relationships are about being respectful and having a getting the boundaries right when it came to formality and informality and the exercise of power. In context where these relationships arise, '[o]bedience is more likely to be enduring rather than grudging, information will flow more readily between the power-holders and their subjects, trust will develop, and well-being [among prisoners] will be higher' (Liebling 2011: 486). Staff relationships were seen as good when prisoners felt respected and in turn felt they could turn to those staff for help when needed (Liebling 2011). As discussed in Chapter 5 in relation to complaints and resolving problems in prison, most participants referred to seeking out a member of staff as the main way of resolving a problem. However, in the current study, some participants had negative perceptions of professionals and the prison system due to prior experiences and preconceptions about professionals. Some were sceptical of anyone acting in the interests of prisoners. This could hinder trust building and increase the perceived risk of exposing vulnerabilities to oversight bodies. In addition to this, when it came to complaints about staff members, participants felt that prison staff would stick together and in those instances, it would be hard to trust staff to speak on behalf on the prisoner. Participants also spoke about prison as a solitary time, where they relied upon themselves to get through their time in prison rather than trusting others to help them get by. This reflected an attitude held by some participants as not being able to trust others in prison. In addition to staff relationships, participants spoke about inter-prisoner relationships in prison. Rowe (2012: 110) highlights the challenges of forming relationships in prison, especially with other prisoners who may be perceived as untrustworthy. Her participants spoke of the risk involved in exposing vulnerabilities through trusting a stranger. In the current study, participants spoke about the paranoia they felt in prison, as well as concerns about being watched when interacting when inspection bodies or putting in a complaint. Some participants felt that these interactions could be perceived negatively by others in prison, and they may be perceived as being a 'rat'. There was a sense that people would jump to a negative presumption about what you were complaining about. In addition to this, some participants felt that others would take advantage if you asked for help in filling out a complaint form and this could result in trouble for the prisoner.

Relationships are important in prison for learning about life in prison and how everything works; however, due to the low-trust nature of the prison environment participants raised concerns about the potential exploitation of vulnerabilities or negative attitude for using the complaint system or speaking to oversight bodies. These findings provide insight into the role of low-trust environments and relationships in perceptions and the operation of oversight in prison.

7.3.2 Being Perceived as Untrustworthy

Another finding in relation to trust was the experience amongst participants of being perceived as untrustworthy by others. As outlined by Hawley (2012: 18), '[p]eople who are rarely trusted do not have the opportunity to develop their trustworthiness and cannot be expected to respond with alacrity when trust is offered to them'. Therefore, experiences of being perceived as untrustworthy can have significant implications on prisoners' abilities to trust, especially for those who have been subject to long-term distrust (Hawley 2012). This has particular implications for interacting with inspection bodies, as it can have an impact on the perception as to whether or not their voices will be valued and heard. Butler and Maruna (2016) highlight the value people place on feeling heard, as distinct from having their voice included, during proceedings in prison disciplinary hearings. Some participants in the present study felt that their inputs would not be valued due to their prisoner status or due to their specific position within prison, for example, being subject to specific regimes and/or being labelled as troublemakers. This meant that for those prisoners there was a sense of futility in speaking up and pointlessness to sharing their experiences with inspection and monitoring bodies or filing a complaint. This sense of not being seen as trustworthy may have a long history drawing on previous experiences with the criminal justice system more broadly or authority figures and can play a role in how those in prison try to resolve problems. As will be discussed in the next section, trust in the bodies themselves was also a critical factor in how people viewed oversight and the merits or risks of engaging with it. The perceived legitimacy of oversight bodies plays a role in deciding to engage; however, this was mediated by how people saw themselves as worthy of protection, meaning that they were sometimes unwilling to interact with the oversight body even if they had trust in the body due to a sense that they saw themselves as not worthy or voiceless.

This section draws together key findings about participants' sense of trust placed in them. Participants spoke about feeling unworthy of trust, as well as feeling that others would not trust them. The consequences of this feeling of having a lack of trust or value placed on your words and experience is a sense that no one will listen to your concerns, as well as feeling that nothing would change even if you spoke up. As found by Crewe (2009: 178) in UK prisons and illustrated by the findings set out in Chapter 6, those who felt untrusted or ignored in prisons were liable to give up their efforts to interact with the prison system. These feelings resulted in prisoners who were submissive to the prison regime through feelings of pointlessness or futility, akin to attributes found by Carrabine (2005) in relation to fatalism. Similarly in this study, some participants expressed disillusionment with the system and the sense that seeking to interact with oversight bodies was pointless as the system would never change. Crewe (2009: 271) also discussed how those in prison felt a sense of surrogate resistance through helping others to file complaints.

7.3.3 Trust in Oversight Bodies

As discussed in Chapter 6, there was a feeling of a lack of trust amongst prisoners concerning oversight which was manifested across several dimensions. As noted by one participant (06), to understand prison life, it is important not to *'be fooled by the flowers'*, highlighting the importance of interacting with those in prison to gain an insight into life in prison but also the sense amongst some prisoners that the nice appearance of certain parts of the prison could create a misleading perception of prison life to those entering the prison. There was a lack of trust that inspection bodies would be permitted by the prison authorities to do their work properly, as well as a lack of belief in the ability of those bodies to make any real change. Several participants also reported that they did not feel they had an opportunity to ask questions of or seek to speak to the OiP, resulting in a credibility gap, with many feeling that there was no chance of a real encounter with a prison inspection body.

This perceived interference by the prison authorities in how such bodies do their work was also evident in participants' perceptions of the handling of complaints. Central to the lack of the trust in oversight bodies was therefore the sense that bodies were not operating according to certain criteria central to effective oversight, such as independence. Independence is a key virtue advocated for by many scholars of oversight, and considered to involve both structural and de facto elements (Steinerte and Murray 2009). In the absence of strong knowledge of the bodies, noted in Chapter 5 and above, misconceptions can arise surrounding specific functions and powers of the different bodies. Participants felt that bodies were all guided by the prison service in terms of who they spoke to and the areas of the prison which they saw. This created the perception that the prison service could control the image presented to outside bodies and these perceptions undermined their view of the credibility of the process through presenting an inauthentic impression of the prison. This lack of trust arose through prior experiences of interacting with oversight bodies, impressions passed on from other prisoners or a general sense that no one would act with prisoners' interests to the fore. Even those who had experiences of interacting with the oversight bodies were not clear as to why they had been chosen to speak to an inspection or monitoring body, or had a clear idea of how the body operated. However, key to this finding was poor knowledge on the existence or specifics of the various oversight mechanisms and the low-trust environment in the prison which gave rise to a general scepticism and a lack of trust in authorities which was extended to oversight bodies. Despite this low trust, in some cases specific actions such as asking prisoners how they were doing and being present in areas of the prison such as cells, increased trust and credibility, as it communicated care for the well-being of prisoners, as well as visibility concerning the powers of the inspector to access all areas of the prison, in particular areas which may represent a less favourable view of the prison.

In the case of complaints, the absence of trust was stronger, with almost all participants viewing the system as one to be avoided at all costs yet despite this it was still used by 22% of survey respondents. As outlined above and in Chapter 5, key to this was trigger issues such as family contact and healthcare, which participants felt particularly motivated by and willing to use all routes possible to be heard even when they had limited faith in its ability to resolve their problem. As outlined above and in Chapter 6, participants often referred to different ways of resolving issues in prison rather than using the complaint system, such as relying on a trusted member of staff, asking to meet the governor, or simply tolerating the problem for the duration of their sentence. This negative perception of the complaint system meant that the formal complaint procedure was not seen as a legitimate means of resolving complaints by many participants. As highlighted by Beijersbergen et al. (2015), perceived legitimacy and adherence to principles of procedural justice play an important role in the eventual acceptance of outcomes, as well as overall compliance in prison. As can be seen from the findings discussed in Chapter 6, there was an absence of trust in the processes within the complaint mechanism. In the words of Lind and Tyler (1998: 530), trust in authorities is a core component in procedural justice literature and 'people care whether their treatment (and not simple their outcomes) is fair because fair treatment indicates something critically important – their status within the social group'.

Another key finding in relation to trust in the complaint system is drawn from prisoners' relationships with staff. As outlined in Chapter 6, while participants often spoke about a good officer or officers, there was not necessarily a universal experience of respect and trustworthy officers amongst participants. Crewe et al. (2015) note the importance of prison staff relationships, in particular the role of respect in building right relationships with prisoners for a healthy and well-functioning prison environment. In addition to this, staff can be perceived as embodying the institution and their actions can be used to gauge the fairness of the institution (Liebling 2011). The importance of staff-prisoner relationships has been documented in many studies, and is known to affect all aspects of a person's experience while in prison (Liebling 2004). It was clear from the current study that these relationships also played a key role in influencing use and perceptions of the complaints system. Participants raised concerns about potential reprisals for filing a complaint, especially when it was directed against a staff member, as well as the potential to damage an important relationship through complaining. Given the heavy involvement of staff and the lack of an external element in the existing complaint system in Ireland, participants looked to staff behaviour and view of complaints to assess how complaints would be received and dealt with.

These findings have implications for prison experience literature and procedural justice literature. The role of staff relationships in mediating complaints is an important finding which adds to our understanding of the importance of right relationships in the handling of prisoner complaints. As highlighted by Miller (2001), procedural justice principles are important in both formal and informal dealings with authorities. In the current study, this is expanded to underline the role of staff relationships when assessing an internal complaint system and further emphasises the importance of a system perceived as independent. These findings also suggest that further research is necessary on whether these prior relationships influence complaint perceptions in other contexts.

As underlined by Hardin (1996), there is a risk involved in placing your trust in someone. This risk is heightened for those who have more to lose or are in an environment of constraint, such as a prison. Therefore, in order to decide to interact with oversight bodies, those in prison may carry out a risk assessment of the persons' intentions and motivations as set out in Chapter 7, as well as the prisoner's view of the possibility of change, their prioritisation of the issue concerned and the risk of reprisals. Franke et al. (2010: 112) in their study of legitimacy of in a prison in comparison to a bootcamp found that the perceived interest of staff in the development of prisoners was important in increasing legitimacy and motive-based trust in the staff in the corrections bootcamp. Participants by and large did not have sufficient information about oversight bodies, meaning they could not properly assess their interests and motives. As such, it was difficult for participants to develop trust in such bodies, who often fell back on prior experiences with other authorities such as the prison itself in judging oversight bodies, and which sometimes result in the misconstruing of the motives of such bodies. As noted by Behan (2016) in relation to VCs, prisoners felt that members of VCs were political appointees with little interest in the role, and that looking into prisoner complaints was a formality rather than a way to resolve an issue in the prisoner's favour. This concern was also reflected upon by participants in the current study, who queried whether VCs actually investigated a complaint or just agreed with the governor's assessment of the situation.

The next step in the risk assessment was determining whether a body could do anything and whether engaging was therefore worth it. Participants discussed the enforceability of decisions by complaint bodies and recommendations from inspection reports. As outlined in Chapter 6, participants often felt that without enforcement powers the prison service were unlikely to willingly adopt changes to the system. Similarly in Behan's (2016) study, participants felt that inspection was a 'paper exercise' rather than something that could prompt changes in the system. In addition to this, participants felt that complaints would either never be dealt with or would be decided in favour of the prison service. This meant that for many participants change was unlikely to arise from interacting with oversight.

As outlined in Chapter 5, most participants referred to some form of reprisals as a possibility in complaining or speaking up. Similarly, Behan (2016: 169) found that prisoners were concerned about raising complains with the VC due to concerns about reprisals. This was also the case for participants in Calavita and Jenness' (2015: 75) study where concerns for retaliation permeated prisoners' narratives on complaining. As with Calavita and Jenness' (2015: 75) study, concern about reprisals was mostly focused on complaints against staff in the current study. Discussions of reprisals varied widely with participants referring to concerns of being transferred for complaining to more subtle forms of reprisals such as staff members making your life more difficult through opening your door last in the morning or not being helpful in dealing with requests. These concerns were factors in the risk assessment prisoners undertook in deciding whether to engage or speak up about a problem, and added an additional layer to trust building in prisons. As discussed by one participant, the risk of reprisals and paranoia in the prison environment would at least be reflected upon when deciding to speak up. As highlighted by Hawley (2012: 19), when those who are deemed untrustworthy themselves are asked to trust someone, the information needed for a risk assessment to interact is more important. The lack of accurate information on oversight bodies amongst prisoners and the frequent impromptu requests to engage creates challenges in assessing whether or not engagement is worthwhile for the prisoner.

These findings underline the lack of trust currently held by prisoners in Ireland of oversight bodies. They also add to our understanding of decisions to engage through outlining the different factors which prisoners take into consideration. Oversight bodies are assessed for their motives and intentions, in particular whether they care about those in prison. In addition to this, participants were concerned about what results bodies could actually achieve. Finally, the risk of reprisals was discussed by participants. The heightened risk of reprisals in the prison environment was clear here, and concerns around complaints about staff were evident. However, the willingness to complain was mediated by the nature of the complaint with particular issues carrying more weight for prisoners in deciding to interact. These findings further highlight the importance of context in legal mobilisation both in filing complaints and assessing whether to engage with inspection and monitoring bodies.

7.3.4 Wasted Agency and Implications of Low Trust

As noted by Behan (2020: 11), 'imprisonment confines, restricts and prevents an individual from the freedom of choice necessary for agency, building trust, developing social capital and engaging in networks of engagement essential for robust citizenship'. Similarly, as set out in Chapter 6, participants in the current study experienced challenges in building trust and had limitations placed on their agency. As discussed by Crewe (2009), these restrictions increase the significance of staff-prisoner relationships in accessing services available in prison. These limitations can create challenges in engaging with oversight bodies, especially in instances such as those set out in Chapter 5 and above, where prisoners have limited information on the existence of oversight bodies and how they operate. In situations where people have limited agency and concerns about exercising the agency they retain, care will be taken in deciding when to use their agency. Prisoners may prioritise interactions where they have a clear understanding of the benefits and risks of engaging or, as set out in Chapter 6, on specific issues which have increased significance for them. As noted by Participant 19, '*I try push the line as far as I can with the visits and stuff*'. As noted in Chapter 6 and above, family contact was a key area where participants were more likely to speak up or complain when a problem arose and is clearly important to those in prison. This may result in issues perceived as minor or not as important being overlooked or not perceived as worth wasting agency on.

The concept of 'wasted agency' therefore is based on the underlying concerns of those in prison and the perception of how far you can push the line or exercise your agency before the risk of reprisals increases beyond what is acceptable to the prisoner for the right at issue or one's energy is burnt out. Not speaking up is also a form of self-protection from being repeatedly refused one's request or feeling that one's sense of worth is being undermined by those in prison. As set out above, when choosing to engage with oversight bodies, having information on the risks and benefits of interacting are key especially for those in low-trust environments. However, in the case of participants in this study there was limited information on the various bodies and how they operated, and participants therefore found it difficult to assess the benefits of an interaction. As noted by Participant 31, '*I would only go to him if I know … if I had a good chance of winning my case*'. This reiterates the importance of having a clear understanding of the bodies' mandates and how they operate in deciding whether to use the limited agency retained by those in prison on an interaction with an oversight body.

Drawing on Behan's (2016) work, this highlights the finding that if trust decreases, either through misconceptions or lack of knowledge to engage, engagement decreases resulting in a drop in legitimacy as prisoners' views are not being heard in the inspection and monitoring processes. As outlined by Behan (2016: 172) '[i]f there is little trust in these bodies, this reduced the likelihood that prisoners would approach them and undermined their legitimacy is prisoners failed to engage with them'. These findings have implications for the legal mobilisation literature as they further emphasise the importance of context in accessing and mobilising protection mechanisms. Prisoners make calculations in deciding when to act and, in the absence of clear knowledge of these bodies, this assessment is done based on prior experiences or information available to prisoners. This risk-based assessment of engaging in the absence of complete and accurate knowledge of the different bodies, can result in engagement being a wasted of limited available agency and impact on quality of reports and overall perceptions of the situation in prisons. The absence of complaints or issues being raised with monitoring bodies should not, in isolation, be perceived as an absence of issues within the prison.

7.4 Misalignment between Oversight Structures and Lived Experiences of Prison and Penal Culture

Oversight bodies rely on those whose rights they are tasked with protecting to interact with them and provide information on the lived experiences of a particular setting in order to write reports or handle complaints. However, these interactions are not always straightforward and, as set out above, challenges in the prison environment can hinder awareness of and access to these bodies. As noted by Peter Tyndall, Office of the Ombudsman Ireland, 'in the case of, for instance, people who are in prison... for us to sit in our offices and wait for them to come to us does not work'.[1] The findings discussed in this section suggest a disconnect between the idea of these bodies and how they operate at a conceptual level, or as designed within human rights standards, and the lived experiences of those in prison concerning such bodies. Key findings in this regard relate to perceptions of such bodies as bureaucratised, standardising and depersonalising, and therefore at a remove from the lives of those in prison, as well as the ways in which interactions are approached. In addition to this, in combination with how the concept of rights is experienced by people in prison described above, those in prison may not view themselves as vulnerable and in need of protection. This can result in conversations around issues affecting those in prison, whereby oversight bodies hold a much wider concept of rights and vulnerability than those in prison.

7.4.1 Tensions between Resolving Immediate Problems and the Long-Term Goals of Human Rights Protections

Participants were not always clear about the mandates of various human rights-protecting bodies and what could be achieved through interaction with them. As outlined in Chapter 5, in discussing VCs, participants' focus was on their role in handling complaints rather than in carrying out inspections. While complaints are about resolving individual problems, inspection processes have long-term objectives to reform the prison system as a whole. A high prevalence of short sentences and a desire to forget about prison once on the outside meant that the long-term goals of inspection and monitoring were not always viewed as immediate or a pressing need for those in prison. At times, this meant that prisoners did not see a point to interacting with inspection and monitoring as their focus was on getting through their sentence rather than longer-term prison reform. While short-termism in thinking is understandable in the prison environment, deeper considerations were also at play which may explain why participants did not see a great deal of value in the long-term projects of human rights improvements.

As discussed by Behan (2016), prison involves both physical and psychological isolation through which regimes and disciplines used do not enhance communication and cooperation. Instead, prison is designed to encourage complaint citizenship, where obedient behaviour is encouraged rather than those in prison gaining a broader sense of responsibility. The lack of trust experienced by prisoners in wider society, can transform into non-engagement with civic and political institutions due to 'little confidence in the possibility of change either by an individual group or society' (Behan 2016: 112).

7.4.2 Bureaucracy: Increasing Professionalism and Depersonalisation

Inspection and monitoring and complaint procedures in Ireland and internationally have been changing dramatically in recent years. In Ireland, both the OiP and formal complaint procedures are relatively recent additions to oversight in prions. However, some of the findings from this study highlight the challenges in accessing an overly formalistic system for prisoners. Armstrong (2018: 404) raises concerns around the shift in human rights-focused international guidelines to domestic operational documents which seek to create objective tools of measurement and can result in 'a process by which general principles of human rights are technically and institutionally specified as procedures and processes of bureaucracy which largely advantage prison authorities in the struggle to frame State conduct as rights violating or compliant'. While this quote speaks to the ways in which prison authorities respond to rights obligations by means of protocols and procedures, this insight can also be applied to the way in which human rights-protecting bodies work. For some participants, inspection and monitoring and complaints were viewed as mechanisms by which prison authorities could channel problems or prisoner dissent into avenues that, ultimately, would not change very much. Some viewed these processes as merely 'box-ticking' exercises which would not challenge the structures or the system. As such, these kinds of bodies may play a role in legitimating penal power and breaking prisoners through ingraining a sense of powerlessness and futility in speaking up. Often participants felt that they could not be heard in a meaningful way by inspection and monitoring and complaints procedures. As found by Calavita and Jenness (2015: 169) in their study of prisoner complaints, 'participants [prisoners and staff] speak past each other, as their two languages of [humanistic] needs and bureaucratic mandates entail not only distinct vocabulary but altogether different syntaxes of meaning'. This may also apply to the interactions between prisoners and outside bodies.

As outlined in Chapter 5, participants were sceptical of who was involved in carrying out inspection and monitoring in prisons and whether they would understand the challenges and problems of prisons. Participants in particular referred to the need to have people with lived experiences or who came from similar backgrounds to prisoners on the VCs so they would understand life in prison. This concern with the appointment process for VCs was also noted by participants in Behan's (2016: 171) study who felt that they were 'jobs for the boys' rather than being taken up by people who were concerned with the treatment of prisoners. Participants sometimes expressed distrust for authorities and felt that they were far removed from prison life and could easily be fooled by the staff into getting an inaccurate picture of life in prison. For participants, lived experience was invaluable in having insight into the real prison, which was also reflected through participants valuing the input of life sentence prisoners in inspection reports. In communicating needs and problems to oversight bodies, it is necessary to '*look beyond the flowerpots*'

(Participant 06), to gain insight into problems in prison and understand experience of those in prison. Participants were sceptical about inspection and monitoring bodies abilities to gain insight into the 'real prison', as well as the standards which outsiders perceived as acceptable for those in prison.

As well as a feeling that a lack of shared experience inhibited communication between people in prison and rights-protecting mechanisms, it was also clear that formalised, bureaucratised processes involving paperwork was felt to be a means of thwarting proper engagement for people in prison. Prior to 2013, prisoners could file a complaint by using a half sheet, a piece of paper pulled out of an officer's notebook, folded in half, ripped and given to the prisoner, or through VCs or requests at governors' parade to speak to the governor. These options are still available to prisoners and many participants preferred speaking to an officer or the governor rather than filing a complaint. A variety of reasons were given for this such as literacy and difficulties in communicating effectively on paper, as well as concerns about complaints going missing and the need for a decision to be taken quickly on a complaint. The formalisation of the complaint procedure, through a formal written complaint procedure, created difficulties for those with literacy difficulties and the other ways in which those in prison resolved their complaints. However, this feature also highlighted the importance of inter person communication for those in prison, which is in contrast to the shift to a written complaint system within the prison service. As pointed out by O'Donnell (2016: 47) there was a 'squeezing out of the person that accompanies advanced bureaucratization when the rulebook comes to dictate the terms of engagement'.

Crewe (2009: 67) discusses the use of formal complaint procedures as a tool used by staff to manage prisoner complaints when overburdened and unable or unwilling to deal with them themselves. This was reflected in the current study, where participants wanted to be able to speak to someone and explain themselves but felt that a staff member or more importantly a staff member who could make a decision was not always available to them even at the designated time such as governor's parade. This focus on formal, written procedures created a barrier for some prisoners to complain but also represents a disconnect between methods of resolution that prisoners are comfortable with and reforms in the prison system.

In addition to this, interacting through paperwork for complaining was felt by some prisoners to be a depersonalising experience. Participants felt more comfortable communicating directly with a decision maker where they could explain themselves clearly and get a response without concerns about missing forms or being ignored. For some participants there was a sense that in the process of formalising procedures, the micro level of individuals was being lost through the macro level goals of oversight and reforming the system. Some participants felt left behind by the changes to prison process rather than included. As highlighted by Behan (2016), this message of inclusion played a role in prisoners' choosing not to vote due to a sense that politicians and their policies did not reflect the interests of the prisons.

Similarly, in the current study, a sense that reforms were not going to be in the prisoners' interests or that bodies were not truly for prisoners resulted in prisoners choosing not to take part.

In addition to this, Crewe (2009: 114) outlined how the use of paperwork to resolve complaints was perceived as dishonest or disrespectful, as staff could go behind prisoners backs and write something down without a direct face to face interaction. Participants in Crewe's study expressed nostalgia for the old days where requests and complaints were dealt with as face-to-face interactions and prisoners could get a direct response on an issue. Similarly, participants in this study spoke about the challenges in receiving a response through the use of paperwork and how the person giving the response often did not have the power to make a decision or could provide an explanation as to why a decision was made.

7.4.3 Transparency of Processes

The various processes involved in carrying out inspection and monitoring or investigating complaints were not always clear to participants in this study as set out in Chapter 5. Inspection and monitoring bodies have been criticised elsewhere for their lack of methodology and transparency in carrying out their activities (Seddon 2010; Karamalidou 2017). This lack of transparency at times led to a perceived sense amongst some prisoners, that they had not been listened to as many prisoners did not know or could not access inspection reports or had a clear sense of who an inspector spoke to or where they went in prisons when they visited. This led to a sense that visits were controlled by the prison service and that an in-depth view of the prison was not being obtained by those coming into the prison. In the case of complaints, a sense of being forgotten about or that complaints were not taken seriously as those in prison were not always provided with a response or reasons for why complaints were refused. The perception that prisoners were selected by the prison service to speak to the inspector was also raised by participants in Behan's study (2016: 165). Prisoners often felt removed from the inspection process to the lack of follow up on what happened with the information they provided and the eventual report. Some felt that those on inspection bodies were professionals who would not understand the experiences of prisoners and were too close to prison staff.

7.4.4 Perceived Vulnerability

When discussing oversight bodies in prison, in particular the CPT's mandate around torture, participants understood the need for such bodies in general; however, some felt that they did not need them themselves. This feeling was linked to a sense that the standards in their prison were good for prison, and others such as those with disability or who were in different parts of the prison, for instance those in segregation, were more in need. This shows that there are differences in the understanding of vulnerability in the prison context. As is the case in research, oversight bodies may see all people in prison as vulnerable, but not all those in prison agree with this characterisation. It also shows that people in prison often have low expectation as to what are acceptable standards in prisons, as outlined in Section 7.2.2. These different concepts of vulnerabilities can create challenges in speaking up about prison experiences as a prisoner may not see themselves as vulnerable. This speaks to a certain way in which people in prison have impoverished views of the treatment they deserve as human beings, as well as a strong element of stoicism about the conditions they face (Behan 2012; Karamalidou 2017). For some participants, there was a sense that prison was incapable of change and therefore prison was something to be tolerated or put up with it. This also indicates that human rights standards may be meaningless unless grounded in a real sense of deserving by those in prison. However, in addition to this, as outlined above building trust was important and there are a lack of spaces to expose emotions in prison (Crewe et al. 2014). This means that the bravado or tough face prisoners adopt in prison may be maintained in communicating with inspection and monitoring bodies. As experienced by the researcher, some participants started off interviews by saying everything was going well in prison but later on exposed concerns or challenges they experienced. Exposing vulnerabilities is not easy in an environment such as a prison and being perceived as vulnerable may not be desirable for those in prison.

As discussed by Merry (2009: 4), there is a distance between the site of ideas surrounding human rights and the specific situations in which they are deployed. This was reflected in this research through participants who spoke about not feeling understood by oversight bodies. As set out in Chapter 5, one participant spoke about broken windows as a visible issue in prison, but something which did not bother him as he often felt too warm in the prison and the broken window let in cool air. This again speaks to the disconnect between the expectations and perspectives of outside bodies and those in prison. It also provides evidence of the extensive disenfranchisement of people in prison where having a broken window is considered a good solution, when objectively, ventilation would meet a minimum standard. It also tells us of a very practical focus on immediate solutions for people in prison, a consequence of the limited autonomy they have and options they can deploy to improve their situation. This further highlights the misalignment between long-term planning in penal reform and the immediacy of issues for prisoners. As discussed by Calavita and Jenness (2018), prisons are high-stakes environments and the ability of prisoners to think of long-term reform when their agency and resources are limited is a luxury.

This disconnect between the lived experience and the view of the bodies was also found in participants' feelings that it was never possible for an outside body to truly understand their everyday life. For some participants there was a real concern that through a lack of true understanding of life in prison, outside bodies could make things worse rather than better in prison.

7.5 Conclusion

This chapter highlights the existing perceptions of prisoners of oversight bodies in prison and brings together the factors discussed in Chapter 6 to illustrate the challenges created by the prison environment itself to accessing and the operation of oversight bodies. Three key areas of literature were drawn upon and expanded through the findings discussed here. The link between rights consciousness and understanding of rights while in prison was discussed in relation to both awareness and expectations of prison and oversight bodies. These findings, through applying penal consciousness theory, showed how low awareness or sense of rights can impact on knowledge and accessing rights protection. Following this, different facets of trust in prison were discussed, low trust within the prison environment itself, the perception of being untrustworthy amongst prisoners, trust in oversight bodies, as well as limited agency in prison. These findings highlight the important role of trust in an environment itself to promote trust building and how low trust can impact on prisoners' risk assessment in deciding to engage. Finally, the misalignment between oversight structures and prison experiences was discussed. These findings show that those in prison may struggle to interact with formalised bodies, and that in approaching the issue of oversight in prison, the context of the prison environment and the circumstances of those who the bodies are intended to protect need to be considered.

Drawing on the themes discussed in this chapter, the final chapter provides a brief summary and provides recommendations for overcoming these challenges to help with awareness and perceptions of oversight bodies.

Note

1 Committee on Public Petitions 9 March 2021 Available at: www.oireachtas.ie/ga/debates/debate/committee_on_public_petitions/2021-03-09/2/ (Accessed 31 August 2021).

References

Sara Ahmed, *Complaint!* (Duke University Press 2021).

Sarah Armstrong, 'Securing Prison Through Human Rights: Unanticipated Implications of Rights-Based Penal Governance' (2018) 57 (3) *The Howard Journal of Crime and Justice* 401.

Cormac Behan, 'Still Entitled to Our Say': Prisoners' Perspectives on Politics' (2012) 51(1) *The Howard Journal of Criminal Justice* 16.

Cormac Behan, *Citizen Convict: Prisoners, Politics and the Vote* (Manchester University Press 2016).

Cormac Behan, 'No Longer a 'Collateral Consequence': Imprisonment and the Reframing of Citizenship' (2020) *European Journal of Criminology* 1.

Cormac Behan and Richard Kirkham, 'Monitoring, Inspection and Complaints Adjudication in Prison: The Limits of Prison Accountability Frameworks' (2016) 55(4) *The Howard Journal of Crime and Justice* 432.

Karin A Beijersbergen, Anja JE Dirkzwager, Veroni I Eichelsheim, Peter H Van der Laan and Paul Nieuwbeerta, 'Procedural Justice, Anger, and Prisoners' Misconduct: A Longitudinal Study' (2015) 42 *Criminal Justice and Behavior* 196.

Michelle Butler and Shadd Maruna, 'Rethinking Prison Disciplinary Processes: A Potential Future for Restorative Justice' (2016) 11(1) *Victims & Offenders* 126.

Kitty Calavita and Valerie Jenness, *Appealing to Justice: Prisoner Grievances, Rights and Carceral Logic* (University of California Press 2015).

Kitty Calavita and Valerie Jenness, 'Race, Grievance Systems and Prisoners Perceptions of Justice in Three California Prisons' (2018) 15(1) *Du Bois Review: Social Science Research on Race* 153.

Eamonn Carrabine, 'Prison Riots, Social Order and the Problem of Legitimacy' (2005) 45(6) *British Journal of Criminology* 896.

Ben Crewe, *The Prisoner Society: Power, Adaptation and Social Life in an English Prison* (Oxford University Press 2009).

Ben Crewe, 'Soft Power in Prison: Implications for Staff-Prisoner Relationships, Liberty and Legitimacy' (2011) 8(6) *European Journal of Criminology* 455.

Ben Crewe, Alison Liebling and Susie Hulley, 'Staff-Prisoner Relationships, Staff Professionalism, and the Use of Authority in Public-and Private-Sector Prisons' (2015) 40(2) *Law & Social Inquiry* 309.

Ben Crewe, Jason Warr, Peter Bennett and Alan Smith, 'The Emotional Geography of Prison Life' (2014) 18(1) *Theoretical Criminology* 56.

Cristina Dâmboeanu, Valentina Pricopie and Alina Thiemann, 'The Path to Human Rights in Romania: Emergent Voice(s) of Legal Mobilization in Prisons' (2021) 18(1) *European Journal of Criminology* 120.

David M Engel, 'Vertical and Horizontal Perspectives on Rights Consciousness' (2012) 19 *Indiana Journal of Global Legal Studies* 423.

Michel Foucault, *Discipline and Punish: The Birth of the Prison* (Vintage 2012).

Derrick Franke, David Biere and Doris MacKenzie, 'Legitimacy in Corrections: A Randomized Experiment Comparing a Boot Camp With a Prison' (2010) 9(1) *Criminology and Public Policy* 89.

John Gilliom, *Overseers of the Poor: Surveillance, Resistance, and the Limits of Privacy* (University of Chicago Press 2001).

Evi J Girling, 'European Identity, Penal Sensibilities, and Communities of Sentiment' in Sarah Armstrong and Lesley McAra (eds) *Perspectives on Punishment: The Contours of Control* (Oxford University Press 2006).

Russell Hardin, 'Trustworthiness' (1996) 107(1) *Ethics* 26.

Katerine Hawley, *Trust: A Very Short Introduction* (Oxford University Press 2012).

Yvonne Jewkes, 'Men Behind Bars: "Doing" Masculinity as an Adaptation to Imprisonment' (2005) 8(1) *Men and Masculinities* 44.

Anastasia Karamalidou, *Embedding Human Rights in Prison: English and Dutch Perspectives* (Palgrave Macmillan UK 2017).

Alison Liebling assisted by Helen Arnold, *Prisons and Their Moral Performance: A Study of Values, Quality, and Prison Life* (Oxford University Press 2004).

Alison Liebling, 'Distinctions and Distinctiveness in the Work of Prison Officers; Legitimacy and Authority Revisited' (2011) 8(6) *European Journal of Criminology* 484.

Alison Liebling, 'Moral Performance, Inhuman and Degrading Treatment and Prison Pain' (2011) 13(5) *Punishment and Society* 530.

Allen E. Lind and Tom R. Tyler, *The Social Psychology of Procedural Justice* (Plenum 1988).

Thomas Mathiesen, *The Defences of the Weak: A Sociological Study of a Norwegian Correctional Institution* (Tavistock 1965).

Sally Engle Merry, 'Concepts of Law and Justice Among Working-Class Americans: Ideology as Culture' (1985) 9(1) *Legal Studies Forum* 59.

Sally Engle Merry, *Human Rights and Gender Violence: Translating International Law Into Local Justice* (University of Chicago Press 2009).

Dale T Miller, 'Disrespect and the Experience of Injustice' (2001) 52 (1) *Annual Review of Psychology* 527.

Bronwyn Naylor, 'Human Rights and Respect in Prisons: The Prisoners' Perspective' (2014) 31 *Law Context: A Socio-Legal Journal* 84.

Bronwyn Naylor and Stan Winford, 'Implementing OPCAT Through Prison Monitoring: The Relevance of Rehabilitation' (2019) 25(1) *Australian Journal of Human Rights* 113.

Ian O'Donnell, 'The Aims of Imprisonment' in Yvonne Jewkes, Jamie Bennett and Ben Crewe (eds) *Handbook on Prisons* (2nd edn, Routledge 2016).

Prisons and Probation Ombudsman, *Learning From PPO Investigations: Why Do Women and Young People in Custody Not Make Formal Complaints*? (Prisons and Probation Ombudsman 2015). Available at: https://ppo.gov.uk/learning_research/learning-lessons-bulletin-why-do-women-and-young-people-in-custody-not-make-formal-complaints/.

Mary Rogan, 'Discerning Penal Values and Judicial Decision Making: The Case of Whole Life Sentencing in Europe and the United States of America' (2018) 57(3) *The Howard Journal of Crime and Justice* 321.

Abigail Rowe, 'Women Prisoners' in Ben Crewe and Jamie Bennett (eds) *The Prisoner* (Routledge 2012).

Kevin D Sawyer, 'Jailhouse Lawyering From the Beginning' (2021) 68 *UCLA Law Review Discourse* 98.

David Scott, 'Eating Your Insides Out: Cultural, Physical and Institutionally-Structured Violence in the Prison Place' (2015) 221 *Prison Service Journal* 55.

Toby Seddon, 'Rethinking Prison Inspection: Regulating Institutions of Confinement' in Hannah Quick, Toby Seddon and Graham Smith (eds) *Regulation and Criminal Justice: Developing a New Framework for Research and Policy Development* (Cambridge University Press 2010).

Lori Sexton, 'Penal Subjectivities: Developing a Theoretical Framework for Penal Consciousness' (2015) 17(1) *Punishment & Society* 114.

Susan Silbey, 'After Legal Consciousness' (2005) 1 *Annual Review of Law Social Science* 323.

Elina Steinerte and Rachel Murray, 'Same But Different? National Human Rights Commissions and Ombudsman Institutions as National Preventive Mechanisms Under the Optional Protocol to the UN Convention Against Torture' (2009) 25(2) *Netherlands Quarterly of Human Rights* 189.

Gresham Sykes, *The Society of Captives: A Study of a Maximum Security Prison* (Princeton University Press 1958).

Sarah Tait, 'A Typology of Prison Officer Approach to Care' (2011) 8(6) *European Journal of Criminology* 440.

Dirk van Zyl Smit and Sonja Snacken, *Principles of European Prison Law and Policy: Penology and Human Rights* (Oxford University Press 2009).

8 Conclusion

8.1 Introduction

Guided by the existing literature on rights consciousness, penal culture and rights protecting bodies, the overarching aim of this book was to explore prisoners' views and experiences of how oversight bodies operate in prison, as well as identify factors which influenced or impacted on their perceptions and experiences of oversight. Chapters 5 and 6 presented and analysed the key research findings through outlining participants' awareness of and perceptions of the various bodies, as well as identifying barriers in the prison environment to rights consciousness and engaging with the bodies. Chapter 7 moved the discussion forward by bringing these findings together for a deeper analysis of the data and further unravelled the role of the factors discussed in Chapter 6 on the operation of the oversight bodies in the prison environment. This chapter also puts forward recommendations for oversight bodies and the prison service for embedding rights consciousness in prison and building awareness and engagement with oversight bodies. These findings have important implications for how these bodies operate in prisons and the need to build prisoner awareness and rights consciousness to promote engagement and protection. As outlined in Chapter 7, the culture in prisons shapes the experiences and perceptions of existing bodies. Therefore, recommendations will also be given to highlight the role of the prison in facilitating and integrating oversight into prisons. Furthermore, this chapter briefly considers the ethics of prison research and reflections on the researcher's role in this space.

8.2 Untangling Participants' Perceptions and Awareness of Oversight Bodies

Low levels of awareness can create fundamental problems in seeking to engage with the bodies and understanding the specific mandates of each. Learning about bodies when approached or when the bodies are in the prison results in a limited period for prisoners to make an informed assessment about trusting the body. This can create challenges especially in a low trust environment such as a prison where trusting the wrong person can have

DOI: 10.4324/9781003477471-8

significant repercussions. As discussed in Chapter 6, prisons in particular are low trust environments and those who have experienced a lack of trust themselves, may be less likely to place trust in others. Additionally, it may be difficult to place trust in authorities which they have had negative prior experiences, as may be the case for some prisoners, especially if they view the oversight bodies as part of the prison service itself or the wider criminal justice system. Therefore, providing those in prison with accurate information and expectations about the specific roles of different oversight bodies is key to building trust in those bodies.

Expectations were explored in Chapters 5 and 6, both in relation to expectations of the prison system and expectations of oversight bodies. In relation to prison expectations, participants often had low expectations about what prison should be like and what they were entitled to. As highlighted by Sexton's (2015) work on penal consciousness, these expectations in turn impact on perceptions and severity of prison experiences. For example, as discussed in Chapter 6, as a result of the improvements around in-cell sanitation in Irish prisons some participants felt that all of their needs had been met in prison, as the practice of slopping out had been normalised as part of the prison experience setting a low expectation of prison conditions. This in turn can make identifying issue in prison to speak up about either to an inspection body or through complaining challenging, as the perception held by some was that prison was sufficiently good for prison.

As set out in Chapter 3, inspection and monitoring bodies rely on recommendations rather than enforcement powers to negotiate change in prisons. Therefore, it is the prison system which must enact the change and oversight bodies are not directly in control of the process. Some prisoners spoke about the possibility of enforcement powers for oversight bodies and felt without these powers, the prison service would not act on its on to make changes or implement recommendations. It is important when engaging with those in prison that realistic expectations about what can be achieved by inspection and the limitations of their powers are made clear. This will reduce unintended frustrations and disillusionment when the service may not fully implement recommendations in a timely manner. Adding tensions and emotion to an already emotion-laden environment through creating false or misleading expectations should be avoided. Some participants also had low expectations about the oversight bodies and although they chose to engage they did not have high expectations about being heard or changes being made. Meeting these low expectations reinforces the view that even those who say they are there to help prisoners also cannot be trusted. Ensuring realistic expectations is important in this regard, as well as following up with prisoners where possible to include them in the process.

Increasing awareness about the specific mandates also has important ethical implications, as prisoners are informed about who they are speaking to and what happens with the information they provide to the bodies. Informed engagement ensures that expectations are in line with what the bodies can actually achieve and is less likely to negatively impact on a person's perception of the body. Being informed about a body's mandate gives prisoners the necessary knowledge to make an informed choice as to whether or not they want to engage and grant autonomy to the prisoner in sharing personal information about their experiences.

Some prisoners spoke about knowing about the bodies but never 'seeing' them around the prisons or having the impression that they only went to certain parts or spoke to certain prisoners and perceiving the process as being controlled by the prison service. This had an impact on their assessment of the oversight bodies and in particular a failure to be seen as independent or to capture the 'real' prison through their activities. These perceived failures of oversight bodies had an impact on prisoners' sense that inspection was for them and that their rights were effectively protected while in prison. This in turn reduced faith and trust in the process and what it could achieve.

Another key theme identified in the research was the rights consciousness of those in prison. Chapter 6 showed that although prisoners were aware of their rights in some cases, they did not always apply the rights rhetoric nor were they aware of the specificities of rights. Others held a very limited conception of their rights while in prison, only being concerned with rights such as receiving food and having access to fresh air and exercise. Furthermore, some prisoners did not feel worthy of rights or that others perceived them as worthy of rights. As indicated above, this in turn had implications for identifying problems in prison and seeking to engage with oversight bodies, as their expectations of what they were entitled to and what prison should be like were in some cases quite low. As highlighted by Dâmboeanu et al. (2021: 135), 'developing human rights consciousness is not straightforward; it is a slow and complex process, which implies "a shift in subjectivity"' and in some cases a reassessment of ones sense of self and identify as a person worthy of having their rights protected. Additionally, embedding rights and the ability to seek rights protections depends on institutional support (Merry 2003: 381). Institutions play a central role in building rights consciousness and embedding a rights agenda into the prison environment. Experiences of prison, as well as in society more broadly by those labelled as criminals or prisoners, can impact on one's perception of self and whether or not the rights outlined in the law are internalised as real and accessible. Building rights consciousness can take a long time and those in prison often bring their conceptions and expectations of rights with them from the outside. As highlighted by Maguire's (2021) work, carceral spaces are not equipped to challenge these perceptions of self which prisoners bring with them upon entry into prison.

Chapter 6 also discussed the impact of penal culture on prisoners' experiences of oversight in prisons. The environment in which oversight bodies operate can impact significantly on how people engage with the bodies and can hinder or promote seeking out information and engagement with rights protection. Culture can be seen as:

> a pattern of shared basic assumptions that the group learned as it solved its problems of external adaptation and internal integration, that has worked well enough to be considered valid and, therefore, to be taught to new members as the correct way to perceive, think, and feel in relation to those problems.
>
> (Schein 2017: 17)

Culture is built around the environment in which a group of people are in and how they adapt to survive in that space. In the case of prisoner and penal culture, specific facets of the environment such as staff prisoner relationships, inter-prisoner relationships and power dynamics played a role in how those in prison interacted with these bodies. This sharing of culture was also relevant in how prisoners gained information about the bodies, as other prisoners were seen as a key source of information on prison life and rights as outlined in Chapter 6. This can result in the passing on of assumptions and experiences with the bodies which in turn may influence other prisoners' decision to engage. As highlighted by Suntinger and Birk (2021: 19) knowledge of the world is based on our own personal constructions and 'the person and medium of observation influences the results of the observation'. Culture is not easy to change and requires a wide range of actors to facilitate changes to how they operate, including the prison service itself, how staff see their role within the prison and how oversight bodies present themselves to those in prison. This is turn needs to be communicated to those in prison so that a slow cultural shift can arise which allows for knowledge transfer with a recognition of rights and rights protection for all those in custody. Embedding this change is needed at a system wide level, as focusing on one facet or group of people in isolation risks placing them in opposition to the prevailing cultural patterns and failing to create this cultural shift. A particular aspect of prison culture which is important to return to here is a sense of stoicism and creating a tough persona. Some participants spoke of complaining or those who spoke about problems in prison as being 'whingers' or too soft. There was a perception among some participants that in prison it was important to be perceived as tough and to simply get on with one's sentence, rather than complain. While this was related to expectations discussed above and in Chapter 6, this was also related to a sense that letting your guard down would only result in negative repercussions or in making your time in prison harder. As discussed by Jewkes (2005), masculinities prevalent in prisons can make it challenging to show emotions or to create safe spaces where prisoners could discuss their problems. Letting down this front and exposing vulnerabilities was seen as leaving a prisoner open to exploitation. This highlights the importance of confidentiality in the oversight process, to allow for a safe space where prisoners can trust the oversight bodies. Additionally, due to the limited opportunities to speak openly about issues in prison, it may be difficult to open up when prisoners are being asked to assess a body on the spot and do not have sufficient time to gauge whether or not they can trust the body and may find it challenging to reflect on their prison experience. As discussed by Warr, in relation to research interviews, these are different forms of communication which go beyond the traditional prison interactions.[1]

8.3 Limitations of the Research

The research took place across three research sites within the prison campus, which while providing for a variety of experiences with oversight bodies did not account for the variety across all prisons. A full discovery and analysis of the role of each prison's history in the development of prison culture and engagement with oversight bodies was also beyond the scope of this research. Additionally, as a cross-sectional study, the data was gathered at one moment in time from the various individuals, and changes in perceptions over time or the relationship between different factors could not be fully explored. However, the study used random sampling resulting in participants with a broad range of prison experience. The significance of ethnic background was not fully explored, partially due to the small number of participants which could lead to identifiable information, and the overall demographics of those living in Irish prisons. A further study which oversampled from these groups could provide important insight into experiences of these groups, as previous research with foreigners highlights the additional barriers they may face due to language or cultural differences or lower levels of trust among those from ethnic minorities (Boone and Kox 2014).

The study was limited to male prisons, which excluded a discussion of diversity of views due to gender dimensions. There is some evidence from the United Kingdom to suggest that experiences of these bodies may be different among the female prison population, in particular lower usage due to different staff relationships (Prisons and Probation Ombudsman 2015). Further research which focuses on female prison population is needed to explore the differences across experiences of oversight bodies more broadly.

While this study has explored how various factors influence perceptions of oversight bodies, they were largely absent in the thinking of the participants, therefore the role of oversight bodies in shaping participants' views of prison was beyond the scope of this findings. A further study with well-informed prisoners or those who have experience of engaging may provide insight into this.

8.4 Recommendations

The findings show there are significant challenges when it comes to oversight in prisons. A number of recommendations will be considered to enhance the rights protection in prisons and ensure the intended beneficiaries can access the bodies. However, Kemp and Tomczak' (2024) concerns around the need for decarceration alongside efficient oversight should be retained, as prisons should be a means of last resort.

8.4.1 Need to Increase Awareness about Inspections

Prisoners need to be more aware of oversight groups and their mandates. Those who took part in the study were often unfamiliar with the bodies or unclear about their exact role. It would help to tell prisoners and to give them regular reminders about these groups. When first entering prison, a lot of information is received by the new prisoner who may be in a state of shock. Information on inspection and complaints may not be their main concern at that time. Therefore, regular reminders ensure that the information is more likely to be retained and available to prisoners when they need it.

This is particularly important as the ability to carry out surprise visits was the power which prisoners indicated was the most important for a good inspector to have, as discussed in Chapter 5. Therefore, being informed of the different offices and their mandates prior to such visits is key to ensuring that those in prison are not learning about the bodies and making assessments on whether to engage on the spot. As noted by Participant 26, it is important for those in prison to know who those coming into prison are in order to allow prisoners to make the choice to interact. He noted that otherwise people may not learn about specific bodies until after they have already left the landing or prison and this is too late for them to approach them.

Some prisoners spoke about having to seek out information about what bodies were available. This could be a significant barrier for those who already do not trust the system, are unwilling to ask for information and do not know where to ask for information. Another key recommendation linked to increasing awareness is visibility of oversight bodies. In a vacuum where those in prison do not know much about the bodies or how they operate, misconceptions can develop. These can be damaging to the perception of the bodies held by prisoners and can result in prisoners choosing to distance themselves from them or be wary of openly engaging. As outlined in Chapter 5, some participants felt that the bodies only went to certain parts of the prison or spoke to certain people. This is in contrast to the opinion that having unlimited access to all areas and prisoners is a key part of a good inspection process. While oversight bodies may have a process for selecting prisoners that ensures a wide pool of prisoners were spoken with, this was not always clear to those in prison. Increasing transparency in the process of inspection and visibility around the presence of inspection would help in addressing these perceptions and ensure greater access to the bodies.

8.4.2 Need to Promote Trust and Credibility

There is a low level of trust in inspection bodies and the complaint procedures in Ireland, as highlighted by the findings discussed in Chapter 6, and this can be a barrier to making use of them. It is necessary to ensure that prisoners see both the complaints procedures and the bodies themselves as being independent. This could be done by increasing the visibility of oversight bodies and their ability to move freely through the prison. It would also be important that communication between these groups is given priority. As with the IMBs in England and Wales (Scott and Flynn 2014), membership of VCs is characterised by those who are middle-aged and from middle class backgrounds, representing limited commonality with the social backgrounds of those in prison. Increasing diversity among the VC members may help encourage prisoners to engage and increase credibility through seeing those with similar life experiences who are perceived to better understand the problems of prisoners.

Additionally, closing the feedback loop by providing information to prisoners on the implementation of recommendations and access to the inspection report would give prisoners an insight into the process and the sense that their voices had been heard by reflecting their concerns in the report. As highlighted by one participant who accessed the report following an interaction with the Inspector:

> *the Inspector did spot a few things in [the prison] that needed sorting out like, you know and he included it in his report like, which I thought made a big difference, you know what I mean like.*
>
> (Participant 36)

While prisoners are not necessarily the target audience for reports by oversight bodies, providing access to the report may help promote legitimacy of the process among the prison population and dispel perceptions that the process is guided by the prison service and only interacts with certain prisoners or areas within the prison. If necessary, a supplementary or summary report in accessible language could also be developed for those in prison. It also recognises the contribution prisoners make to the process in providing their experiences and insight into prison life to the bodies and moves beyond the perception of prisoners merely as sources of data for the reports. Recognising that they are active participants in the process is important in promoting future engagement and awareness of the process, as well as in respecting the contribution they make to the reporting process. Reports may also feed into prisoners' sense of self-worth and build their expectations around how prison should be.

Hearing back from complaints with a reasoned decision would help ensure that incorrect assumptions regarding the handling of a complaint are avoided and, in line with literature in the area of procedural justice, help those whose complaint has been rejected to understand the decision-making process and the reasons for the outcome.

8.4.3 Improve Access to the Complaint System and the Office of the Inspector of Prisons

As discussed in Chapter 5, prisoners highlighted the challenges to accessing the complaint system and engaging with the OiP. As highlighted by Kirs

(2021) 'accessible information about the right to complain is at the heart of a fair and efficient procedure'. Literacy played a role in accessing oversight bodies, in particular the complaint system as some felt they could not express themselves clearly when writing a complaint. Literacy also played a role in engaging with inspection bodies, as participants spoke about not being able to express themselves properly and professionals not being able to understand issues which might affect them in prison. Issues which may seem relatively minor to someone on the outside such as delays in receiving post or accessing the landing phone to call a family member, take on additional significance in the prison context, where resources are limited, and prisoners rely on the prison service for access to fundamental needs. A complaint system should take into account the users of the system and include an option to orally submit complaints through a trusted person.

Some prisoners spoke about specific groups of prisoners being important in highlighting issues and seen as representatives for prisoners. In particular, these were prisoners serving particularly long sentences, such as those serving a life sentence and those who took part in Red Cross activities.

As in Jenness and Calavita's (2018) study, outcomes from complaints take on an additional significance in the prison context. However, procedural justice elements, such as voice, neutrality, trust and respect discussed in Chapter 4 remained important (Jackson et al 2010). The prison literature on procedural justice suggests that a better sense of procedural justice can increase trust in prison, overall well-being, and lower levels of misconduct, self-harm and those released committing further offences (Beijersbergen et al 2015). While the specific role of complaint procedures in the overall sense of procedural justice in prison has not been explored, it is clear from the findings that principles of procedural justice were important to those in the research. Ensuring that responses to complaints are perceived as procedurally just means that prisoners are more likely to trust the person giving the response and handling the complaint, to feel respected and have faith in the response and how the complaint was dealt with, and is more likely to feel that they have been heard and considered. The findings discussed in Chapter 5 show that the attributes of a good complaints model upon which prisoners place more importance are speed, independence of review and reasoned rejections. The desire found here for independent review of complaints should be listened to, not only by the Irish authorities in their design of a new complaints system, but by all those involved in the administration of such mechanisms. Human rights frameworks stress the importance of effective complaints mechanisms. These findings should also be heard by those designing and administering such systems to ensure that such systems are 'genuinely available', 'accessible', 'trusted' and 'effective' in order to fulfil the potential human rights instruments suggest complaints procedures have.[2]

A particular concern with the Irish system as outlined in Chapter 5 and noted in reports by the OiP and the CPT as highlighted in Chapter 3 relates to the significant delays within the complaint system. Delays can communicate a lack of respect for those submitting complaints, as well as the issues which they are complaining about, and can contribute to a sense of not being heard in prison. Delays in dealing with complaints, as discussed by Naylor (2014) and above, can also impact on the usage of the complaint system by those serving shorter sentences. Given that shorter sentences are a feature of the Irish prison population, it is important that complaints are dealt with in a timely manner to ensure that even those serving short sentences can use the system. Delays in responding to complaints as discussed by Bierie (2013), may also be linked to increases in prison violence due to a sense of frustration at not being heard. Also as highlighted in Chapter 5, a significant portion of prisoners preferred to resolve issues themselves, which may be a result of feelings that the system does not work or that the complainant will not hear back within a meaningful time frame. The Irish prison service has incorporated specific timelines into its complaint policy and adherence to these are important to build trust and faith in the system. In cases, where further investigation is needed and a delay does arise, it is important to inform the complainant and keep them updated about the status of their complaint.

Another concern referred to by participants was in relation to reprisals or repercussions for speaking up about problems in prison or complaining. Whether a real or perceived threat, this can have significant implications on prisoners' willingness to engage with oversight bodies or submit a complaint, as well as seeking out information on their rights or oversight bodies. Looking for information or speaking up was felt by some participants to earn you a label of being a troublemaker. Participants spoke about the risk of being transferred to a different prison or reprisals which would be difficult to identify such as being unlocked last in the mornings. Given the inherent power dynamics in prisoner staff relationships, oversight bodies and the prison service should take steps to both mitigate the risk of reprisals, as well as reassure those who have concerns about speaking up. As explored in Chapter 7, this had implications for the kinds of problems which prisoners were willing to draw attention to themselves for, in particular being willing to tolerate conditions themselves but filling complaints or speaking to bodies when issues arose around their family communication or visits.

8.5 Reflecting on the Research Process

Embarking on research in an underexplored area can be a daunting experience; however, it is also critical to develop our understanding of people's experiences in prison and especially bodies designed to protect their rights. As highlighted above, limited data and research has been conducted to data on the Irish Criminal Justice System, although the field is growing in recent years, and the insights provided here and elsewhere provide important groundwork to build on by later research and researchers. It is important prior to entering the field to be aware of the potential challenges and limitations to researching in a particular environment.

Prior to commencing this project, the author was aware of the underdevelopment of criminological data in Ireland and the infancy of in-prison research in this jurisdiction. In order to ensure access was granted and the specifics of the research were considered feasible, numerous meetings were held with key stakeholders in the area. The research was also conducted as part of the PRILA project, which included a prison officer, Ray O'Keeffe, who provided invaluable insights into the operation of prisons and navigating the field.

Entering the field also required gaining permission from both the researcher's institution and the prison service itself. As a significant amount of data was required, applications for the required permissions and approvals were made at the very start of the study. This was of utmost importance due to the lack of precedent in this area of criminological research in Ireland. These processes can be time consuming and starting early ensures that the researcher had sufficient time to gather and analysis the data due to the time constraints of the project and funding. Protocols and arrangements were all agreed in advance of any data being collected or analysed making the research process easier to navigate, and a wealth of feedback was received from all those involved in the research project. Importantly, completing primary research in prisons requires a researcher to be aware of their underlying assumptions of the criminal justice system, as they will shape the way data is collected and analysed, as well as how their decisions may impact on research findings (Liebling 2001). During the project, the researcher also engaged in fieldwork with other members of the PRILA team which provided additional insights into the field. The researcher also conducted familiarisation tours prior to embarking on fieldwork to enhance her ability to remain neutral during data collection and analysis. This is important to the integrity of the research being conducted, as well as the participants involved.

8.6 Closing

In recent years there has been a growth oversight and an increasing guidance on how to carry to oversee places of detention in international conventions and rules such as OPCAT, UN Mandela Rules and the CoE EPRs; however, the actual experience of those who these bodies are designed to protect remains relatively underexplored. This book addresses that gap in knowledge through advancing the understanding of living experience of oversight. It is important to understand what rights protection looks like for the most vulnerable to ensure that mechanisms are accessible and understanding of the environment in which they operate.

Despite oversight bodies, such as the VCs, being active in Ireland for over a century and various discussions taking place within the government on reforming and abolishing these bodies at different stages, there is a lack of information on how those in prison perceive and experience them. Understanding these experiences are key to informing policy in this area and ensuring reforms reflect the lived experiences of those in prison in this area.

Oversight bodies in Ireland, similar to elsewhere in Europe and across the globe, have faced a range of hurdles in their operation, such as lack of resources and a lack of political interest in prisons, which has implications for the allocation of resources and responses to problems and implementing reforms (Rogan 2014). As noted in Chapter 3, despite a commitment to introducing the Ombudsman to the prisoner complaints system in 2016 and similarly signing OPCAT in 2007 Ireland has yet to implement either of these changes to the prison oversight framework in Ireland. Advancing knowledge on the experiences of those in prison of rights and rights protection highlights the importance of effective rights protection in prison and the need to build awareness of and remove barriers to access rights protection. However as highlighted by Goffman (1986: 14), '[h]e who would combat false consciousness and awaken people to their true interests has much to do, because the sleep is very deep'.

Notes

1 Jason Warr, Quid Pro Quo in Prison Research, Comparative Penology. Available at: www.compen.crim.cam.ac.uk/Blog/blog-pages-full-versions/blog-18-jasonwarr
2 CPT, *27th Annual Report of the CPT* (Council of Europe 2018).

References

Karin A Beijersbergen, Anja JE Dirkzwager, Veroni I Eichelsheim, Peter H Van der Laan and Paul Nieuwbeerta, 'Procedural Justice, Anger, and Prisoners' Misconduct: A Longitudinal Study' (2015) 42 *Criminal Justice and Behavior* 196.

David Bierie, 'Procedural justice and prison violence: Examining complaints among federal inmates (2000–2007)' (2013) 19(1) *Psychology, Public Policy, and Law* 15.

Miranda Boone and Mieke Kox, 'Neutrality as an Element of Perceived Justice in Prison: Consistency versus Individualization' (2014) 10 *Utrecht Law Review* 118.

Kitty Calavita and Valerie Jenness, 'Race, Grievance Systems and Prisoners Perceptions of Justice in three California Prisons' (2018) 15(1) *Du Bois Review: Social Science Research on Race* 153.

Cristina Dâmboeanu, Valentina Pricopie and Alina Thiemann, 'The Path to Human Rights in Romania: Emergent Voice(s) of Legal Mobilization in Prisons' (2021) 18(1) *European Journal of Criminology* 120.

Erving Goffman, *Frame Analysis: An Essay on the Organization of Experience* (Northeastern University Press 1986).

Jonathon Jackson, Tom Tyler, Ben Bradford, Dominic Taylor and Mike Shiner, 'Legitimacy and Procedural Justice in Prisons' (2010) 191 *Prison Service Journal* 4.

Yvonne Jewkes, 'Men Behind Bars: "Doing" Masculinity as an Adaptation to Imprisonment' (2005) 8(1) *Men and Masculinities* 44.

T Kemp, P Tomczak, The Cruel Optimism of International Prison Regulation: Prison Ontologies and Carceral Harms (2024) 49(3) *Law & Social Inquiry* 1683–1714.

Eszter Kirs, *Complaint Procedures and the Right to Information in Prisons: A Handbook for National Preventive* (Ludwig Boltzman Institute Fundamental and Human Rights 2021).

Alison Liebling, 'Whose Side Are We On? Theory, Practice and Allegiances in Prisons Research' (2001) 41(3) *British Journal of Criminology* 472.

David Maguire, *Male, Failed, Jailed: Masculinities and 'Revolving Door' Imprisonment in the UK* (Springer Nature 2021).

Sally Engle Merry, Rights Talk and the Experience of Law: Implementing Women's Human Rights to Protection From Violence (2003) 25(2) *Human Rights Quarterly* 343–381.

Bronwyn Naylor, 'Human Rights and Respect in Prisons: The Prisoners' Perspective' (2014) 31 *Law Context: A Socio-Legal Journal* 84.

Prisons and Probation Ombudsman, *Learning from PPO Investigations: Why Do Women and Young People in Custody Not Make Formal Complaints*? (Prisons and Probation Ombudsman 2015).

Mary Rogan, *Prison Law* (Bloomsbury 2014).

Edgar Schein, *Organisation Culture and Leadership* (3rd edn, Wiley 2017).

David Scott and Nick Flynn, *Prisons & Punishment: The Essentials* (Sage 2014).

Lori Sexton, 'Penal Subjectivities: Developing a Theoretical Framework for Penal Consciousness' (2015) 17(1) *Punishment & Society* 114.

Walter Suntinger and Moritz Birk, *Systemic Thinking in Preventive Human Rights Monitoring: A Dossier for National Preventive Mechanisms* (Ludwig Boltzman Institute Fundamental and Human Rights 2021).

Index

Note: Page locators in **bold** and *italics* represents tables and figures, respectively. Endnotes are indicated by the page number followed by "n" and the note number e.g., 111n5 refers to note 5 on page 111.

FSC
www.fsc.org
MIX
Papier | Fördert gute Waldnutzung
FSC® C083411

Kolibri 360 GmbH
Ferdinand-Jühlke-Straße 7
99095 Erfurt, Deutschland
produktsicherheit@kolibri360.de